ROOM'S DICTIONARY OF DISTINGUISHABLES

Also by Adrian Room

Room's Dictionary of Confusibles
Place-Name Changes since 1900: A World Gazetteer

ROOM'S DICTIONARY OF DISTINGUISHABLES

Adrian Room

ROUTLEDGE & KEGAN PAUL
Boston, London and Henley

First published in 1981
by Routledge & Kegan Paul Ltd
9 Park Street, Boston, Mass. 02108, USA,
39 Store Street, London WC1E 7DD and
Broadway House, Newtown Road,
Henley on-Thames, Oxon RG9 1EN
Set in Linoterm Baskerville by
Rowland Phototypesetting Ltd, Bury St Edmunds, Suffolk
and printed in the United States of America by
Vail Ballou Press, Inc., Binghamton, New York
© Adrian Room 1981

British Library Cataloguing in Publication Data

Room, Adrian
Room's dictionary of distinguishables.
1. English language — Synonyms
and antonyms
I. Title
423'.1   PE1591   80-42285
ISBN 0-7100-0775-2

'What is the difference between a riddle and two elephants sitting on a bun?'
'One is a conundrum and the other is a bun-under-'em.'

(Schoolchildren's conundrum, of considerable vintage. For the actual difference between a conundrum and a riddle, see **pun**.)

INTRODUCTION

We live in a world in which there are a number of grey areas. Not only are there an infinite number of divisions between the well-defined extremes of black and white, but there are several shades between the contrasting colours, primary or political included, of red and blue. Nothing, it seems, is one hundred per cent 'this' or wholly and demonstrably 'that', but very often 'this' with a bit of 'thatness', or 'that' tending towards the 'this'.

Even in the actual scientific world of primary colours, red, green and blue lights can, when properly selected and mixed, produce any hue, even white, grey and purple.

And this is the sort of difficulty we are up against. First, we have to determine at what stage white becomes so dark that it can no longer be called 'white'. Second, we must decide what to call it if it is no longer dark enough to be called 'black'. 'Grey', you say? Yes, but at what point does 'white' become 'grey', and 'grey' itself darken into 'black'? Or, since now in the last quarter of the twentieth century it is a multicoloured glow that lightens the darkness of our sitting rooms, and no longer a black and white one, what precise combinations of red and blue and anything else will produce the shades we know as 'purple', 'mauve', 'magenta', 'puce' and the like? What in fact *is* the difference between 'purple' and 'mauve'? When is a door not a door?

The factual question and the age-old riddle pose problems that may not have ready answers.

This dictionary tries to distinguish in such cases. It deals in the main with two types of word: common everyday words, such as 'boat' and 'ship', 'rabbit' and 'hare', 'world' and 'earth', and words that, while forming part of most people's active vocabulary, are usually regarded as belonging to a particular specialisation, branch of learning or region of study, as 'acid' and 'alkali' from chemistry, 'carnation' and 'pink' from horticulture, and 'panther' and 'puma' from the world of zoology.

Such pairs of words have a common link. Both a boat and a ship are vessels for travelling over the water, both a carnation and a pink are sweet-smelling garden plants of the genus called *Dianthus*, both a panther and a puma are large members of the cat family. But what is the difference between the two in each case? And could it be that a panther actually *is* a puma? The dictionary aims to make the distinction clear.

In many cases, of course, a distinction needs to be made not just between two words or concepts but among more than two. The dictionary entry that deals with the panther and the puma, for example, also considers them in relation to the leopard, jaguar and cheetah, thus sorting out the members of a fivefold yet far-flung animal family.

This present dictionary is rather more straightforward, perhaps, than its predecessor, *Room's Dictionary of Confusibles* (Routledge & Kegan Paul, 1979). Confusibles are words that not only have a common semantic link but also look alike, sound alike, and are even spelled similarly. Distinguishables have an association in meaning only. Moreover, a confusible can be any part of speech, whereas distinguishables — at least, the ones in this dictionary — are always nouns. But otherwise the approach made to the words is much the same in both books, although with distinguishables the emphasis is necessarily more on definition than example.

To compensate, perhaps, for the absence of verbal illustrations, pictorial ones have been provided instead, especially in cases where it is felt they will help to clarify a written description by means of a visual accompaniment. And if it is enough for some readers to distinguish between x and y by merely taking a glance at the illustrations, and not bothering to read the text, what does it matter: the dictionary will have distinguished, and achieved its aim!

A very few pairs of distinguishables included here are, admittedly, rather less common than others. But perhaps the rarest pair, 'appoggiatura' and 'acciaccatura', which so nearly made it as confusibles in the previous dictionary, could no longer be denied entry, on grounds of pure melodiousness. (They even have an appropriately delicate illustration to accompany them.) And those terrible twins, 'type I error' and 'type II error', have also been granted a (strictly limited) portion of space, if only to serve as grim warnings of the art of lexicography at its basest, and as superb examples of the ridiculous in the world of technical jargon.

A casual flip-through of the main pages of text will no doubt reveal some gaps, and the reader may feel cheated that his own pet pair of distinguishables is not represented. But while any book is a finite thing, and therefore certain distinguishables will indeed not have been included, some apparent gaps may not be gaps at all, since the distinguishables that seem to be missing are not really distinguishables. The following categories, thus, I have not regarded as distinguishables, and so they will not feature in the book:

1 Words that are true synonyms, as **binoculars/field-glasses**, **harmonica/mouth-organ**.
2 Words that are simply British English *v.* American English, as **lift/elevator**, **pavement/sidewalk**.
3 Words that have a 'non-standard' equivalent, such as a dialect form, colloquialism, slang term or the like, as **lapwing/peewit**, **football/soccer**, **dollar/buck**. In this category come the once notorious 'U' and 'non-U'

pairs, as **napkin/serviette**, **writing-paper/notepaper**, lavatory/toilet.

4 Words that simply have alternative spellings, as **jail/gaol**, **faint lines/feint lines**.

In short, where *a* actually *is b* – a pavement *is* a sidewalk to Americans, just as it is a *trottoir* to a Frenchman, and binoculars *are* field-glasses – there is nothing to distinguish, at any rate not in meaning, and such words will not be in the dictionary.

Even here, though, there are one or two instances where I have deviated from this principle, notably where words that are commonly regarded as being entirely synonymous are not really so, or used not to be so, or where the difference in actual designation is sufficiently interesting for the words to be entered. Examples are **viper/adder**, and **witch doctor/medicine man**.

As for the genuine distinguishables that are missing, it can only be said that this is probably because they are so well known that it would be insulting to the reader, even if he is not a native English speaker, to include them. A silly example is **cat/dog** (both popular pets); a more realistic example is **mush-room/toadstool** (types of fungus that respectively can and cannot be eaten). However, the pairs **frog/toad** and **herring/kipper** are in the book, and to those readers who indignantly state that they *do* know the difference between the two, and they can't believe that there are people around who *don't* know the difference, I make no apologies. For every one person who can confidently identify a reptile as a frog, not a toad, I am sure there are at least ten who would hesitate to do so, and not simply out of squeamishness. Even if you do feel that you know the difference between a **boat** and a **ship**, why not read the entry that deals with these two types of vessel? You may be in for something of an eye-opener.

As mentioned, the actual range of words covered ranges from the everyday to the specialised. This means that the actual types of word or words also vary, so that there are some proper nouns and names (**Paul Pry/Peeping Tom**, **Maginot Line/Siegfried Line**), a few titles (**Republican/Democrat**, **Lordship/Worship**), and one or two abbreviations (**GCE/CSE**). In the definitions of many words, too, account is taken of American as well as British usage: see, for example, **border/frontier**, **lawyer/barrister/attorney**.

The arrangement of entries and order of words within the entries is basically similar to that used in the *Dictionary of Confusibles*. The entries themselves run in normal alphabetical order, with the words dealt with in an entry, either as a pair or a larger group, being given in what is normally order of frequency. Thus, **balcony**, for example, is regarded as a more common word and thing than **verandah**, and so comes as the first word in the entry. There are several cases, however, where either the more important or 'greater' word comes first, as **lake** before **pond**, and **charm** before **talisman**, or where the order is arbitrary or purely conventional, as **acid** before **alkali**, **Republican** before **Democrat**. Such arbitrary order will obviously apply the most often when the words concerned are opposites of some kind. In actual fact the order itself matters little, since every word or phrase that does not stand in first place in an entry is cross-referenced to the first headword in its appropriate alphabetical place.

In a few cases an identical word will head more than one entry. **Port**, for example, is the first headword of two entries. In such cases the cross-reference to this word has a brief description of it so that the reader will know which entry he must turn to for the sense that interests him. See, for example, the cross-reference **channel**, which leads to **sound**. It is briefly defined as 'narrow stretch of water' to distinguish it from the other **sound**, 'thing heard', to which **noise** cross-refers. Where on the other hand identical words do not appear as the leading headword of an entry, they will cross-refer to their respective entries in the normal way, these cross-references being given alphabetically. See, for example, **abbey**, which cross-refers respectively (and alphabetically) to **cathedral** and **monastery**, where its meanings differ somewhat.

But why a *Dictionary of Distinguishables* at all? If you are not sure of the difference between *x* and *y*, why not look them up in an ordinary dictionary? There are two main reasons why such a procedure may not produce the desired result, and solve the uncertainty that prompted the enquiry. The first is that it will always be necessary to look up both words separately, and then carefully compare the information given. This is time-consuming and tiresome. The second reason why such a course of action may not tell you what you want to know is simply that the dictionary itself may not be the right one for your purpose. Indeed, if it is a smallish one it may not distinguish at all, since it is enough to state, under their respective headings, that a gale is a 'strong wind' and a tempest a 'violent wind', thus leaving you to ponder on the significance, if any, of 'strong' and 'violent'. In fact, since many distinctions are concerned with purely factual information, of a more or less detailed nature, it may well be more satisfactory for you to turn to an encyclopedia – which may not only be not readily available but will almost certainly tell you far more than you need to know, making your search for a basic distinction between *x* and *y* a frustrating one.

The aim of this present dictionary is thus to present the distinctions all ready and served up, with just the right ingredients, for the reader to savour and consume. He will be told the minimum of what he needs to know in order to sort out the two words, and in some cases, especially where the concepts are more complex or abstract, rather more than the minimum. And for checking purposes, although he will of course know it already, the general association between the two or more words is given in the form of a concise definition in parentheses after the headwords of each entry.

4

Distinguishables, therefore, is something of a new type of dictionary. Apart from its straightforward practical value, too, it has a general overall objective – that of reminding us that more often than we care to admit we do actually fail to distinguish between two similar words, ideas or concepts. We say 'I had a good crossing on the boat' when perhaps we should have said 'ship', vaguely regard a baronet as the son of a baron, wonder if our occupation is the same as our trade or profession, and are rather uncertain about whether a coronary is the same as a stroke, or even what it is anyway. Does it matter that a road and a street are not quite one and the same thing, or that not all pies are tarts, or all tarts pies? The dictionary exists because it is felt that if words are to have any precise meaning at all, such distinctions do indeed matter. The English language is one of the richest and most expressive in the world, and the more carefully and thoughtfully we use its words, the greater the strength and expressiveness of the language become. The more careful and thoughtful and selective a reader and writer of English is, too, the more effective and commanding and influential does he become. It is not more words we want – we have plenty enough as it is – but more precise words. And put at its simplest and most basic, it can hardly be helpful or meaningful to say x when we mean y, simply because we cannot, or will not, distinguish.

In an age of computers, let us not neglect our prime and considerably older form of communication – words. They can be just as effective, and they are much cheaper to operate.

Readers of the dictionary may like to know where the various pairs and groups of distinguishables were unearthed. Many of them came out of every-day standard dictionaries, such as the *Concise Oxford Dictionary*, or general reference works, such as Roget's *Thesaurus of English Words and Phrases*. Others came just as they occurred, 'out of the air', and in this respect I would like to thank Margaret Dickson, who suggested some very good candidates, tracked down either in rather pedantic textbooks in the library or jotted down as they occurred, and when they occurred, on a note-pad. I would also like to thank Mrs Joyce Watson for carefully typing out the completed draft of the manu-script. And last but definitely not least I would like to thank Oxford Illustrators who have provided such attractive and helpful drawings to complement the text.

Petersfield, Hampshire   Adrian Room

DICTIONARY

abbey see (1) **cathedral**, (2) **monastery**

abdomen see **stomach**

abolition/dissolution/prorogation
(ending or annulling of something)
The terms are used for the ending of something that has been legally or politically sanctioned or established. 'Abolition' means ending for good, and is used in particular of slavery and capital punishment – both of which were suddenly found to be shameful and entirely undesirable. 'Dissolution' is used more of the breaking up or dispersal of something, especially parliament for a new session, or historically the suppression

('Dissolution') of the monasteries by Henry VIII in the 1530s. 'Prorogation' is the discontinuing of the meetings of parliament without a 'dissolution', that is, the official ending of one session, when parliament 'stands prorogued', until the day of meeting of a new session. The 'prorogation' of parliament usually extends from late July or early August to October or November, when another session will begin.

absolution see **acquittal**

accent see **dialect**

acciaccatura see **appoggiatura**

accordion/concertina (portable musical instrument with reeds and bellows)
The 'accordion' first appeared in Vienna in the 1820s. The early models had buttons at both ends – unlike the modern 'piano accor-

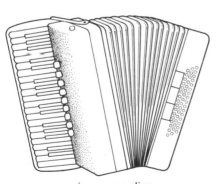
piano accordion

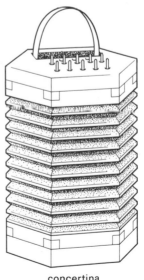
concertina

7

dion', which has a piano-style keyboard for the right hand – and were so-called 'single action', meaning that the instrument's reeds, arranged in pairs, gave one note on the press or push and another on the draw or pull. Later models, and always the 'piano accordion', have 'double action', meaning that both reeds in a pair are tuned to the same note so that both the press and the draw of the bellows will give an identical note. The 'concertina' appeared a few years after the 'accordion' in London, with its characteristic hexagonal bellows and buttons, never a keyboard, at both ends. 'Concertinas' are almost always 'double action', with the reeds producing the same note when the bellows are either compressed or expanded. There is, however, a type of German 'concertina', known in its more sophisticated form as an 'Anglo-German concertina' (just an 'Anglo' to professionals), which is 'single action', like the early 'accordions'. On both English and German 'concertinas' alternate notes of the scale are produced by the right hand and the left, but in the so called duet-system 'concertina' a complete chromatic scale is provided for each hand. Although largely superseded by the 'accordion' in the twentieth century, the 'concertina' must not be under-rated: Tchaikovsky has four of them in the score of his second orchestral suite, opus 53.

account/bill/invoice/statement
(document stating debit, credit or balance)
An 'account', in commercial terms, is a record of money or goods or services received and expended, as typically an 'account' settled with a firm monthly by a private customer. A 'bill' – as if we didn't know – is a note of charges for goods delivered or services rendered, payable either on receipt or entered in an 'account'. An 'invoice' is a list of goods sent or services performed, with prices and charges. Firms usually indicate if an 'invoice' also serves as a 'bill'. A special type of 'bill' is a 'bill of exchange'. This involves the payment of money and is an official order in writing, signed by the person giving it, to pay a particular sum to a specified person or to the bearer – that is, to the person who presents it. A well known form of 'bill of exchange' is a cheque. A 'statement' is a formal record of a customer's or client's liabilities and assets, or of an amount due to a tradesman or firm. A bank 'statement' – in full, 'statement of account' – records transactions made through a bank, by cheque and otherwise, over a given period, the balance, or amount one has in the bank ('when overdrawn marked OD'), being noted on the occasion of each transaction.

ache/pain (sensation of bodily discomfort)
An 'ache' can be dull or sharp, and is usually fairly persistent, as a 'headache', 'toothache' or 'backache'. A 'pain' is usually sharp rather than dull, but is sudden and normally of short duration, as a 'pain' in one's leg from cramp or in one's ankle from a sprain. 'Pain', too, may be mental or emotional, as the 'pain' of parting, but 'ache' – apart from 'heartache' – is usually a physical thing. English spelling is capricious, heaven knows, but why can't 'ache' be spelt 'ake'? The answer is that it once was, at least the verb was, while the noun, spelt as now, was actually pronounced 'aitch'. This went on till 1700, when the noun, keeping its spelling, came to be pronounced the same way as the verb 'ake'. (Compare the similar pair of 'make' and 'match' – where, however, the noun is still pronounced with a 'tch'.)

achievement/exploit/feat (special accomplishment)
An 'achievement' often implies a number of setbacks and difficulties, all of which had to be dealt with and overcome, resulting finally in success. An 'exploit' connotes bravery of some kind, or an act performed with ingenuity or even cunning. The word comes to English from the Latin, via French, meaning 'something unfolded', almost so that one sees it as a flowering or blooming, which can be looked back on and admired. A 'feat' implies the carrying out of something difficult, usually a single act of some kind, as a 'feat' of showmanship or of strength. It's a word not frequently used in English, no doubt because of the rather ludicrous image conveyed by such a phrase as 'Walk in space – astronaut's great feat'. In the original Latin it means, rather prosaically, 'something done'.

acid/alkali (corrosive chemical substance)
Chemically, the two are opposites, as shown by litmus paper, which is turned red by an 'acid' and blue by an 'alkali'. Since they are chemically opposites, the one therefore neutralises the other, which is why a primitive way of reducing the irritation of an insect bite ('acid') is to put washing soda on it ('alkali'). In a complementary way, too, an 'acid' reacts chemically with an 'alkali' to form a salt. The first known 'acid' was vinegar. Chemically (again), the definition of an 'acid' is a substance which in solution in an ionising solvent (usually water) gives rise to hydrogen ions. An 'alkali' is a base – today the more common word in chemistry – that is soluble in water, when it forms a caustic or corrosive solution, as caustic soda (sodium hydroxide) or ammonia. The word, like a surprising number of words starting 'al-' (alcohol, algebra, alcove) is Arabic, and means 'the calcined ashes': 'alkalis' were formerly obtained from wood and bone ashes.

acquittal/exoneration/absolution (freeing from blame)
An 'acquittal' is a release from a particular accusation. The word has a legal ring to it, and in law it actually means a setting free not only from the guilt of an offence but also from the suspicion of an offence. (Someone who has been officially acquitted of a criminal offence may plead *autrefois acquit* or 'formerly acquitted' if subsequently charged with an offence that is legally the same.) An 'exoneration' is a clearing from the blame of an offence – even when the person concerned has actually admitted to the act. The word is of Latin origin, meaning 'disburdened'. An 'absolution' has something of a religious overtone: the formal act of a priest pronouncing the forgiveness of sins to those who are penitent and confess them. Of the three words here, however, 'absolution' is the most general in meaning.

Act/Bill (type of parliamentary law)
An 'Act', in Parliament, is properly a 'Bill' that has been passed by both the House of Commons and the House of Lords and assented to by the Queen. A 'Bill' is a draft 'Act' of Parliament which can be presented to either House, either as a Public 'Bill' (the majority), which involves measures relating to public policy, or as a Private 'Bill', which relates to matters of individual, corporate or local interest. (The latter is not the same as a Private Member's 'Bill', which is a Public 'Bill' introduced by a private member, that is, an MP who is not a minister.) A 'Bill' is passed by three readings in the House in which it was presented, and is then sent to the other House. When it has passed through these stages and received the Queen's formal assent, it becomes an 'Act' – in legal vocabulary, a statute. However, under the provisions of the Parliament 'Acts' 1911 and 1949, a 'Bill' passed by the House of Commons may receive the royal assent and become an 'Act' without the agreement of the Lords.

addenda see **supplement**

adder see **viper**

admission see **confession**

advice note/delivery note (document indicating that goods are on their way)
An 'advice note' is sent by the supplier to the customer before the invoice (see **account**). It is sometimes sent in advance of the goods, or alternatively together with them. A 'delivery note' is similar, but it always accompanies the goods and is often in duplicate, the recipient signing one copy and returning the other. The signed copy is then taken by the deliverer back to the vendor as evidence that the goods have been delivered.

aerodrome/airport/airfield (place where aeroplanes take off, land, and are housed and serviced)
An 'aerodrome' is a general word for an 'airfield' that is usually a smallish, civil and private one. An 'airport' is a large 'aerodrome', especially one for public passengers, and often of international status, with several large buildings. 'Airport' is very much a twentieth-century word, arising on an analogy with a sea **port**. An 'airfield' is much more than just a field, of course. The word particularly applies to service (RAF) air bases. The term gained popularity after the Second World War. Churchill, in his *The*

9

Second World War, wrote, 'For "aerodrome" either "airfield" or "airport" [should be used]', adding, 'the expression "airdrome" should not be used by us'. So far, it has not been.

aerospace see **airspace**

African elephant/Indian elephant
(species of elephant)
These are two vintage distinguishables, eminently suitable for quizzes and general knowledge contests. 'The African elephant is distinguished from the Asian elephant by its larger ears and flatter forehead', says *Everyman's Encyclopaedia*. Probably the ears are the obvious feature: the 'African elephant's' ears come right down over its shoulders, while the ears of the 'Indian elephant' are strikingly small by comparison. The 'African elephant'

note ears

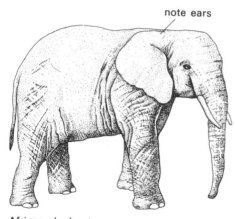

African elephant

Indian elephant

is also in fact rather a darker grey, and inclined to be fiercer. It is also rarer than its Asiatic cousin. A further, delicate distinction is that the 'African elephant' has two sensitive 'finger-tips' at the end of its trunk, whereas the 'Indian elephant' has only one.

airfield see **aerodrome**

airport see **aerodrome**

airspace/aerospace (space in which aircraft fly)
The two terms are confusingly similar. 'Airspace' is the territorial air – the equivalent of territorial waters – that lies above a country and that is within its jurisdiction. One thus has 'violation of "airspace"' when an aircraft of one country flies through the air over another country who will not permit such an incursion for political or strategic reasons. 'Aerospace' is the umbrella term for the region of flight of aircraft *and* spacecraft, that is, flight in the atmosphere and outer space. More commonly the word is used of the technology of such aviation. The expression is American in origin, although Britain uses it in this sense and indeed had a Minister for 'Aerospace' in the Conservative government of 1970–4.

ale/bitter/mild/stout/lager (type of beer)
The word 'ale' is now a historic one for beer except as used commercially or as a trade name, such as India Pale Ale ('IPA'), a pale or light beer originally brewed for export to India. 'Mild' and 'bitter' have names accurately reflecting their respective tastes: 'mild' beer is not strongly flavoured with hops, 'bitter' is. ('Mild and bitter' is a mixture of the two, which rather seems to negate the point of the flavouring.) 'Stout' is a strong, dark beer with roasted malt or barley, while 'lager' is 'continental beer', a light kind of beer which properly is kept in a cold store (German *Lager*, 'store') for some months to mature and then drunk chilled. All beers have long been a staple drink in England, with 'stout' something of a connoisseur's beverage (Guinness is a well-known brand of it), and 'lager' increasing in popularity from the 1970s.

alkali see **acid**

allegiance see **loyalty**

alligator see **crocodile**

alternating current/direct current (type
of electric current)
'Alternating current' (AC) is the one most
commonly found in the home and in commercial use. The voltage 'alternates', that is,
the flow reaches a maximum in one direction
then decreases and reverses until it reaches a
maximum in the opposite direction. This
cycle is repeated continuously. 'Direct
current' (DC) has a flow that does not
change direction. This is the current
produced in batteries and fuel cells. It lost
out commercially to AC in the 1880s because it cannot be transmitted over long
distances at a high voltage and then trans-
formed economically at a low voltage. DC
made something of a comeback in the 1960s
and is sometimes used today in conjunction
with predominantly AC systems. (In 'underground' or 'hippie' jargon 'AC/DC' means
'bisexual', the reference being to an electric
appliance that can operate on both types.)

alto see **treble**

amplifier see **loudspeaker**

amps see **volts**

amulet see **charm**

anger/fury/rage/indignation (strong
sense of annoyance)
These are specialised types of temper.
'Anger' often involves a strong feeling of
revenge for a wrongdoing, and may be suppressed or suddenly expressed. 'Fury' is
great 'rage' – which itself is violent 'anger'.
This leaves 'indignation', which usually implies a moral or 'proper' 'anger', especially
when directed against something unworthy
or outrageous.

angle/tangent (point where one line meets
another or leaves it)
An 'angle' is a space between two meeting
(straight) lines. A 'tangent' is a line that
meets a curved one at a point and has the
same direction at this point, so touches it.
Both words are used figuratively, as the

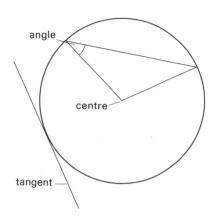

'angle' or viewpoint from which something
is considered, or a speaker or writer who
goes off at a 'tangent' – suddenly diverges
from the matter in hand. (In this latter
phrase, the line is seen as leaving the curve,
not meeting it.) See the illustration for the
literal terms.

anorak/parka (warm weatherproof jacket
with a hood)
The 'anorak' originated in the Arctic as a
Greenland Eskimo word for the skin or cloth
hooded jacket worn in the icy polar regions.
It is now the word for a similar jacket, often
a blue or green quilted one, used for everyday wear as an outdoor coat. A 'parka' is
similar, but tends to be used for specific
purposes such as mountaineering. It, too, is
an Eskimo word in origin, but from much
further east, from the Aleutian Islands, off
the south-west coast of Alaska. The garment
is in fact more of a thick smock, slipping over
the head, than the 'anorak', which usually
has a front fastening, as a zip. Genuine
Eskimo 'parkas' are much longer, too, reach-
ing to the thighs or even knees. Many so-
called 'parkas' today, however, are simply
glorified 'anoraks', although they usually
have a fur-lined or fur-fringed hood and thus
resemble the Eskimo original, which is fully
lined with caribou, seal or other fur.
(Eskimo women wear 'parkas' that have an
extra hood in which a small child can be
wrapped.)

antiseptic see **disinfectant**

anxiety see **apprehension**

apostle/disciple (follower of Christ)
'Apostle' is the word used in the Gospels, and in subsequent writings, to refer specifically to the twelve chief 'disciples' chosen by Christ: Peter, Andrew, James, John, Philip, Bartholomew, Thomas, Matthew, James the Less, Thaddaeus, Simon and Judas Iscariot. (After the suicide of Judas, Matthias was voted in to replace him.) Traditionally, too, Paul and Barnabas are regarded as 'apostles', since they, together with the twelve 'disciples', fulfilled the technical requirement for bearing the title: they had 'seen the Lord'. The word actually derives from the Greek for 'one sent', 'ambassador'. The term 'disciple' is synonymous with 'apostle' in many ways – all the above were both 'disciples' and 'apostles' – but the word is used less specifically to apply to any follower of Christ, whether he had actually seen Him or not. The word means simply 'learner', 'pupil'.

apothecary see **chemist**

appendix see **supplement**

appoggiatura/acciaccatura (type of musical grace-note)
Two admittedly rather specialised words, but which are pure music to look at, to say ('ap-poj-yat-*oo*-ra', 'atch-yac-cat-*oo*-ra' – Italian style), and of course to hear played professionally. An 'appoggiatura' is a grace-note that normally takes half the time value as the note on which it leans (Italian *appoggiare*, 'to lean'), although it steals the emphasis of this main note, which follows gently like the resolution of a discord, as it often is. An 'acciaccatura' is a grace-note

appoggiatura

acciaccatura

that in theory is timeless, and so squeezed in as quickly as possible before the main note is played – or even played at the same time as the main note, then immediately released. (The origin here is Italian *acciaccare*, 'to crush'; the note is sometimes called a 'crush-note', which is not anything like as evocative.)

apprehension/anxiety (feeling of concern)
'Apprehension' usually involves a greater or lesser degree of fear or uneasiness, with at the same time an implicit hope that what may come will not after all turn out for the worst, as a feeling of 'apprehension' when opening a reply to one's letter to the tax inspector. (With 'neat' fear one almost always expects the worst, but 'apprehension' may mean that one will get away with it.) 'Anxiety' suggests a rather lengthy state of 'apprehension', possible at not such a keen level. The word is actually related to 'anger'.

apricot see **peach**

apron/pinafore (garment worn in front of the body to protect the clothes)
The 'apron' is essentially the garment of the housewife and mother – to whose 'apron'-strings spoilt children or hen-pecked husband can be tied. The word is like 'adder', that is, it should be 'a napron' rather an 'an apron'. (It derives from Old French *naperon*, meaning 'small table-cloth'. For more about 'adder', the word and the beast, see **viper**.) A 'pinafore' or 'pinny' is similar, but is usually worn by a young child – of either sex – to protect its clothes, as when eating or messily playing. More decoratively, it can be worn as a fashionable garment by girls or women over a dress. Compare, in this respect, a 'pinafore' dress, which is one without a collar and sleeves worn over a blouse or jumper. 'Pinafores' were originally 'pinned afore', i.e. pinned on to the front of the dress.

aqueduct/viaduct (type of bridge, often with a series of arches)
An 'aqueduct' is for water only. The word particularly applies to Roman bridges of this type, some of which still exist and are still used for carrying water, as the fine one at Segovia, Spain. A 'viaduct' is designed to

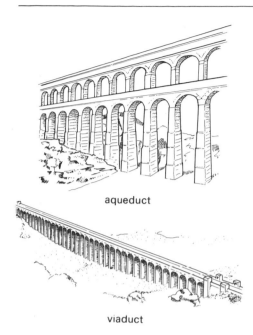

aqueduct

viaduct

carry a road or railway over a ravine or valley. Holborn 'Viaduct' in London, about a quarter of a mile long, was built in 1867–9 over the valley of the 'Hole Bourne', or part of the River Fleet, to connect Holborn Circus with Newgate Street.

arbour/bower (shady or private retreat)
An 'arbour' has its sides and roof formed mainly by trees or climbing plants, as a type of natural summer-house. The word actually comes from Old French *erbe*, 'herb' (as modern French *herbe*, 'grass'), but the initial 'e-' became 'a-' by association with Latin *arbor*, 'tree'. A 'bower' is simply a place with closed-in foliage, whether natural, as an 'arbour', or man-made, as a summer-house. It would be agreeable if the word were related to 'bough' or 'flower', but it actually derives from a Germanic word meaning 'dwelling-place'. The street and section of New York known as The Bowery gets its name not from 'bower' but from the Dutch word for 'farm', *bouwerie*, to which the street originally led. (The farm was owned by the Governor, Peter Stuyvesant.)

archdeacon see **dean**

aristocrat see **autocrat**

arrogance see **vanity**

artery see **vein**

arthritis see **rheumatism**

Asdic see **radar**

ashes see **cinders**

asphalt see **tar**

ass see **donkey**

assassin see **murderer**

assault see **attack**

astrology see **astronomy**

astronomy/astrology (study of the stars)
'Astronomy' is the word for the scientific study of the stars in particular and celestial bodies generally. 'Astrology', which has been enjoying something of a cult revival in western society from the 1970s, is the science or art – considered by many to be no science or art at all – of judging the occult influence of the stars and planets on the lives of humans. In ancient times 'astrology' embraced what is now called 'astronomy', and was divided into natural 'astrology', which consisted in calculating the movements of the heavens, and judicial 'astrology', which studied, as 'astrology' does today, the supposed influence of the stars on human life and destiny. It is perhaps rather surprising that 'astronomy', not 'astrology', has come to be the word used for the scientific study: there are far more '-ologies' in science than '-onomies'. The 'astro-' element in each, of course, means 'star'.

atomic bomb/hydrogen bomb (type of thermonuclear bomb)
The 'atomic bomb', or atom bomb, has a force that comes from nuclear fission, e.g. uranium (235) or plutonium, which when combined form an assembly which starts an uncontrolled chain reaction. Its first – and most inglorious – military use was when dropped on Hiroshima after the Second World War (6 August 1945). The 'hydrogen bomb' derives its power from fusion. It is a

13

fission, or atomic, bomb surrounded by a layer of hydrogenous material. The temperature resulting from the explosion of the fission bomb causes the fusion of the hydrogen nuclei to form helium nuclei. It is many more times more powerful than the 'atomic bomb', and as yet has never (D.G.) been used in warfare. It has, however, been tested by the major powers.

atomic number/atomic weight (unit of measurement of a chemical element)
The 'atomic number' is the number of protons in the nucleus of an atom of a given element, for example for oxygen it is 8, for hydrogen 1, for gold 79, for radium 88. The 'atomic weight' is the average weight of the atoms of a given specimen of an element measured in atomic mass units, one of which approximately equals 1.7×10^{-24} grammes. For oxygen the atomic weight is thus 15.9994, for hydrogen 1.0079, and for uranium, the heaviest naturally occurring element, 238.029. Today the preferred term for 'atomic weight' is 'relative atomic mass', as since 1961 the carbon-12 atom has been the usual basis of calculations, not the oxygen-16 atom.

atomic weight see **atomic number**

attack/assault (act of force, armed or unarmed)
An 'attack' is a generally forceful act directed against somebody or something, whether physical or verbal (which in a sense could be even more damaging). An 'assault' is an 'attack' that is specifically hostile, whether literally or figuratively. Legally an 'assault' is 'an attempt or offer to beat another, without touching him' – which means that ' "assault" and battery' involves the actual 'beating'.

attic/loft/garret (small room at the top of a house)
An 'attic' is usually up in the roof of a house, where it is a small room with a skylight. Where it exists, it is often used as a boxroom or 'junk room', unless enterprisingly converted into an extra bedroom or study or 'pad'. (An 'attic' under a mansard roof is itself called a mansard – a mansard roof being one that has two slopes, the lower

steeper than the upper.) A 'loft' can be an alternative word for an 'attic' – in America it may mean an upper room in general, or even a whole storey – but normally is the word for the space or area approached by a trap-door that lies directly under the roof and often containing the main water tank and various other plumbing or heating arrangements. It, too, can frequently be converted into a proper room, and at the least insulated to preserve the heat in the rooms below it. A 'garret' is a less common word for a rather mean or wretched 'attic', traditionally or romantically sometimes regarded as a place for impoverished painters and poets. Thomas Chatterton, the young 'Gothic' poet of the eighteenth century, indeed led such a life – and tragically poisoned himself in a Holborn 'garret' when still only seventeen.

attorney see **lawyer**

auction bridge see **contract bridge**

audience see **audition**

audition/audience (important interview)
An 'audition' is a trial arranged for a would-be performer by an impresario or agent. An 'audience' is an interview granted by a monarch or other high personage to an individual. Both words are literally a 'hearing', as 'audible' and the more common sort of 'audience' that listens to a performance.

autocrat/plutocrat/bureaucrat/aristocrat (kind of ruler or person in authority)
An 'autocrat' is an absolute ruler, such as a monarch who holds and exercises powers of government by an inherent right, with no restrictions. A 'plutocrat' is a member of the wealthy ruling class (if there is one). A 'bureaucrat' is one of the officials who rule, especially a remote civil servant or minister, and one who operates by a fixed routine rather than by a rational or considered policy. An 'aristocrat' is a member of the nobility or of the upper classes, especially someone who is distinguished by his genteel manners or general 'superiority' in habits, dress, speech and the like. The four 'crats' (the element is Greek for 'power', 'rule') have names that denote their distinguishing characteristics, respectively 'on one's own', 'wealth', 'office', and 'best'.

autogyro see **helicopter**

automatic see **pistol**

BA see **BOAC**

baboon see **gorilla**

BAC see **BOAC**

back/rear (location of something behind
something else)
'Back' has the implied opposite 'front', and
often indicates a position both behind something and outside it, as a small garden at the
'back' of a house (and a tiny lawn at the
front). 'Rear' usually refers to the final or
end section of something, as the 'rear' of a
train or a 'rearguard' bringing up the 'rear'
of an armed force (as the opposite of the
vanguard).

balcony/gallery/circle/dress circle
(section of the auditorium of a theatre
situated above the stalls, that is, above
floor level)
Going upwards, the 'circle' is a curved section of seats on the first or a higher floor,
which may be divided into two such sections, the lower being called the 'dress circle'
(in which evening dress was once *de rigueur*)
and the higher the 'upper circle'. Above the
'circle' comes the 'balcony', which is also
effectively – and may even be called – the
'upper circle'. In a cinema the 'balcony' is a
fairly general word for any seats upstairs.
Highest of all is the 'gallery', traditionally
the cheapest and most vociferous section of
the audience. However, the highest tier may
be called the 'balcony', not the 'gallery',
especially in a smaller theatre, and in the

USA the 'balcony' turns out to be what in a
British theatre would be the 'dress circle'.
Cinemas, too, may settle for a 'circle' of
some kind instead of a 'balcony'. The terms
are thus entertainingly imprecise and vari-
able. See the illustration for a visual arrangement.

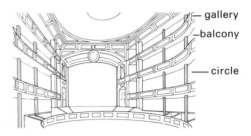

balcony/verandah (platform in front of a
house on which one can walk or sit)
A 'balcony' is almost always a suspended
platform with railings or a parapet outside
an upper floor window. A 'verandah' (or
veranda) is an open portico or gallery at the
front of a house or along the side with a roof
supported on pillars. The word is of Hindi
origin: the structure is a special feature of
houses in India.

ballad/ballade (kind of narrative poem or
song)
There is a technical difference between these
two very similar terms, and this is in the
verse form. A 'ballad' has stanzas or verses of
four lines, of alternating four-feet and three-
feet length, and with only the second and
fourth lines rhyming. The first stanza of
Charles Causley's literary (and modern)
'ballad' 'Mother, Get Up, Unbar the Door'
illustrates this:

> Mother, get up, unbar the door,
> Throw wide the window-pane,
> I see a man stand all covered in sand
> Outside in Vicarage Lane.

A 'ballade', by distinction, usually has three
stanzas of eight lines, with the same three or
four rhymes throughout, and ending with an
envoi of four lines, the whole rhyme scheme
thus being ABABBCBC BCBC. Further-
more, the last line of the first stanza serves as

a refrain repeated in the last line of each stanza and of the *envoi*. Thus a somewhat complex form! The 'ballade' was revived with a certain degree of success in modern times by G. K. Chesterton and others. To illustrate the rhyme-scheme, here is a stanza from his *A Ballade of an Anti-Puritan*:

> They spoke of progress spiring round,
>   Of Light and Mrs. Humphry Ward—
> It is not true to say I frowned,
>   Or ran about the room and roared;
>   I might have simply sat and snored—
> I rose politely in the club
>   And said, 'I feel a little bored;
>   Will some one take me to a pub?'

ballade see **ballad**

ban/bar (prohibition or restriction)
A 'ban' is a formal or authoritative prohibition, or one made by public opinion. A 'bar' is a kind of temporary 'ban', as an obstruction or objection. Of course, both a 'ban' and a 'bar' can be lifted, but one almost expects a 'bar' to be. Legally, a 'bar' is an objection which nullifies an action or claim, or a stoppage of an alleged right of action.

banjo see **guitar**

bank card see **credit card**

bankruptcy see **insolvency**

banquet see **feast**

bar see **ban**

baritone see **tenor**

baron/baronet (one of lowest ranks of the nobility)
A 'baron' in Britain holds a title that is either hereditary or, as laid down by the Life Peerages Act of 1958, for life only. 'Barons' are known as 'Lord X', where X is either a surname, often the title-holder's own, or the name of a place historically linked with his family. A 'baronet' is a member of the lowest hereditary British order, and ranks below a 'baron'. The wives of both – in the case of a 'baron', the baroness, therefore – are called 'Lady X', the X being the same as their husband's name. 'Barons' exist or existed also on the European continent, although the title in both France and Germany is given only by courtesy. The word originally meant simply 'man': compare modern Spanish *varón*, meaning 'male', 'man'. For some more elevated noble ranks see **duke** and **marquis** and also, for a more general view of the nobility, **lord**.

baronet see **baron**

barrel-organ/hurdy-gurdy (musical instrument played by turning its handle)
The two names have a popular and a specific meaning. The 'barrel-organ', to the man in the street (literally), is, or was, the street piano played in the time-honoured way by an Italian with a pet monkey. (It largely disappeared after 1922 when Mussolini came to power and recalled all Italians engaged in street music.) This same instrument was also known as a 'hurdy-gurdy', which is also, however, the name of quite a different instrument: a sort of violin with a rosined wheel acting as a circular bow. This sounded two drone strings by being turned with the right hand, while the left hand played piano-type keys. Meanwhile the 'barrel-organ' proper was an instrument with a pin-studded cylinder (or barrel) turned by a handle, and a mechanism for opening pipes or striking metal tongues. As such it was not a street instrument but one originally used in churches in the late eighteenth and early nineteenth centuries. The 'barrel-organ' of the street piano kind had a barrel, it is true, but was certainly not an organ in the accepted sense of the word.

barrister see **lawyer**

basin see **bowl**

basketball see **netball**

battalion see **corps**

battle see **war**

bay/gulf/bight/inlet/cove (bow-like expanse of water)
A 'bay', the most common word, does not necessarily have to be landlocked, i.e.

approached by a strait (see **sound**). It can have quite a shallow curve, as the 'Bay' of Biscay. 'Gulf' implies a deeper recess, however, with a narrower width of entrance. Most 'gulfs' are fairly large or important in some way, as the 'Gulf' of Mexico which gave its name to the 'Gulf' Stream. A 'bight' is a less common word for a curve or recess of the coast or a river bank. German 'Bight', a sea area for shipping forecast purposes, is the stretch of sea off the north-west coast of Germany. An 'inlet' is much smaller: a small arm of the sea, almost a creek. A 'cove', which tends to have pleasant seaside or smuggling associations, is a small 'bay' or recess in the shoreline of the sea, a lake, or a river, especially a sheltered one. One might expect it to be related to 'cave' or 'cover', but it actually comes from an Old English word *cofa* meaning 'chamber'.

bazaar see **fête**

BEA see **BOAC**

beach see **shore**

beginning/start (initial stage or part of something)
'Beginning' is a general word, as the 'beginning' of the month (the first few days of it) or the 'beginning' of a programme (the opening moments of it). 'Start' implies the distinct, perhaps sudden, first phase or opening action of something, as the 'start' of a race (the important moment when the participants suddenly begin to move) or the 'start' of a new career (the first part of a milestone in one's life). 'Start' is one of the few common words beginning with 'st-' that does *not* have something to do with standing still – as these last two words and others such as 'state', 'stick', 'stop' and 'stubborn'.

belly see **stomach**

belt/zone (region with special characteristics)
A 'belt' is a strip or band of land or territory, as a green 'belt' that encircles a city to prevent sprawling development, or a commuter 'belt' or dormitory 'belt' further out from a city, where those who work in the city live and from which they travel daily. The word

is a fairly informal one, and the actual idea of 'strip' may be rather vague. It is quite vague in 'zone', which is the formal word for a region of any shape – although often circular. Examples might be a danger 'zone', a smokeless 'zone', the British 'zone' in Berlin, or the so-called Torrid 'Zone', between the Tropics of Cancer and Capricorn. However, 'zone' actually derives from the Greek word for 'belt' or 'girdle', so the 'strip' concept is basically there. 'Zone', incidentally, is not related to 'zodiac', even though the latter is a 'heavenly belt'.

bias see **prejudice**

bight see **bay**

bill see **account**

Bill see **Act**

billiards/snooker/pool (game of 'poking balls about a smooth table to score by sending them into small pockets', J. B. Pick, *The Phoenix Dictionary of Games*, Phoenix House, 1954)
'Billiards' is the game with three balls: a red, a white, and a spot-white (white ball with a spot on), with each player aiming to strike his own ball (white or spot-white) to hit the red and his opponent's and, preferably, pocket the red in so doing. 'Snooker' has all the coloured balls: fifteen red (scoring one each), one each of yellow (scoring two), green (three), brown (four), blue (five), pink (six) and black (seven) and one white ball, the latter used as a cue ball by the players in turn. A player is 'snookered' – a term that has come to be used figuratively in the sense 'stymied' (the golfing equivalent), 'frustrated' – when a ball he is not 'on' lies between the ball he is aiming at and his cue ball. 'Pool' exists in two varieties, English and American. 'English pool' is played by two to ten players on a billiard table, each player having a cue ball that is a different colour to those of his opponents. The object of the game is to pocket the ball aimed at and so take a 'life' – and also to avoid being pocketed. The name of the game derives from the fact that the players pay an agreed amount into a pool, which is taken by the last player to remain in the game. 'American

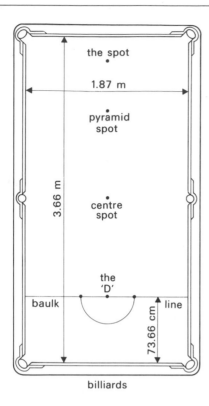

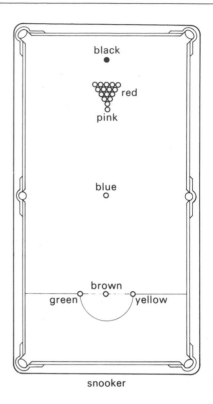

billiards   snooker

pool', or 'pocket billiards', diverged in the nineteenth century from English 'billiards' to become a game in which fifteen numbered and coloured balls are potted in turn, with one point scored for each pot and the game finishing when an agreed total, usually 150, has been reached. (Initially the balls are placed in a triangle, as in 'snooker'.)

billow/breaker/roller (wave at sea)
A 'billow' is a great, surging wave – and poetically the sea itself. The word is not related to 'bellow' or 'pillow' but is of Scandinavian origin. A 'breaker' is an ocean wave with a breaking crest – this is the wave used for surfing. A 'roller' is a long, swelling wave that 'rolls' in towards the coast.

bison see **buffalo**

bitter see **ale**

bitters see **vermouth**

bitumen see **tar**

black humour/sick humour (type of 'warped' humour)
'Black humour' aims to present tragedy or bitter reality in comic terms. It often treats sad or macabre subjects (death, divorce, serious illness, murder) in this way. Classic examples of black comedies in the twentieth century are Edward Albee's *Who's Afraid of Virginia Woolf?* (1962, film version 1966), dealing with the intense 'love-hate' relationships of a middle-aged, alcoholic couple, with few holds barred, and the plays of Joe Orton such as *Entertaining Mr Sloane* (1964) and *Loot* (1966) which involve, among other things, a funeral, murder, blackmail and homosexual eroticism. 'Sick humour' also deals in the macabre and in human misfortunes, but at a less intense level and with more of a pathological 'twist'. It is most common in the form of the 'sick joke', the most original of which can usually be savoured in the 'raconteurs' corner' of a pub on a Friday or Saturday night. Cynics – or sober realists – see both phenomena as symbolic of the ever-increasing moral dis-

orientation and decadence of western society in the twentieth century.

black magic/white magic (type of supernatural power)
'Black magic' is evil magic, evoking devils. It involves the use – or abuse – of supernatural powers for selfish ends, as in sorcery, necromancy (making predictions by communicating with the dead) and the raising of the dead generally. 'White magic' is good magic, evoking angels, and involves the selfless use of supernatural powers to promote the good of others. (There is also natural magic, which evokes no personal spirit.) So, at any rate, say the experts on these things. But 'black magic' is the kind most down-to-earth mortals will have heard of and been attracted to, if only because of brand-name associations.

Blackshirts/Brownshirts (members of militant organisation)
The 'Blackshirts' were the Italian Fascists. Neo-Fascists and other offshoots of this organisation also frequently wear a black shirt as part of their uniform. In Britain the 'Blackshirts' of Oswald Mosley's British Union of Fascists were notorious in the 1930s. The 'Brownshirts' were Hitler's Stormtroopers, otherwise the SA. The term is sometimes used loosely of any Nazis.

blancmange see **jelly**

blast-off see **lift-off**

blink see **wink**

blizzard see **storm**

bloater see **herring**

Blue Book see **White Paper**

BOAC/BEA/BAC/BA (aircraft or airway company)
'BOAC', the British Overseas Airways Corporation, was founded in 1939. In 1972 it merged (formally in 1974) with 'BEA', British European Airways, founded in 1946, to form 'BA', British Airways. 'BAC', the British Aircraft Corporation, was set up in 1960, as a merger of the aircraft and guided weapons interests of the Bristol Aeroplane Company (20 per cent), English Electric (40 per cent) and Vickers (40 per cent). It has produced many important names in the aerospace industry, including the Viscount, Vanguard, VC10, One-Eleven and, best known of all, the Concorde, which is now flown jointly by 'BA' and Air France. Disconcertingly, however, 'BA' is also British Aerospace, a nationalised corporation, which was formed in 1976 and acquired the assets of 'BAC' as well as those of Hawker Siddeley and Scottish Aviation. So *it* now produces the Viscount, etc. . . .

boa constrictor see **python**

boar see **pig**

boat/ship (vessel used for travelling on water)
'A "boat" is small, a "ship" is large' is as far as most people are prepared to distinguish. In general true, of course – although one can be more precise. As distinct from a 'boat', a 'ship' is a relatively large sea- or ocean-going vessel, usually over 500 tons in weight. Of sailing vessels, a 'ship' has three or more masts with square rigging. There are two notable exceptions to the 'small-large' distinction. Submarines are officially 'boats' (compare the term 'U-boat' as applied to German submarines in the First World War, itself derived from the German *Unterseeboot*). The other exception relates to the ore-carrying vessels, ore 'boats', that ply on the Great Lakes of the USA. When it comes to methods of propulsion, 'boats' can be propelled by any of the four methods: oars, paddles, sail or power (as steam or engine). 'Ships', on the other hand, are propelled virtually exclusively by sail or power only. 'Boat' is, however, often used loosely to apply to any vessel, especially to a passenger one, as in 'What sort of cabin did you have on the "boat"?' In spite of a certain overlap between different types of 'boat' and 'ship', usage is more or less standardised for many vessels. Thus one has a fishing 'boat', rowing 'boat', motor 'boat', ferry 'boat', paddle 'boat', 'lifeboat', 'houseboat', 'speedboat', 'gunboat', motor torpedo 'boat' (or MTB), 'showboat' and, as a once popular type of aircraft, flying 'boat'. An early form of mail

'boat' was a packet 'boat' – which in fact gave the French word (*paquebot*) that today means 'passenger liner'! Most 'ships' are more specialised in their function, so that one has a 'warship', 'battleship', hospital 'ship', 'lightship', slave 'ship', container 'ship' and, by transference, 'airship' and 'spaceship'. The overlap occurs for sailing 'boats' or 'ships', 'steamboats' or 'ships', passenger 'boats' or 'ships' and, historically, the 'Q-boat' or 'ship', otherwise the mystery 'ship' – a 'warship' disguised as a tramp steamer in the First World War with the aim of decoying German submarines.

boater see **panama**

boating see **sailing**

bog see **marsh**

boogie-woogie see **swing**

boot/shoe (item of outer footwear)
In general, a 'boot' comes above the ankle – well above it for most Americans – and a 'shoe' stops below it. 'Shoe', moreover, is a general word for any variety of footwear, indoor or outdoor, that does not cover the ankle, as slippers, sandals, plimsolls, clogs and brogues. Most 'boots' have a fairly specialised use, either professionally or functionally, as army 'boots', football 'boots' and

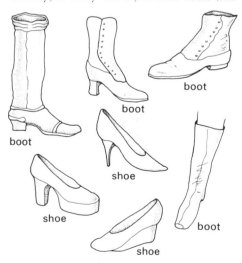

boot

boot

boot

shoe

shoe

shoe

boot

wellington 'boots', or for fashion wear, as 'snakeboots' and kinky 'boots'.

booty see **loot**

bop see **swing**

border/frontier (line or boundary marking the limit of a territory)
A 'border' is close in meaning to a boundary, except that it often includes territory on either side of a boundary, as the 'Border', geographically if loosely so called, between England and Scotland, Northern Ireland and the Irish Republic, and, in America, between the USA and Mexico – hence, in the latter case, 'south of the "border"'. A 'frontier' is similar, but usually implies that the territory beyond the 'border' is different in some way, in terms of geography, politics, language or culture. Perhaps the most familiar is the 'frontier' that is the boundary of a country, with its customs officers, checkpoints and, usually, 'frontier' guards. In the USA, the 'frontier' is that part of the country which forms the 'border' of a settled or inhabited region, so that beyond it lies something of a wilderness or, seen differently, a virgin land. Davy Crockett became internationally known – perhaps more thanks to Disney than to history – as 'king of the wild "frontier"'. He was active on the 'frontier' in western Tennessee in the early nineteenth century.

borstal see **remand home**

bough see **branch**

bower see **arbour**

bowl/basin (round dish for liquids or solids)
A 'bowl' is a deep 'basin', especially one for food, as a breakfast 'bowl' or fruit 'bowl', or for liquid, as a wine-'bowl' or, less palatably, washing-up 'bowl'. It is thus both wide and deep, like the grave envisaged by the girl whose true love had abandoned her for the pleasures of a tavern in the town. A 'basin', by comparison, is more wide than it is deep, as a hand-'basin', slop-'basin', or wash-

'basin'. Sometimes the difference is small, as between a sugar 'basin' and sugar 'bowl', which are virtually interchangeable. The words also have a geographical sense, when a 'bowl', more an American term, is a 'bowl'-shaped region, as the Western Dust 'Bowl', and a 'basin' a land-locked harbour or the area drained by a river and its tributaries, as the Thames 'basin'.

bowling see **bowls**

bowls/skittles/ninepins/bowling (game in which a heavy ball is rolled down a course to strike a target)
'Bowls' (in the USA 'bowling') is the game in which biased or weighted balls ('bowls') are rolled over a smooth green to bring them as near as possible to the jack, a small white ball, or to knock an opponent's bowl out of the way as a tactical manoeuvre. 'Skittles' is a game popular at fairs and fêtes (where it may go under such a name as '"bowling" for a pig'), in which nine wooden pins at the end of an alley are to be bowled down with a wooden (unweighted) ball. 'Ninepins', therefore, is an alternative (mainly British) name for this game, and a version of this went to America some time ago, whence it mysteriously returned as 'tenpins', otherwise tenpin 'bowling' or just 'bowling' – the automated game in which hard rubber balls are bowled down lanes to strike machine-operated pins. But how did nine come back as ten? The explanation is simple: 'ninepins' was declared illegal under American law; a tenth pin was therefore added; tenpins by any count is not 'ninepins'; tenpin 'bowling' evades the law! Tenpin 'bowling' caught on in Britain in a big way in the 1960s, when many alleys or 'bowls' were constructed on former theatre or cinema sites. 'Bowling', it will be noticed, is a general name for all four sports (as well as the term for the special delivery of the ball by a bowler in the game of cricket).

boxer see **bulldog**

bracken see **ferns**

brain see **mind**

brains see **mind**

brains trust/brain trust (group of experts vouchsafing an opinion)
A 'brains trust' is a group of experts or 'brains' who give impromptu answers to questions – not necessarily giving any information, but quite often simply engaged in discussion. The phrase became familiar from the wartime radio *Brains Trust* – a panel of Sir Julian Huxley, Professor C. E. M. Joad and Commander Campbell, under the chairmanship of Donald McCullough – who answered questions put to them by the public. The term was borrowed from the American 'brain trust' of the 1930s, which was a group of experts called in to advise Roosevelt in his first administration. This corresponded to what is now known in Britain as the 'think tank', the nickname for the Central Policy Review Staff initiated in Edward Heath's government (1970–4) and since retained. (The term 'think tank' is also of American origin.)

brain trust see **brains trust**

brambles/briers (collection of thorny or prickly plants or bushes)
'Brambles' are specifically blackberry bushes. (The word is related to 'broom'.) 'Briers' (or briars) normally means the thorny branches of the wild rose from which also hips come.

branch/bough (limb of a tree)
A 'branch' can be any limb of a tree; a 'bough' is one of the main ones, which in turn may have its own 'branches'.

brandy/cognac (type of spirit)
'Brandy' is a spirit distilled from wine or, sometimes, fermented fruit juice (as apple 'brandy', plum 'brandy' or cherry 'brandy'). The word is properly 'brandywine', from Dutch *brandewijn*, 'burnt (i.e. distilled) wine'. 'Cognac' is French 'brandy', usually regarded as the finest of all 'brandies'. Properly it is distilled from the wine of the region around Cognac, a town in western France.

brass/bronze (metal alloy)
'Brass' is a yellow alloy of copper and zinc; 'bronze' is a brown-coloured alloy chiefly of copper and tin, and known from very early

times. The instruments of 'brass' mentioned in the Bible, however, were in all probability made of 'bronze', since it is not known what the exact composition of the metal was.

bravery see **courage**

breaker see **billow**

bridle see **rein**

briers see **brambles**

brigade see **corps**

brim see **rim**

Britain see **England**

British Isles see **England**

brochure/pamphlet (type of booklet or leaflet)
A 'brochure' is normally a commercial publication, for example of a travel agency or a motor dealer. A 'pamphlet' is either a small, unbound discourse on some subject, especially a political or religious one, as a tract or a manifesto, or, loosely, any leaflet, even a single sheet. The word suggests an exotic or erratic spelling of 'leaflet', but it actually comes from *Pamphilet*, which was the popular name of a twelfth-century comic love poem in Latin entitled *Pamphilus, seu de Amore* ('Pamphilus [that is, "love-all"] or about Love'). *Brochure* is French for 'stitching'.

broker see **stockbroker**

bronze see **brass**

broom see **gorse**

Brownshirts see **Blackshirts**

buffalo/bison (ox-like animal)
There are three kinds of 'buffalo': *Bubalis bubalis* of Asia, originally from India, valued as a draught animal, *Syncerus caffer*, or Cape 'buffalo', of South Africa, and *Bison bison*, of North America, and thus the American 'buffalo' – or 'bison' (or wild ox). This is the one that turned William Frederick Cody in-

to 'Buffalo' Bill, the champion 'buffalo' killer of the Plains of Kansas. His total haul was 4,280 in eight months, or around eighteen a day, which must have meant at least one unfortunate 'buffalo' before breakfast as a starter. Seen objectively, the Indian 'buffalo' is a heavy animal with coarse black hair and long, curving horns; the Cape 'buffalo' is less heavy and has horns that are very broad at the base, where they almost meet; the American 'buffalo' (the 'bison') has a humped body and small horns.

buffer/bumper (device for deadening the impact or reducing the force of a blow to a vehicle)
'Buffers' usually come in pairs, especially on railway vehicles or at the end of a track. A 'bumper', in contrast, is found on cars and other road vehicles, where it is designed to reduce damage in a collision. However, in the USA railway 'buffers' are 'bumpers', while 'bumpers' on a car are fenders – a word that can also, however, mean the wings or mudguards of a car or other vehicle.

buffet see **café**

bugle see **cornet**

builder/mason (constructor of houses and buildings)
A 'builder' usually means a master craftsman, especially one contracted to build houses. A 'mason' is a craftsman who works in stone. He does not build buildings, but bits of buildings, i.e. masonry or stonework. It would be logical if the word came from 'mansion' or French *maison*, 'house', but in fact it rather unexpectedly derives from Latin *maccare*, 'to beat', and may, perhaps, be related to 'mattock'.

bull see **ox**

bulldog/boxer/bull-terrier (dog with a bull-like or pugnacious face)
Actually, 'bulldogs' are not so called because they look like bulls but because they were bred for baiting bulls. The breed has come to typify tenacity, determination and courage, characteristics seen also in Winston Churchill, who was popularly likened to the

animal. The original 'boxer' was a dog called Flocki shown in Munich in 1895, the offspring of a bullfighting terrier bitch and a 'bulldog' called Tom. Today the breed is taller and more slender than the 'bulldog', but like it a good guard and an affectionate companion. (Why 'boxer'? Does it look like one? The name may come from the dog's manner of 'boxing' with its forepaws when it begins to fight.) A 'boxer' was thus a cross-breed, and so is a 'bull-terrier', which is a cross between a 'bulldog' and a terrier, and famous as the original 'Bill Sykes tyke' of pits and rat haunts. It is characteristically an all-white dog, and of a somewhat brutal-ised appearance. There are also so called 'coloured' 'bull-terriers' – ones with brindle or black predominant.

bullock see **ox**

bull-terrier see **bulldog**

bumper see **buffer**

bun/roll/scone (small bread or cake)
A 'bun' is usually soft, round, and sweet, and often contains currants. A number of varieties exist, as an iced 'bun', with icing on top, Bath 'bun', spiced, with currants inside and iced, Chelsea 'bun', rolled with cur-rants, and the like. A 'roll' can be round or long – as a bridge 'roll', which is smallish and soft – and is customarily served with the soup or starters at lunch or dinner, when it is eaten with or without butter and, in polite society, torn asunder with the fingers rather than neatly cut with a knife. The 'scone', which has Scottish associations, if only through the Stone of Scone – which is not a type of rock-cake or edible at all, but a coronation stone from Scone, near Perth – is a cake of barley-meal or oatmeal or wheat-flour, with or without currants, traditionally baked on a griddle and eaten with a little butter and, although somewhat gilding the lily, sometimes a little jam. Scots tend to say the word to rhyme with 'con', although south of the border it often rhymes with 'cone', a pronunciation still regarded in some circles as 'non-U'.

burberry see **raincoat**

burden see **load**

bureaucrat see **autocrat**

burglary see **theft**

burlesque see **parody**

burrow see **den**

business see **occupation**

bust see **sculpture**

butter/margarine (yellow, creamy foodstuff used in cooking and as a spread)
Advertisers do their best to assure us that there is only a minimal difference between 'margarine' and 'butter' ('Fancy calling Stroke margarine!'). Some 'margarines' do in fact contain a small percentage of real 'butter', although 'margarine' is legally not 'butter' at all, but a 'butter' substitute. The chief difference between the two is not in their appearance or even use, but in their content: 'butter' is made from the fat of an animal's milk, usually a cow's, when this milk, or its cream, is churned. 'Margarine' is made from edible vegetable oils and animal fats in cultured skimmed milk. Furthermore, while 'margarine' may con-tain preservatives, it is illegal for any pre-servatives to be used in 'butter'. Can there really be anything in common between 'marge' and the attractive girl's name Margaret? The answer is yes: they both basically mean 'pearl'. It was originally wrongly thought that all oils and fats, in-cluding the ones used to make 'margarine', contained so called 'margaric acid', which is pearl-white in colour. In many ways, and especially nutritionally, since by law it is now compulsorily fortified with vitamins A and D, 'margarine' today is a very worthy substitute for 'butter', and so called 'soft' 'margarine', which is cholesterol-free, has found favour in many households. (Whether the 'g' in the word is pronounced 'soft', as in 'tangerine', or 'hard', as in 'marguerite', is a matter of taste, as the substance itself is.)

buttercup/celandine (plant with yellow flowers found in fields and woods)
The 'buttercup' is a member of the genus *Ranunculus*, which also includes anemones and marsh marigolds. It has five green

sepals (which form the calyx, or envelope of the flower) and five fullish yellow petals. The 'celandine' is properly a member of the poppy family, although the lesser 'celandine' is a member of the 'buttercup' family. It has three sepals and usually eight petals and is often found near water, which the 'buttercup' does not necessarily prefer. The petals of the lesser 'celandine', too, are noticeably slimmer than those of the 'buttercup'.

butterfly/moth (flying insect with large showy wings)
The difference is this: 'butterflies' are usually day-flying creatures and brightly coloured with knobbed or club-shaped antennae ('feelers'), and hold their wings vertically when at rest. 'Moths' are normally nocturnal and dull-coloured, with spindle-shaped, threadlike or comblike antennae, and hold their wings (with one or two exceptions) flat when at rest. On closer examination, moreover, most 'moths' will be found to have a connecting hook for fastening their wings together, which 'butterflies' do not have. The type of 'butterfly' known as skippers are entomologically halfway between the two.

note antennae

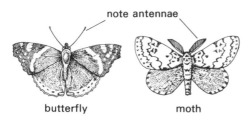

butterfly   moth

by-pass/ring road (road avoiding a town or its centre)
A 'by-pass' is a main road that 'passes by' a town or other congested area and provides an alternative route for through traffic. A 'by-pass' that goes right round a town (with the appropriate turn-offs to a motorway or other main route) is called a 'ring road'.

cabaret see **musical**

cabinet-maker see **carpenter**

café/buffet/cafeteria (public place for meals, snacks and refreshments)
The origin of the 'café' is in the coffee-houses of France (French *café* meaning 'coffee', and a word familiar as part of the name of a well-known instant variety). With such a fine gastronomic pedigree – French is the language of gourmets *par excellence* – it is perhaps surprising that the word has descended to mean little more than just an inexpensive snack-bar, a 'caff', in fact. There are some restaurants of note, however, that preserve the classy tone of the word, as the long established 'Café' Royal in London. A 'buffet' – the word is also French in origin, literally meaning 'stool', but now 'sideboard' – is also found at both ends of the social scale, as a 'buffet' supper, where guests serve themselves from groaning tables or even sideboards, or a station 'buffet', which is really a kind of cosmopolitan, but typically British, 'café'. (A 'buffet' car on a train serves snacks, as distinct from a dining car, which is a rail-running restaurant.) A 'cafeteria', in essence, is a 'café' where customers serve themselves by fetching their food and drink from a counter and carrying it to a table. The word is rather loosely used, though, and some 'cafeterias' offer excellent waitress service and no self-service at all. The word is American-Spanish for 'coffee-shop'.

cafeteria see **café**

calf/heifer (young cow)
A 'calf' is the word for the young of a cow, male or female, in its first year. A 'heifer' is a young cow in general, or in particular one that has not had more than one 'calf'. For young horse words see **colt**.

camouflage see **disguise**

china/pottery/porcelain (type of earthenware)
'China' was a term used originally to distinguish 'porcelain' from China from European 'pottery'. Subsequently the word came to apply to both without distinction. 'Pottery' is literally anything made out of clay by a potter on a wheel – especially, of course, a pot – but the word is properly used for all ware that is opaque, whereas 'porcelain', now regarded as the 'true' 'china' Worcester, Wedgwood, and the like, is translucent. Both 'pottery' and 'porcelain' are further divided by experts into, respectively, earthenware (fired at a temperature below 1200 degrees C) and stoneware (above 1200 degrees C) for 'pottery', and hard-paste and soft-paste 'porcelain' – where the 'hard' and 'soft' refer not to the degree of 'hardness' and 'softness' of the clay but to the degree of firing necessary in the kiln. Hard-paste, being necessary in the kiln. Hard-paste china, too, contains kaolin – a fine white porcelain, too, contains kaolin – a fine white clay originally from the Chinese mountain of Kauling (its name meaning 'high hill'). 'Porcelain' is one of the most unusual words in the English language, since it ultimately comes from Italian porcellana, 'little sow' (small female pig) via French porcelaine meaning shell', 'porcelain'. The association is a bizarre one: a cowrie shell is translucent, and at the same time resembles a sow's back. One wonders precisely whose fantasy led to such original comparisons.

chorus (group or band of singers)
A 'chorus' is a fixed or regular group of singers a church 'choir', school 'choir', 'Bach Choir', and so on, which may or may not have soloists. A 'chorus' is a special band of singers who usually gather to perform a particular piece, as an opera or oratorio in which there will, by contrast, be several principal singers. However, the words are sometimes used more or less interchangeably and The Oxford Companion to Music, unexpectedly, does not distinguish between them.

chop (slice or cut of meat)
A 'chop' is basically a slice of meat that includes a rib and is cut from the loin. A 'cutlet' is cut from the neck, when it becomes a 'chop', or from a part that is similar to a 'chop', or from a part that resembles a 'chop'. The word is doubly misleading in origin, since it comes not from 'cut' but from French côtelette, which in turn comes from Latin costa meaning 'rib' – which, today at any rate, it does not contain.

chorus see **choir**

chrysalis/cocoon (case protecting an insect pupa)
A 'chrysalis' is either the case or the whole pupa, especially, of course, of a butterfly or moth. The rather learned word derives from the Greek for 'gold', the colour of certain 'chrysalises' (or chrysalides, or – rather too correctly – chrysales). A 'cocoon' is usually silky, and especially applies to the case of a silkworm, from which, in fact, the silk actually comes (which is why the wretched pupating creature is plunged into hot water, so that its carefully wound case can be as carefully unwound). However, even a 'cocoon' is strictly speaking a 'chrysalis', since it is a pupa.

church/chapel (place of worship, for some a regular one)
In Britain, at any rate, 'church', meaning both the building and the body of Christians, has an 'establishment' connotation. But then the Church of England, which is the one meant, is indeed quite literally the established church of the land, so the connotation need not be a derogatory one. But if 'church' does mean 'them', then 'chapel', which normally means a Nonconformist building or body, must be 'us', so what about those for whom 'church'-going is 'us'? The split (or distinction) will probably be of little significance to members of either – for them religious worship is what really matters – yet the division is there, if only when it comes to an intermarriage: 'His people are "church", but hers are "chapel"!' There are, however, Anglican 'chapels', such as the separate place of worship, with its own altar, in a large 'church' or cathedral – where the 'chapel' dedicated to the Virgin Mary is called the 'Lady Chapel' – or the building or room that is the place of worship in a school or institution, and non-Anglican 'churches', as, obviously, Roman Catholic ones. A division can often be found in virtually any section of society – if that is what you are looking for.

cannabis/marijuana (hallucinogenic drug prepared from hemp)
According to the World Health Organisation, 'cannabis' does not encompass resin alone – which would be hashish (Cannabis indica) – but is a general term for the flowering or fruiting tops of the hemp plant, its leaves, and sometimes its stems and seeds, used as a drug by being smoked, drunk (in an infusion) or eaten. 'Marijuana' is the name of a specific type of 'cannabis' plant – Cannabis sativa, sometimes called American 'cannabis' – that unlike 'real' 'cannabis', which comes mainly from India or North Africa, is grown in the western hemisphere. 'Marijuana' is usually smoked and is relatively mild compared to 'real' 'cannabis' as used in other countries. Most American 'marijuana' is grown in Mexico. Although hallucinogenic, both drugs are technically regarded as non-addictive or non-habit-forming, i.e. as 'soft' drugs, not hard drugs.

cannon see **gun** (both entries)

canon see **dean**

cantata see **oratorio**

canter see **trot**

canyon see **ravine**

cap see **hat**

capsule see **probe**

car see **coach**

carcass see **corpse**

caretaker/curator/janitor/custodian (official appointed to look after premises)
A 'caretaker' either takes charge ('caretakes') in an owner's absence or, more commonly, is the person who looks after a public building such as a school or office block. The latter sense is a British one, corresponding to the American 'janitor'. A 'curator' is the keeper or 'custodian' of a museum, where a 'custodian' is one who has the custody of special records, documents or particular historical objects. A 'custodian' is also, however, one who guards or is specially responsible for people who are 'in care' in some way, as prisoners or a ward, although in the latter case the term is normally in fact 'guardian'.

cargo see **freight**

caricature see **cartoon**

carnation/pink (garden plant with sweet-smelling white or pink flower)
A 'carnation' is a cultivated clove 'pink', that is, the clove-scented 'pink' botanically known as Dianthus caryophyllus. (The Sweet William, or bunch 'pink', belongs to this family.) The 'pink', therefore, is a general name for the plant of the genus Dianthus that has not only white or pink flowers, but crimson or variegated ones. How did the 'carnation' get its name? Originally, perhaps, it was 'coronation', although one theory claims it derives from Latin carnatio, 'flesh-colour' (compare 'carnal' or 'carnage'). The reference is not to real flesh, but to the rather more lurid colour of flesh in paintings.

carpenter/joiner/turner/cabinet-maker (specialist in woodwork)
A 'carpenter' is a craftsman in wood or woodwork, especially of a rough, solid kind, as in a house or boat. A 'joiner' makes furniture, house fittings, and other woodwork that is lighter than that of a 'carpenter'. (He joins, basically with glue, rather than builds.) A 'turner' is a craftsman who works with a lathe, and a 'cabinet-maker' is not just someone who makes cabinets but who is a skilled joiner. The first three words (not 'cabinet-maker', which is a seventeenth-century word) denote ancient crafts, which is why they also occur as surnames (although the surname Turner denotes someone who may have worked in materials other than wood, such as metal or bone).

carriage see **coach**

cartoon/caricature (amusing or grotesque drawing)
Originally and properly, a 'cartoon' was a full-size drawing on stout paper as a design for a painting, tapestry, mosaic, or the like (see, for example – literally, if possible – the

Leonardo da Vinci 'cartoon' of the *Virgin and Child* in the National Gallery, London). The word then came to mean a full-page illustration, especially a satirical one on politics, in a newspaper or magazine (see some of these in early numbers of *Punch*). Eventually it came to be used of any amusing or witty drawing, with or without a caption, a sequence of which is a 'strip cartoon', telling a story or recounting an incident or episode. Another spin-off is the 'animated cartoon', or just 'cartoon', as perfected, for example, by Walt Disney in the cinema. A 'caricature' is a grotesque representation of a person – less often, a thing – exaggerating his characteristic traits. This may well be in the form of a 'cartoon', of course. 'Caricature' can also apply to any representation like this, as a written account or a mime. The word is not related to 'character' but comes from Italian *caricare*, literally 'to load' (compare English 'charge'). 'Caricatures' are, after all, 'loaded' portraits. 'Cartoon' is also Italian in origin, meaning 'large card' (compare English 'carton').

catalogue see **list**

cathedral/abbey/minster (large or important church)
A 'cathedral' – in full, 'cathedral church' – is the principal church of a diocese, where the bishop has his throne or seat (Greek *kathedra*, 'chair') and in whose city he lives, in either a palace or a more modest residence. An 'abbey' is the term either for a religious community (see **monastery**) or for an important church as, notably, Westminster 'Abbey', which was once attached to a religious house. (Officially, Westminster 'Abbey' is neither a 'cathedral' nor an 'abbey', but a collegiate church. It was built on the site of a monastery called the 'west "minster"' – that is, a 'minster' that was west of the city of London. It must not be confused with Westminster 'Cathedral', which is the principal Roman Catholic church in England.) A 'minster', then, is the title of certain large or important churches that were originally associated with a monastery. A noted example is York 'Minster' – actually a 'cathedral' and famous for its grandeur and fine medieval stained glass – which was built on the site of a monastery.

cave/cavern (hole under the ground or in the side of a hill or cliff)
A 'cavern' is a very large 'cave', often regarded as containing something worth having – or avoiding – as a vast underground chamber where treasure is stored or danger lies hidden. A 'cave', the more common word, is a more mundane thing, where primitive man lived or some bears still do live, although Aladdin's 'cave', where he found his magic lamp, is rather more out of this world.

cavern see **cave**

celandine see **buttercup**

cellar see **vault**

centre see **middle**

cerise see **violet**

certificate see **degree**

chain store/multiple store (shop that is one of several similar owned by one company)
A 'chain store' may specialise in one main item of goods, as one of the many shoe shops that belong to a particular company, or sell a range of goods. A 'multiple store' will always sell a range of goods (a 'multiple' choice), such as Woolworths or the Co-op.

chairman see **president**

channel see **sound** (narrow stretch of water)

chapel see **church**

charm/talisman/amulet/mascot (object believed to bring good luck)
A 'charm', in general, is anything worn to avert evil or bring luck or otherwise aid its owner. A 'talisman' is similar – it is supposed to have the power to work wonders – but specifically is an inscribed stone or ring said to ensure safety or bring good fortune. An 'amulet' is a 'charm' worn to ward off evil, but not necessarily to bring good luck. A 'mascot' is a person, animal or thing supposed to bring luck to an individual or

group of some kind, as a regimental 'mascot' (traditionally, and rather bafflingly, a goat) or a team 'mascot' (a small boy footballer who wears the team strip and features in team photographs). Many people, from schoolchildren taking exams to racing drivers in contest on the track, have a 'lucky "mascot"' such as a cuddly toy or other whimsy that they take with them to bring them success and frustrate the knavish tricks of their rivals.

chart see **map**

check/mate/checkmate (final or near final position in chess)
'Check' is the call to inform your opponent that his king is exposed to a direct attack. 'Mate' and 'checkmate' mean the same, although 'mate' is the term normally used in chess, with 'checkmate' often having a figurative meaning. This is the call you make to announce that your opponent's king is in an inextricable 'check', so that the game is over – you have won. The ordinary verb 'to check' meaning 'to stop' derives from this, but 'checkmate' does not mean that you have 'checked your mate' or something: it is a distorted rendering of the Persian *shah mat*, 'the king is dead'.

checkmate see **check**

cheesecloth see **muslin**

cheetah see **leopard**

chef see **cook**

chemist/apothecary/pharmacist (dealer in medicinal drugs)
A British 'chemist' is an American 'druggist', just as a British chemist's shop is a drug-store across the Atlantic. The American term is more realistic, in fact, since a 'chemist' is also the term for one skilled in chemistry, which a 'chemist' (as found in the High Street) is very likely not. An 'apothecary' is a now obsolete term for a 'chemist' (or druggist). However, in Britain the Society of 'Apothecaries' still exists as a body authorised to license students to practise medicine by passing its special examination. Perhaps the British 'chemist' should be renamed a 'pharmacist', who is not

only skilled in pharmacy (the preparation and dispensing of drugs) but a pharmaceutical 'chemist' – that is, the 'chemist' we usually mean, with the shop that sells drugs

cheque card see **credit card**

chicken pox/smallpox (contagious di with red spots)
'Chicken pox' is a fairly mild disea monly contracted by young child often occurring in epidemics. 'Sma much more unpleasant thing: an disease with fever and pustules leave permanent scars. The the 'pocks' they produce. The 'chicken pox' and the farm false one (although the nam ingly, be sometimes used, USA, for fowl pest). 'Chi 'child', a usage not n compare Macduff's 'all in *Macbeth*. 'Smallpox' general sense – just named to distinguish syphilis (also called

child/infant/min person)
The meaning of different statut Act, 1958, fo young person Education A above com sixteen). I young pe one who discreti manag perso was wer the L t

only skilled in pharmacy (the preparation and dispensing of drugs) but a pharmaceutical 'chemist' – that is, the 'chemist' we usually mean, with the shop that sells drugs

choir/ch
A 'choir' singers, a the Bach may not ha group of si form a pa oratorio, in soloists or P words are so changeably, *Music*, rather tinguish betwe

chop/cutlet (sl
A 'chop' is norr cludes a rib-bon 'cutlet' is usually will be a neck-' contains no bone.

churchwarden see **sidesman**

chutney see **pickle**

cider/scrumpy/perry (sparkling alcoholic drink made from fruit)
'Cider' is made from fermented apple juice. 'Scrumpy' is a rough brew of 'cider' famous in the West Country, where cider-apples are widely grown. 'Perry', a more or less exclusively British drink, is made from the juice of pears. 'Cider' is produced in a number of different varieties, drier and sweeter, and not all are necessarily sparkling. In the USA, moreover, 'cider' usually means *un*fermented apple juice, i.e. non-alcoholic.

cinders/ashes/clinker (residue of a fire)
'Cinders' are usually reasonably 'solid' or substantial, and may contain matter that is still combustible. 'Ashes' are essentially powdery (and usually grey), and cannot be further subjected to combustion. 'Clinker' – not so called because it 'clinks' but deriving from a Dutch word – is a fused, solid mass of incombustible matter remaining after the burning of coal (unlike 'cinders', which are generally smaller, and can be the remnants of coal, wood, or any combustible matter). A further distinction between 'cinders' and 'ashes' is that 'cinders' may be either hot or cold, while 'ashes' are nearly always thought of as cold or 'dead'.

cipher see **code**

circle see **balcony** (section of the auditorium of a theatre)

city see **town**

class/form (set of pupils in a school)
'Class' is a general word used in both primary and secondary state schools, although 'class' is normally reserved for primary or junior schools and 'form' often used in secondary, especially grammar, schools, as the fifth 'form' or sixth 'form' (the most senior). In independent schools 'form' is generally preferred to 'class' at any level, although there are always exceptions. The difference is thus one of usage.

clavichord see **harpsichord**

claw/talon (pointed nail on the foot of an animal or bird)
A 'claw' is a general term, so that cats, dogs, lions, starlings and eagles, to name a few, have 'claws', and so by extension (literally) do lobsters, crayfish and the like. A 'talon' is the 'claw' of a bird of prey, as a vulture or hawk. It should really mean little more than 'heel', or at most 'hind "claw" of a bird', as it does in French and a number of other languages. The meaning '"claw" of a bird of prey' is peculiar to English.

clearway see **motorway**

clerihew see **limerick**

clinker see **cinders**

coach/carriage/car (passenger vehicle as unit of a railway train)
'Carriage' is the general and popular word, as a 'first class "carriage"' or a 'crowded "carriage"'. 'Coach' is a more official word, and normally the one used by railway authorities, as in announcements about 'the front three "coaches"'. A 'car' is a specific type of 'carriage', as a dining or restaurant 'car', buffet 'car' or sleeping 'car'. In the USA, 'car' is used in a wider sense to mean 'carriage', a 'railroad "car"'.

coast see **shore**

coat/jacket (outer garment usually with sleeves and buttoning or fastening down the front)
A 'coat' is a general word for a top garment usually designed for outdoor wear, as an 'overcoat', 'raincoat' or car 'coat'. Many 'coats', however, have specific uses indoors, as a 'housecoat', morning 'coat' or 'waistcoat'. The latter is not even (usually) a top garment, and a 'petticoat' is certainly not – although it once was the word for an outer skirt. All 'jackets' are 'coats', which is why the two words are often used interchangeably, but unlike 'coats' they are normally short, whether for outdoor or indoor wear, as a donkey 'jacket', lumber 'jacket' and shooting 'jacket' (outdoor), or dinner 'jacket', sports 'jacket' or bed-'jacket' (indoor).

cockle/mussel (edible shellfish)

'Cockles' are smaller and rounder – or more exactly more heart-shaped. They vary in colour from brown to red or yellow and are usually found under a layer of sand. 'Mussels' are twice as long as 'cockles' and are found sticking to rocks, and to one another, in large colonies. They are dark blue or dark greenish-brown in colour. Both are regarded as tasty delicacies, but to define the difference between them in this respect one would have to ask an expert, such as the Irish girl Molly Malone, who 'wheeled her wheelbarrow through streets broad and narrow, Crying, "Cockles" and "mussels"! alive, alive, oh!' (But perhaps she merely sold them and never sampled her own wares?)

Cockney see Londoner

cocoon see chrysalis

cod/halibut (fish yielding oil from its liver)

The 'cod' is a standard-shaped, i.e. cylindrical, fish important for food. 'Cod' liver oil is a useful source of vitamins A and D. The 'halibut' is a large flatfish, with its eyes and colouring on one side only. Its liver oil yields mainly vitamin A.

code/cipher (secret symbols or language for messages)

A 'code' is essentially a system of signals, using letters, figures, word groups or symbols, while a 'cipher' is a form of secret or disguised writing, or the key to it. In cryptology, a 'code' system is a specialised form of substitution in which whole words, long phrases, and even sentences are replaced by arbitrary equivalents, such as other words, groups of letters or figures, or combination of these. A 'code' book or 'permutation table' would be used for encoding or decoding messages. A 'cipher' system involves a variety of devices, such as transposition of letters, the use of grilles, and substitution (as figures for letters). A very simple 'cipher' system would be so-called monoalphabetic substitution, where one letter of the alphabet stands for another (as B for A, C for B, and so on). Ships' signalling flags are a form of 'code', with the Blue Peter, for example, meaning 'Am about to sail', and Nelson's

Cipher

L	E	X	I	N
G	T	O	A	B
C	D	F	H	K
M	P	Q	R	S
U	V	W	Y	Z

1. Message: **AM FOLLOWING ON NEXT TRAIN**

2. Plain-text: **AM FO LX LO WI NG ON NE XT TR AI NX**

3. Cipher: **GR QF EI XG YX LB BX LX EO AP HA LI**

Cryptogram

4. **GRQFE IXGYX LBBXL XEOAP HALI**

Code

One-part code

```
A B A B A – A
A B A C E – Abandon-ing-s
A B A D I – Abandoned
A B A F O – Abate-ing-s
A B A G U – Abated
A B A H Y – Abeyance
A B E B E – Abide-ing-s
A B E C I – Abide
. . . . .  –  .................
Z Y Z Y Z – Zone-s
```

Two-part code

Encoding

```
K A B O L – A
S T O L G – Abandon-ing-s
E X I F O – Abandoned
Z U M R A – Abated
A B A B A – Abeyance
R O A B Y – Abide-ing-s
. . . . .  –  .................
B I K U R – Zone-s
```

Decoding

```
A B A B A – Abeyance
A B A C E – Procedure
A B A D I – To purchase
A B A F O – Commenced
A B A G U – Do not think
A B A H Y – Recorded
. . . . .  –  .................
Z Y Z Y Z – According to
```

famous message 'England expects . . .' expressed in a series of flags. (He intended the second word of the message to be 'confides', but this was not in the signal book and would have had to be represented by seven flags. He therefore changed it to 'expects', for which a single flag existed.)

cognac see **brandy**

college of advanced technology see **technical college**

college of education see **teacher training college**

colony/dominion/protectorate/ dependency (country or state dependent to some degree on another)
'Colony' these days does not normally mean 'country occupied by and ruled by another', but in the United Kingdom is usually taken to mean 'British Crown colony', officially defined as 'a territory belonging by settlement, conquest or annexation to the British Crown'. This means fully or partially self-governing 'colonies' such as Belize, Bermuda and Hong Kong where a British Governor is appointed. A 'dominion' was the former title (before 1939) of the self-governing territories of the British Commonwealth, as Canada, Australia and the (then) Union of South Africa. The term was abandoned in 1947 when these became members of the Commonwealth. A 'protectorate', too, is a term that now no longer exists. Strictly speaking, it applies to a weak state protected by a stronger one, or technically, 'a territory not formally annexed, but in respect of which . . . Her Majesty has power and jurisdiction'. The last of the British 'protectorates' were the Solomon Islands, which were granted their independence in 1978. A 'dependency', in British parlance – more correctly a Crown 'Dependency' – is a term applied to the Isle of Man and the Channel Islands. These are not strictly speaking part of the United Kingdom, but have their own legislative assemblies and systems of local administration, and their own courts. At the same time they have a special relationship with the United Kingdom because of their geographical proximity to it and their long connection with the British Crown. They are thus not fully 'dependent' from the point of view of government, but 'dependent' more on good will – and the tourist trade.

colt/foal/filly (young horse)
A 'colt' is a young male horse, usually from when it is taken from its dam to four or five years old. A 'foal' is a young horse generally, or even a young donkey. A 'filly' is a young female horse, with the same specifications as for a 'colt'. (Rather unexpectedly, the word is not related to French *fille* but is of Germanic origin.) For young cow words see **calf**.

column see **pillar**

comedy/farce/slapstick (stage play of a light, amusing character)
'Comedy', the opposite of tragedy, can be satirical, but usually represents everyday life and has a happy ending. 'Farce' can be properly distinguished from 'comedy' by its tendency to derive amusement through the ingenious manipulations of a series of intricate situations in which stereotyped or 'stock' human characters are involved. The plot is often an amatory one (a 'bedroom farce'), with the main subjects in and out of wedlock – and bed. Some 'farces' have become famous, as the so-called Aldwych 'Farces' in the 1920s and 1930s, mostly by Ben Travers, and the Whitehall 'Farces' of the 1950s and 1960s, managed by Brian Rix. Many present-day domestic 'comedies' on television are 'farces' of a lesser rather than greater degree of originality. A special type of 'farce' is 'slapstick', which usually involves good, low, knockabout fun, with much physical action (custard pies, pratfalls, silly walks and the like) and general rumbustiousness. 'Farce' and 'slapstick' are words that have interesting origins. 'Farce' comes from Latin *farcire*, 'to stuff' (compare, at a much more sophisticated level, the *haute cuisine* term *farci*). The idea was that such 'comedies' were 'stuffed' into interludes or intervals as 'fill-ins'. A 'slapstick' was a special type of stick, consisting of two flat pieces of wood hinged together, which when slapped on someone's backside produced a resounding 'crack' but inflicted minimal physical discomfort.

31

comet/meteor/meteorite (bright, moving object in the sky)
A 'comet' is quite often confused with a 'meteor', but in fact is nothing like it. It is a hazy, star-like patch in the sky with a lengthy tail pointing away from the sun, round which it slowly moves in a near oval orbit. The brightest 'comet', and one of the best known, is Halley's, which reappears every 75 years. Its last appearance was in 1910. A 'meteor' is the 'shooting star' or fireball. 'Meteors' generally move in streams round the sun, although they are often observed singly. They are caused by particles called 'meteoroids' entering the atmosphere at high speed and becoming luminous by compression of the air. 'Meteors' usually burn up before they reach the earth's surface, but if they are not completely consumed, the surviving fragment of rock or metal is called a 'meteorite'. Most 'meteorites' are quite small, but large ones have caused spectacular craters in Arizona, for example, and in Siberia. 'Comet' comes from the Greek for 'hairy', a reference to its tail, while 'meteor' derives from Greek 'lofty', 'high in the air' – whence also, of course, 'meteorology' as the term for the scientific study of the weather.

command see **order**

commission see **committee**

commissioner for oaths see **solicitor**

committee/commission (body set up to carry out a special function)
A 'committee' is usually formed by and out of a larger body to carry out, investigate, report, research, debate or the like a special matter that probably concerns the whole of the larger body, as an executive 'committee' or a complaints 'committee'. A special type of 'committee' is a working party, which is specially set up to investigate a particular problem or question. A 'commission' is not necessarily appointed by a larger body but is set up to perform special duties and almost always report on its findings. Often it is a 'once and for all' body: when it has completed its mission it is disbanded. A 'committee', on the other hand, although its members may change, runs for a lengthy period, especially a standing 'committee', which may even be a permanent one.

commonplace/platitude/truism
(unoriginal or trite or obvious statement)
A 'commonplace' is a statement made so often that it is far from original, in other words an everyday saying, as the pathetic 'These things are sent to try us'. It was originally a notable saying, in fact, and entered in a 'commonplace book'. A 'platitude' is a dull or trite statement made solemnly as if fresh or profound but actually rather boring and stale, as many hackneyed sayings and catch phrases. A 'truism' is similiar, in popular usage: an obvious truth, as the hackneyed statement 'You only die once'. Properly, though, it is a much more interesting thing: a proposition that states nothing that is not already implied in one of its terms. An example might be, 'I don't like to go to bed too late', which really means 'I don't like to go to bed later than I like to go', since 'too late' means 'later than I like', 'too late for me'. However, 'commonplaces' and 'platitudes' and 'truisms' turn up regularly in our daily conversation.

communism see **socialism**

company see (1) **corps**, (2) **firm**

competition/contest (act of rivalry in which one aims to win)
A 'competition' almost always suggests an undertaking – usually a sporting one – in which one has an active 'opposition' and hence strives to do one's best. A 'contest' can be an individual attempt to gain an objective or to hold on to what one has gained, although by implication there will be an opposing force of some kind. A 'contest', too, suggests more of an effort or struggle than a 'competition', more of a trial of strength, or even of countering the claim or position of another.

comprehensive school/secondary modern school/grammar school (type of secondary school)
'Comprehensive schools', which in England and Wales comprise just over three quarters of the total, are state schools that take pupils, usually at age eleven, without re-

ference to their ability or aptitude – without any kind of entrance test or exam, in other words – and provide a wide, supposedly 'comprehensive' range of secondary education for all or most of the children in a given district. (In Scotland secondary education is almost entirely comprehensive or non-selective.) 'Secondary modern schools' provide mainly a general education with a practical bias, while 'grammar schools' concentrate on a specifically academic course. Both of these allocate places after an aptitude test – the infamous 'eleven plus' – and both are gradually being phased out. As a result of the gradual abolition of those 'grammar schools' that are direct grant schools, however, many schools of this type have decided to become fully independent, i.e. to join the private sector of education and charge fees to all pupils. A number of 'grammar schools' are thus also familiar as 'public' schools (which in typically convoluted British parlance means just the opposite).

computer programmer/systems analyst
(person working with computers)
A 'computer programmer' writes the set of instructions or program to the specifications of the 'systems analyst', who thus analyses the program in computing terms and writes the specifications for the programs that follow. Put another way, and as something of an over-simplification, the 'analyst' plans what the computer must do, and the 'programmer' instructs the computer to do it. Many 'programmers', of course, are also 'analysts', but not all 'analysts' are 'programmers'. Both are sometimes called 'liveware' (see **hardware**).

conceit see vanity

concert/recital (performance of a musical
work)
'Concert' is a general word derived from Italian *concerto* meaning performing together, as a symphony 'concert'. A 'recital' is a more intimate thing, a programme given by one player or singer, or perhaps by two, as in a violin and piano 'recital'; it is always more personal and on a smaller scale than a 'concert'.

concertina see accordion

confession/admission (acknowledgment
of guilt or offence)
The two are very close, but a distinction can be made. A 'confession' is usually of something 'bad', as a fault, crime, debt, dread or guilty secret. An 'admission' is also this, but has a suggestion of 'allowing', and can imply a personal, unprompted resolve to tell the truth, especially of a lesser evil. 'I admit that it was all my fault', one might say. But an interrogator, especially one investigating a serious crime, says 'Confess!'

conjuror/magician (one skilled in the art of
magic)
A 'conjuror' (also spelt 'conjurer') is a person who practises sleight of hand, not necessarily so that the quickness of the hand deceives the eye, but with manual dexterity. A 'magician' is more of an all-rounder. The word is not only a general one for a 'magic-maker' but also has mystic or even religious connotations, since it derives from the magi or ancient Persian priestly astrologers, of whom three, the Magi, or Three Wise Men, came from the East to Bethlehem to bring offerings to the infant Jesus. For more about magic see **black magic**.

constellation/nebula/galaxy (mass of
stars)
A 'constellation' is the area of sky round a group of stars having an imaginary outline, when seen from the Earth, that gives them their name, as Ursa Major, otherwise the Great Bear, or seen through other eyes Charles's Wain (or even, seen more irreverently, the Bent Saucepan). Astronomers now recognise eighty-eight constellations that more or less cover the sky. A 'nebula' and a 'galaxy' need to be rather more carefully distinguished. A 'nebula' is a bright area in the heavens due either to a 'galaxy' or to a large cloud of distant stars. Today, increasingly, the term tends to be used for visible condensations in interstellar space, while all extra-galactic systems are 'galaxies', which admittedly is something of a paradox. In common use, however, a 'galaxy' is one of two things: either (as the 'Galaxy') another name for the Milky Way (Greek *galaktos* means 'milk'), or one of the

many independent systems of stars, gas, dust and so on that exist in space, especially the one (again, the 'Galaxy') that contains the earth. The confusion between the two is partly due to the fact that 'galaxies' were first described as 'nebulae', since they were only hazy or nebulous objects in telescopes. Later, but not much more helpfully, they were known as 'island universes' or 'extra-galactic "nebulae"'. Apart from our own 'galaxy', only two are visible to the naked eye. These are the Magellanic Clouds in the southern sky, which look like two detached portions of the Milky Way. (They are named after the explorer Magellan, who circumnavigated the world.)

consulate see **embassy**

consultant/specialist (doctor experienced in a particular field of medicine or surgery)
A 'consultant' is so called because he is consulted not by his patients but by his colleagues in the hospital where he works, since he has specialised knowledge. A 'specialist' is a doctor, usually in a hospital, who devotes his attention to a particular class of diseases, for example an orthopaedic 'specialist'. A 'specialist' may thus be a 'consultant', which in hospital appointments is regarded as a senior rank of medical officer.

contempt/disdain/scorn (strong disapproval)
'Contempt' is disapproval combined with disgust or mockery, especially of something regarded as 'beneath one'. 'Disdain' is similar, but has more of an overtone of moral correctness and of a standing attitude towards something. The word is related to 'deign', that is, something one does not deign to consider. 'Scorn' is open 'contempt' or undisguised mockery.

contest see **competition**

contract bridge/auction bridge/whist
(card game for four players)
'Contract bridge' is a development of 'auction bridge' that originated in France as *plafond* ('ceiling') before the First World War. The 'contract', basically, is an undertaking to make a stated number of tricks. The main difference is that in 'contract

bridge' the side that wins the bid can earn only the actual number of tricks bid towards the game, all additional points being credited above the score line. In 'auction bridge' ('auction' from the bidding) all the tricks won, whether bid or not, score towards the game. 'Whist' is perhaps the doyen of full-pack partnership games: the object is to score tricks, a trick being gained by the partners who play the highest card of a suit, or the highest trump card. Each trick over six counts one point, with partners scoring five points for a game and two games for a rubber. 'Whist' was the forerunner of bridge, which was superseded by 'auction bridge' in 1911 with this in turn giving way to 'contract bridge' in 1928. 'Whist' is still flourishing (in 'drives') in town venues and village halls up and down the country.

contralto see **treble**

conundrum see **pun**

convalescent home see **nursing home**

cook/chef (one who prepares food professionally)
Both 'cook' and 'chef' can be used as titles (forms of address), although presumably not so many people today are in a position to say 'I'll have a word with "cook"'. (The designation was originally always masculine, in fact.) The French word 'chef' – implying 'head' 'cook', so that there are other 'cooks' working under him – was first used in English to mean the head 'cook' in the kitchen of a large household. The broad difference today, of course, is that anyone can be a 'cook', even if just for a *mauvais quart d'heure*, but a 'chef' is always a full-time professional.

cooker see **oven**

coppice see **wood**

copse see **wood**

corn/grain/wheat (staple agricultural crop)
'Corn' is the tricky word, since its meaning and usage varies geographically: in England it generally means 'wheat', in Scotland

and Ireland 'oats', and in North America 'maize'. Moreover, it can mean the same as 'grain', i.e. the actual edible fruit or seed of a cereal, as well as a collective word for a whole crop before or after harvesting, as a 'field of "corn"' – which might mean 'wheat' *or* oats *or* maize, or any food-grass. 'Wheat' is a specific cereal plant: the one with the four-sided head used for making flour for bread and regarded as highly nutritious. So all 'wheat' is 'corn', and all 'corn' is 'grain', and most 'grain' is 'wheat'. No wonder all flesh is as grass.

cornet/bugle (instrument of the trumpet family)

The 'cornet' is halfway in size between a trumpet and a 'bugle', with the same open (unstopped) notes and compass as a trumpet, and the same method of operation – valves opened and closed by pistons. It is associated chiefly with brass bands and solitary players on street corners. The 'bugle', very much a military instrument, is roughly the same length as a trumpet but has a wider bore. It differs from both the 'cornet' and the trumpet in that it has no valves, and so can basically produce not much more than five open notes, in ascending order: middle C, G, C, E, G. These are enough, in fact, to play Reveille, 'Come to the cookhouse door, boys', and a number of other military orders. Its name comes from

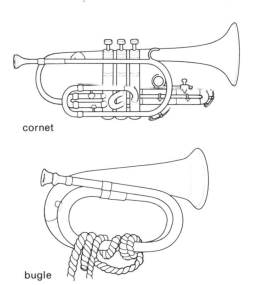

cornet

bugle

Latin *buculus*, 'young ox', from whose horns the instrument was originally made.

coronary see **stroke**

coronet see **crown**

corporation see **firm**

corps/division/brigade/battalion/ company/regiment/troop/squadron/ platoon/section/squad (military formation)

The 'corps' is the largest unit of an army, usually comprising two or more 'divisions' and additional support arms. The next largest unit is thus the 'division'. This is a major formation containing the necessary arms to sustain combat. Smaller than a 'division', and usually commanded by a brigadier, is a 'brigade', which will also have its support arms and services. One of three units (usually) in a 'brigade' is a 'battalion', which in turn is comprised of two or more subordinate units, normally 'companies' or 'regiments'. A 'company' will be commanded by a major or captain and a 'regiment', usually, by a colonel. Of these two latter units, therefore, the 'regiment' is the 'higher ranking'. It is also the chief permanent recruiting and training unit of the army and for tactical control it is itself organised into 'companies', 'battalions' or 'squadrons', much as a 'brigade' is. For some time a 'regiment' was roughly equated with a 'battalion', however (not a 'brigade'), and the two terms were used interchangeably. In most modern armies, though, the 'regiment' is the higher unit. (In 1957 the US Army in fact eliminated its infantry 'battalions' and 'regiments', replacing them with 'battle groups'. A further reorganisation, begun in 1961, called for the restoration of infantry 'battalions' as self-sufficient units of 800 to 900 officers and men, each 'battalion' being divided into four 'companies'.) A 'troop', meanwhile, is a subdivision of a cavalry 'regiment' of about 'company' size, usually commanded by a captain. A 'squadron' is the principal division of a cavalry 'regiment' or armoured formation and is of sufficient size to contain two or more 'troops'. A 'platoon' is the subdivision of a 'company' and is normally under the command of a lieutenant and divided into three 'sections'. Finally, a 'section' is divided into two or more 'squads', the army's smallest units, each of which has typically a dozen men. The exact function, size and ranking of each unit varies from country to country and period to period, so that it is impossible to give precise figures for the number of men in any one unit or to say what the exact composition of a formation will be. Such factors vary with changing tactical and strategic requirements. Moreover, increasing disbandments, amalgamations and arms reductions further complicate the picture. Thus the grading given here is mainly one of size, from biggest to smallest.

corpse/carcass (dead body)
A 'corpse' is the dead body of a human; a 'carcass' the dead body of an animal. For once, therefore, a neat and straightforward distinction. The word 'carcass' suggests 'case – in fact it is sometimes spelt with a final 'e' instead of double 's' – but its origin is something of a mystery. *Webster* suggests possibly Persian *tirkash*, 'arrow-bearing', which is ingenious. (But might not the initial 'car-' have something to do with 'flesh', as in 'carrion'?)

corridor see **passage**

cortège see **suite**

couch/sofa/settee/divan (upholstered seat for two to four persons)
A 'couch' has a back and sometimes arm rests. A special sort of 'couch' is the one found in doctors' surgeries and psychiatrists' consulting rooms, which has a raisable head end – and on which one lies, not sits. A 'sofa' usually has comfortable, padded 'arms' or ends and a comfortable back. (The word is not related to 'soft' but comes from the Arabic, in which it is the term for a part of the floor raised so as to make a seat.) In the USA a large 'sofa' is often known as a davenport, especially when it can be converted into a bed. The name is said to be that of the original maker. A 'settee' is virtually the same as a 'sofa', although it may not have ends. It's a 'non-U' word, says Professor Ross, in *Don't Say It*, as is 'couch'. (Presumably he sanctions 'sofa'.) A 'divan'

normally has no back or arms. Properly, it is the word for a long, low seat against a wall, as in the Middle East. These days it often doubles up as a spare or 'guest' bed or 'put-you-up', when it is called a 'divan bed'. 'The thing itself', says the Professor, 'used to be non-U but is perhaps no longer so' (judgment made in 1973). The word is directly related to the French for 'customs', *douane*, and ultimately derives from Persian *diwan*, 'court', 'bench'.

count see **duke**

courage/bravery/valour/fortitude
(quality of fearlessness, pluck or hardihood)
'Courage' is the basic quality of mind that enables one to face danger, difficulties, threats, pain or other unpleasant obstacles without fear. 'Bravery' is 'courage' combined with daring and boldness. 'Valour' is continuous active 'bravery' in the face of personal danger, with the implication that such 'bravery' is of an enhanced nature. Hence the inscription 'For "Valour"' (rather than 'For "Bravery"') that appears on the Victoria Cross. 'Fortitude' is 'patient' courage, especially under such testing conditions as privation, temptation, hunger and the like, or what is sometimes regarded as the triumph of mind over matter.

course see **field** (area of play)

court see **field** (area of play)

courtesy see **politeness**

cove see **bay**

covert see **den**

cradle/crib (baby's bed or cot)
A 'cradle' is a bed mounted on rockers to send baby to sleep (in theory). A 'crib' is properly a receptacle for animal feed with bars, hence a small bed with latticed or barred sides. A combination of both meanings of 'crib' gives a third use of the word for a model of the manger-scene at Bethlehem as found in churches at Christmas-time.

craving see **longing**

credit card/cheque card/bank card
(special card authorising the obtaining of
goods or cash)
A 'credit card', issued chiefly through banks
but also by commercial organisations, is
mainly used for the settlement of an account
or services, as in a shop, hotel, restaurant or
garage. Familiar types of 'credit card' are
the Access, Barclaycard and American
Express ones. A 'cheque card', or 'bank
card' (or banker's card), is a 'payment
guarantee' card issued by a bank to enable
the holder to cash a cheque up to £50 at any
bank or to support payment by cheque. A
Barclaycard, for customers of Barclays Bank
only, acts not only as a 'credit card' but also
as a 'cheque card'. Holders of 'credit cards'
are issued with a monthly account which, if
not settled fully within a specified period
(usually 25 days from the date of the statement), attracts interest.

cretin see **idiot**

crew cut/Eton crop (hair style in which
hair is cut very short)
A 'crew cut' of which skinheads affect(ed) an
exaggerated version, is a style in which a
man's or boy's hair is cut short all over. The
term apparently originates, as do many
colourful phrases in the English language,
from the USA, where at one time the boat
crews at Harvard and Yale universities went
in for close-cropped hair. An 'Eton crop' is,
though, of ultra-British origin. It is – or was,
since it was mostly in vogue before the
Second World War – a style in which a
woman's hair was cut short all over and
sleeked, like that of the pre-war, but rarely
post-war, Eton boy.

crib see **cradle**

cricket see **grasshopper**

crime/offence (wrongdoing, lawbreaking)
In general usage, a 'crime' is a more serious
thing than an 'offence'. Legally, a 'crime' is
either an act which is forbidden by law, or
the omission to perform an act which is
commanded by law, and as such is often
contrasted with a civil injury, which is the
violation of another's right. 'Crime', too, is a
violation of man-made laws, whereas an

'offence' can be against a divine law, as an
'offence' against morality.

crisis see **emergency**

crocodile/alligator (large fearsome reptile
living in rivers)
The 'crocodile' lives in the rivers of tropical
Africa (especially the Nile), Australia and
America. The 'alligator' is less cosmopolitan. It exists in only two species: the first
inhabits the Mississippi and other large
rivers of America, the second is found in
China, in the Yangtse Kiang. Geographical
disposition apart, there is a physical distinction between the creatures. The 'alligator'
has a broad head, a depressed, blunt
muzzle, and unequal teeth, whereas the
'crocodile' has a narrower head, a rounder,
sharper nose, and equal teeth. Though one
may feel disinclined to examine them too
closely, it is the teeth, in fact, that provide
the ultimate difference: the 'alligator' has
two teeth – one on each side of the lower jaw
four back from the front – that are elongated
and fit into sockets in the upper jaw when its
mouth is closed; with the 'crocodile' these
two teeth project outside its snout. Those
experienced in these things additionally
claim that 'crocodiles' are livelier than 'alli-
gators' and so more likely to attack a supposedly hostile human. But the dental
distinction is the foolproof one.

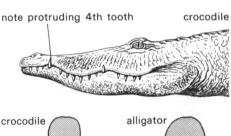
note protruding 4th tooth   crocodile

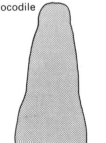
crocodile

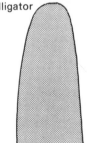
alligator

cross-ply tyres see **radial tyres**

crow/rook/raven (large black bird)
The 'crow' is smaller – about 20 inches long – and less heavily billed than the 'raven'. It feeds chiefly on the ground, where it walks around rather sedately. The 'rook' belongs to the same family as the 'crow' (*Corvidae*) and is roughly the same size. It can be distinguished from it, however, by its gregarious nature – it lives with its many companions in rookeries – and the white skin at the base of its bill and its 'trousers'. The 'raven', also in this family, is the largest of the three – up to 26 inches long. As a scavenger, it is often found where the others are not, for example on beaches, in the mountains, or in a town. Its colouring is more blue-black than pure black, like the 'crow', and its voice is deeper. It is from their voice or call, in fact, that all three birds get their name: compare words such as 'caw', 'croak' and 'creak', also imitative. (Not so easy to see this origin in the 'raven', but it always was a devious bird.)

crown/coronet/tiara (head covering worn as sign of royalty, nobility, or elegance)
The 'crown' is the more or less sumptuous bejewelled head-covering worn by a monarch, as a king, queen, emperor or tsar. A 'coronet', as its diminutive ending suggests, is a small 'crown', especially one worn by a peer or peeress. A 'tiara' does not necessarily denote rank, but may be worn, as a type of ornamental 'coronet', above the forehead, on formal occasions such as dances or banquets or receptions. In this sense it is an exclusively feminine adornment. The pope, however, always wears a 'tiara' on certain important occasions: it is a form of triple 'crown', one surmounting the other, of traditional bee-hive shape and gemmed with three diadems.

crumpet/muffin (type of tea-cake eaten hot with butter)
Both are toasted and eaten with butter, with the American 'muffin' being the equivalent of an English 'crumpet'. English 'crumpets' are in general smaller, thicker, and denser than 'muffins' and are almost always eaten as tea-cakes in winter, whereas 'muffins' were also eaten for breakfast and were not so seasonal in their appearance. (A hundred years ago both were equally popular for tea-parties, which came to be known as 'muffin'-worries and 'crumpet'-scrambles accordingly – that is, a special variety of bun-fight.) 'Muffin' now has something of a romantic ring to it, while 'crumpet' has taken on a new meaning to denote 'sexually attractive woman' or, loosely, 'sex' in general. How this happened – why 'crumpet'? – is not too clear, but there is obviously an association, mainly figurative, with the attributes of the cake when ready to be consumed (as 'hot', 'juicy', 'luscious'). Compare the use of other comestibles in a similar way, as 'cheesecake' and 'bun'.

crustacean see **mollusc**

crypt see **vault**

CSE see **GCE**

cupola see **dome**

curate see **vicar**

curator see **caretaker**

curling see **hurling**

currant see **raisin**

current account/deposit account (type of bank account)
A 'current account' is the standard 'pay in and withdraw' account, using cheques, standing orders and the like, for which the bank may charge. A 'deposit account' is one that earns interest – usually 2 per cent below Minimum Lending Rate (which used to be called Bank Rate) – and in theory not able to be drawn on without notice. Depositors have a pass book recording their balance. A bank customer may well have both types of account, although if his 'current account' goes 'into the red' the bank will not set this right by transferring from his 'deposit account' unless it is so instructed.

custodian see **caretaker**

cutlet see **chop**

cuttlefish see **octopus**

cyclone see **whirlwind**

daffodil/narcissus (pale yellow spring flower)
There are many forms and hybrids of 'daffodil' and 'narcissus', but the 'true' or wild 'daffodil', with its long 'trumpet', is the species of 'narcissus' classified as *Narcissus pseudonarcissus*. This means that 'narcissus' is also a name of many applications, but it more narrowly applies to the species *Narcissus poeticus*, which is heavily scented with white petals, a small orange-rimmed corona and a short 'trumpet'. The name, as well as the flower, is poetic because of its association with the mythological Greek youth who fell in love with his own reflection in the water, subsequently pined away (or threw himself in), and was changed into the flower. Yet the name of the flower does not derive from the yearning young Greek but comes, it seems, from the plant's numbing properties – 'narcissus' the narcotic, in fact. Another member of the 'narcissus' family is the jonquil, of which there are various kinds, but all having clusters of flowers and short, broad coronas.

dais see **rostrum**

damp/moisture/humidity (slight wetness)
'Damp' usually suggests an undesirable and possibly superficial wetness, especially one that can be treated or removed, as rising 'damp'. 'Moisture' implies a natural or acceptable wetness, as the 'moisture' of the soil or the lips. 'Humidity' is a term for a measure of the amount of 'moisture' in the air.

dandruff/scurf (small flakes of dead skin in the hair of the head)
There is very little difference between the words. If any, it is that 'scurf' is the word for the actual scales or small shreds of dead skin (which are in fact being cast off all the time), and 'dandruff', the medical term for which is seborrhoeic dermatitis, is the condition of having 'scurf' on the scalp. ('Scurf' must not

be confused with 'scurvy', a much more serious disease caused by a deficiency of vitamin C formerly attacking sailors who lived without any fresh vegetables.)

day nursery see **nursery school**

dean/archdeacon/canon (clerical dignitary)
A 'dean' controls the services in a cathedral, and with the chapter – 'canons' of the cathedral – supervises its fabric and property. The title also applies to the head of Westminster Abbey (not properly a cathedral) and certain other churches, such as St George's Chapel, Windsor. In the Roman Catholic Church, 'dean' is the title of the head of the Sacred College of Cardinals, in Rome. In the Church of England, a 'rural dean' is the head of a group of parishes in a particular diocese. The term is not exclusively ecclesiastical, though, since in many universities and colleges the 'dean' is the title of a fellow who has special disciplinary and advisory responsibilities. (At Oxford and Cambridge he is specifically responsible for undergraduate discipline.) It can also be the title of the head of a university faculty or department. In origin, the word comes from Latin *decem*, 'ten': the *decanus* was the chief of a group of ten. An 'archdeacon' – literally, 'chief of the deacons' – ranks next below a bishop in the ecclesiastical hierarchy and has administrative authority delegated to him by a particular bishop. He generally supervises the discipline of the clergy under him and administers church property. He holds a territorial title, for example, 'Archdeacon of Lindsey'. A 'canon' is a member of the clergy belonging to a cathedral or collegiate church. 'Residentiary' 'canons' comprise the chapter of the cathedral. As such, they are members of a permanent salaried staff responsible, under the dean, for the maintenance of the services, upkeep of the fabric and the like. 'Nonresidentiary' 'canons' are unsalaried but may have certain privileges and responsibilities: the title can sometimes be awarded as a kind of honorary promotion for dedicated service.

dedication see **devotion**

deep-freeze see **refrigerator**

deer see **stag**

degree/certificate/diploma (formal academic qualification or the document that attests this)
A 'degree' is a university qualification awarded on successful completion of a three-year course or longer. As such it is usually in the form of a 'pass' or 'honours' 'degree', with different classes in some universities, and is officially a first 'degree', otherwise a BA. A subsequent 'degree' would be an MA – a so-called higher or further degree – although a specialised qualification obtained subsequently might be a 'diploma'. Such specialisation is a distinguishing feature of a 'diploma', although today many former 'diplomas' are now termed 'degrees', with 'diploma' reserved for a less academic qualification – or one generally regarded as less academic. Also, a 'diploma' is the equivalent of a 'degree' as awarded by a non-university institution, for example a technical college. A 'certificate' is often, of course, simply a formal record of a person's birth, marriage, death, medical condition and the like, although it can apply to the attainment of proficiency in the academic sense, as GCE and CSE. In this sense it is close to 'diploma'. If both a 'certificate' and a 'diploma' are awarded in a particular field of study, then the 'diploma' is usually higher and awarded at the end of a longer course. Compare, in this respect, the Ordinary National 'Certificate' (ONC) at higher education level, awarded after two years part-time, and the Ordinary National 'Diploma' (OND) gained at the end of a full-time or sandwich course that involves wider and deeper study than the ONC.

delivery note see **advice note**

Democrat see **Republican**

den/lair/covert/burrow (home of a wild animal)
A 'den' is the word for the home of any wild beast, especially one that is a cave, as for a lion or tiger. A 'lair' is not so much a dwelling place as a lying place, that is, a place where a wild animal can rest. A 'covert', too, is not a home in the full sense of the word, but a place of shelter, and in particular a thicket where game animals can hide, or where they happen to be hidden anyway. A 'burrow' is a hole excavated for living in by an animal such as a fox or a rabbit. Some 'burrows' have special names depending on the animal inhabiting it: a badger's 'burrow', for example, is a set (or sett).

denims see **jeans**

department/faculty/school (section of a university)
A 'department' deals with a particular field of study, as for example a 'Department' of English. As such, it usually forms part of a 'faculty', so that the 'Department' of Chemistry, for example, might form part of the 'Faculty' of Science. It follows that a 'faculty' is engaged in the study of a major field of learning, such as theology, the arts, law, music, medicine, science, engineering or agriculture. Birmingham University, for example, has five 'faculties': Arts, Science and Engineering, Medicine and Dentistry, Law, and Commerce and Social Sciences. In the USA both words are extended to mean the staff of the respective section. In some universities several related 'departments' are grouped together as a 'school'. At Leeds University, for example, the 'School' of Chemistry consists of the 'Departments' of Inorganic Chemistry, Organic Chemistry, and Physical Chemistry. This use of the word 'school' originated in the Middle Ages at Oxford, where subjects were arranged in 'schools', not 'faculties' – a practice that continues there even today.

dependency see **colony**

deposit account see **current account**

depth see **height**

design see **plan**

despot see **dictator**

destiny see **fate**

detention centre see **remand home**

developed countries see **developing countries**

developing countries/underdeveloped countries/developed countries (class of country determined according to its economic status)
The 'developing countries' – a term now generally favoured instead of 'underdeveloped countries' – are those that have a relatively low *per capita* income compared with the 'developed countries' of North America and western Europe. In most 'developing countries' the majority of the population are engaged in agriculture, with other distinctive features being low rates of literacy, the observance of traditional customs, and the absence of a middle class. Most 'developing countries' are in Asia, Africa, Latin America, and Oceania, and many of them are former colonies. A collective term for them, especially from the viewpoint of countries not politically aligned with communist or western (capitalist) countries, is the 'Third World'.

devotion/dedication (loyalty to someone or something)
'Devotion' implies a personal attachment, often an earnest or caring one, and a loyalty in which one is not only involved but wishes to be involved. 'Dedication' has more an implication of duty and perseverance, of a personal committal that may be from choice or from altruistic or external motives. 'Devotion', too, often connotes enthusiasm, while 'dedication' suggests a rather lofty single-mindedness. Perhaps the different shades of meaning can be seen best reflected in the basic senses of the words: 'devotion' is related to 'vow', 'dedication' to 'declare'.

dialect/accent (form of speech differing from the standard)
Broadly, a 'dialect' has different *words* from the standard form of the language, while an 'accent' has a different *pronunciation*. The distinguishing features of a 'dialect' are thus its different grammatical structure and different vocabulary, as found, for example, in the Cornish 'dialect' or the Kentucky 'dialect'. A 'dialect' will, however, almost certainly be spoken with a particular 'accent', especially by a native of the place – although it is perfectly possible to speak standard or 'received' English with a regional 'accent' such as a Yorkshire one.

diameter see **radius**

dictator/despot (absolute ruler)
A 'dictator' is a ruler who has absolute control in a government, either without hereditary right or without the free consent of the people. Hitler, Mussolini and Franco are traditionally regarded as 'dictators'. The term 'despot' extends a little wider to denote any absolute ruler, especially one who is a noted tyrant or oppressor. Both words are near-synonyms for autocrat.

diesel oil see **petrol**

difference/distinction (perceivable dissimilarity or disparity)
The 'difference' between two things is the complete or partial lack of identity between them, usually as perceived by one of the senses – they look different, sound different, etc. The 'distinction' between one thing and another is the dissimilarity between them perceived as the result of analysis and/or discrimination, as this dictionary attempts to do. One can in fact have a '"distinction" without a "difference"', which is a way of talking about a discrimination that is artificial or false.

dilemma see **predicament**

dinner see **lunch**

diploma see **degree**

diplomacy see **tact**

direct current see **alternating current**

direction see **order**

director see (1) **president**, (2) **producer**

disciple see **apostle**

discovery see **invention**

disdain see **contempt**

disease see **illness**

disguise/camouflage (concealment of identity)
'Disguise', a fairly general word, usually

41

implies changed dress or at the least a false beard or a wig and dark glasses. 'Camouflage' is a more specialised thing: the disguise of military vehicles, weapons and the like (including weapon-carrying aircraft and ships) by means of smoke screens, patchy paintwork, artificial greenery or foliage, and so on. The design of such 'camouflage' is selected in such a way that the camouflaged object blends with its background and thus is difficult to detect. Animal 'camouflage' works in much the same way, so that the wings of a moth, say, will merge with the bark of the tree on which it is resting, making it less conspicuous to possible predators. It is a popular misconception, incidentally, that the chameleon changes its colour as a form of 'camouflage' to match its background: its colour changes are the result of environmental factors such as light and temperature or of 'emotions' such as victory or defeat in battle with another chameleon. 'Camouflage' is a French word in origin meaning, simply, 'disguise'.

disinfectant/antiseptic (medically cleansing or sterilising agent)
A 'disinfectant' is a chemical agent that destroys bacteria, whether for personal or household use. An 'antiseptic' is an agent that counteracts sepsis by 'preventing' the growth of bacteria. Some agents, of course, are both, which presumably is the ideal combination.

dissolution see **abolition**

distemper see **whitewash**

distinction see **difference**

divan see **couch**

division see **corps**

dizziness/giddiness/vertigo (sensation of whirling or revolving)
'Dizziness' is usually experienced in the head, resulting in a dazed state (the words are similar, but not actually related) and tottering steps or an unsteady stance. 'Giddiness' emphasises the rapid whirling motion experienced when looking down from a height, for example, with a sudden sensation

of unsteadiness or even nausea. 'Vertigo' is the medical term for either of these, or even both together, whether the cause is physical or psychological. All three are equally unpleasant.

doctor/surgeon/physician (medically qualified practitioner)
A 'doctor', formally a 'physician', usually means a general practitioner (GP), that is a 'doctor' advises and prescribes medicines and treatments for all kinds of diseases and conditions, as opposed to a consultant or specialist. In the USA, the term 'doctor' can also be applied to a dentist or a veterinary surgeon. A 'surgeon', who has also received a full medical training, practises surgery, usually of one speciality or another. He is addressed in Britain as Mr (not 'doctor'). In the Navy and the Army all medical officers are called 'surgeons'. A 'physician' is the technical and old-fashioned name for a 'doctor' and in fact means a teacher. For a list of local 'doctors' in the telephone directory's yellow pages you must search under 'physicians and surgeons' since there is no classification under 'doctor'.

doe see **stag**

dolphin/porpoise (small member of the whale family)

dolphin

porpoise

The 'porpoise' is usually smaller than the 'dolphin' and is chubbier in shape, with a blunt snout rather than a beak-like one. Both creatures are intelligent, the 'dolphin' to the extent that it is sometimes said to have a learning ability second only to that of man, performing complex tricks for public entertainment in dolphinariums.

dome/cupola (rounded roof on a church or other building)
A 'dome' is a rounded vault with a base that is circular, elliptical or polygonal. A 'cupola' is a small 'dome' that either forms the roof or simply adorns it. For a fine example of a 'dome', see St Paul's, London, or St Peter's, Rome. For some typical 'cupolas', see the bulbous roofs of virtually any Greek or Russian Orthodox church – and also the Royal Pavilion at Brighton.

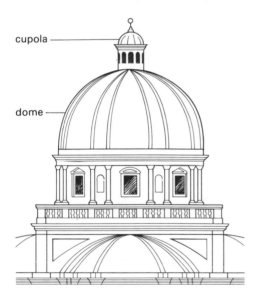

cupola

dome

dominion see **colony**

don/fellow (senior member of a university or college)
A 'don' is a rather vague word to mean any senior member of a college, especially one at Oxford or Cambridge, whether a college head, a 'fellow', or a tutor. It can be used rather disparagingly to denote a stuffy or bombastic academic, as Hilaire Belloc's

'Remote and ineffectual Don'. Rather surprisingly for an 'establishment' word, the term originates in the Spanish title (meaning something like 'lord'), as in Don Quixote or Don Juan. A 'fellow' is the term for an incorporated (i.e. 'regular') senior member of a college. It can also be used of a graduate receiving a stipend for a period of research and, in some universities, of a member of the governing body. A 'fellow', too, is the title of the senior member of a learned society, as a 'Fellow' of the Royal Society. It is rather an unusual word in having both a formal, academic meaning (senior member) and an informal, familiar one (bloke, chap, 'fella'). Its origin is unexpected, also: a 'fellow' was once a 'fee-layer', one who laid down money in a joint undertaking.

donkey/ass/mule (animal like a small horse renowned for its stubbornness or stupidity)
A 'donkey' is an 'ass', and an 'ass' is a 'donkey': they are one and the same beast. Originally 'donkey' was regarded as a slang word, even as late as the early nineteenth century; originally, too, it rhymed with 'monkey'. Today it is the more common name for the animal, which differs from a horse not merely in just being smaller but in having a tuft of hair at the end of its tail, no warts on its hind legs, and, especially, the presence of stripes, although not in the domestic 'donkey'. A 'mule' is properly the offspring of a he-'ass' and a mare, or, popularly, of a she-'ass' and a stallion (which properly is a hinny). The 'hybrid' sense of 'mule' is also seen in the related word 'mulatto', which is the word for the child of a white-skinned person and a black. 'Donkeys' are proverbially stupid or stubborn, but not always actually so. Through biblical associations they are also regarded as patient and humble creatures. In the USA 'donkey' is preferred to 'ass' since the latter word also means 'buttocks' and even 'sexual intercourse' ('piece of ass').

doom see **fate**

dove see **pigeon**

doves see **hawks**

doze/snooze (short or light sleep)

A 'doze' is a light or short sleep in the day-time, often an unintentional one, or at any rate semi-unintentional, as a 'doze' in the sun in the garden or a brief nap in a stuffy office after a satisfying pub lunch. (Compare 'to doze off', which usually implies an unin-tended falling asleep.) A 'snooze' is possibly a more deliberate nap: 'Well, I'll just go and have a little "snooze", I think.' Moreover, 'doze' half implies a dropping off to sleep, whereas 'snooze' relates more to the actual period of sleep itself. The word's origin is uncertain, but it may be something to do with 'snore' or 'somnolent'.

Dracula see **Frankenstein**

dramatist/playwright (writer of plays)

A 'dramatist' writes mostly dramas (in effect, a play of any kind, not necessarily a serious one) or dramatic poetry. A 'play-wright' also writes plays ('wright' meaning 'maker', not 'writer'), but often combines his play-writing with another activity, as 'actor and playwright' or 'novelist and playwright', or perhaps regards himself, or is regarded, as less of a professional or 'dedicated' writer of plays than a serious-minded, full-time 'dramatist'. Perhaps the difference is similar to that between 'lyricist' and 'song-writer': it's really a question of how one views the activity and the person who does it.

dress/frock/gown (main garment worn by a woman or girl)

'Dress' is the general word for the garment that in essence combines bodice and skirt. It is also, of course, an even more general word for the clothing of both sexes, especially when the clothes are formal, as 'morning dress'. 'Frock' is virtually the same as 'dress', but a more restricted word, and used in particular of girls' 'dresses', as a party 'frock' or a pretty 'frock'. Narrowly, the word means the long 'gown' worn by a monk, or priest formerly – hence 'unfrocked', of a priest who has been officially deprived or relieved of his status in the church. 'Gown' is used in specialised instances (as in the last sentence) for the long, loose, flowing garment worn as part of an official costume or 'dress', as a judge's 'gown', surgeon's 'gown', or a university student's 'gown'. More com-monly, though, it is the word for a 'dress' that is elegant or fashionable, especially a long one.

dress circle see **balcony** (section of the auditorium of a theatre)

dresser see **sideboard**

driving licence/vehicle licence/road fund licence (type of licence needed for a vehicle to travel on a public road)

A 'driving licence' is the one that must be held by the driver of a vehicle. It is normally either a 'full' licence, held until he is 70 years old, or 'provisional', valid for one year while he is learning to drive (that is, before he has passed his driving test). This is the licence that is 'endorsed' for traffic offences. A 'vehicle licence' and 'road fund licence' are one and the same thing – a licence that must be bought periodically, usually annually or quarterly, permitting a vehicle to be on the road. The holding of this licence is indicated by the licence disc that is usually displayed in the bottom left-hand corner of the wind-screen.

drove see **flock**

duke/earl/viscount/count (rank of the nobility)

A 'duke', the highest of the four, can be either a royal 'duke', who is a prince, or ruler of a duchy (there are at present only four royal 'dukes' in Britain: of Edinburgh, Cornwall, Gloucester and Kent, all distinc-tive 'royals'), or the title of a nobleman of the next highest rank after a prince, and next above a marquess. (There were twenty-six dukes in Britain in 1980, from Abercorn to Westminster.) An 'earl' holds the next rank below a marquess. His wife is called a countess (for 'counts', read on). A 'viscount' ranks below an 'earl' (or a 'count') and next above a baron. The title is also held by the son or younger brother of an 'earl' or 'count'. 'Counts' as such no longer exist in Britain, although they do in France, as *Comte*, or Germany, as *Graf*, or Italy, as *Conto*. In fact after the Norman Conquest, 'earls' were called 'counts' for a while, and it is just one of the quirks of British history and the English language that although we still have counties and countesses, there are no 'counts' to oversee either.

dusk/twilight (time between daylight and darkness)
'Dusk' is a darker stage of 'twilight', when things cannot be clearly discerned. Loosely, 'twilight' is the period between sunset and darkness – or, less often, between night and sunrise. Astronomically, it begins when the Sun's centre is 18 degrees below the horizon, which is the angle at which no light from the Sun can reach an observer. Civil 'twilight' begins when the Sun's centre is 6 degrees below the horizon. This is usually half an hour to an hour after sunset, and determines lighting-up time (which for sake of convenience is from half an hour after sunset to half an hour before sunrise). The word literally means 'two lights', but it is difficult to see why. One possibility may be in the light being halved, or divided by two, or perhaps it is regarded as a light that occurs twice daily.

duty see **tax**

dwarf see (1) **goblin**, (2) **midget**

dynamite/gelignite/TNT (type of high explosive)
'Dynamite' is the oldest of the three. It was invented and named in 1866 by Alfred Nobel – founder of the Nobel Prizes – as a powerful ('dynamic') high explosive of nitroglycerine mixed with some absorbent substance such as kieselguhr (a type of sand). 'Gelignite' is a gelatin type of 'dynamite', with less nitroglycerine but with an oxidant such as potassium nitrate. Its chief use is for blasting. 'TNT', or *trinitrotoluene* – otherwise $CH_3C_6H_2(NO_2)_3$ – arrived in the twentieth century and has a use that can be military or general. Its chief advantage over its two rivals is that, although exploded by detonators, it is unaffected by ordinary friction or shock.

earl see **duke**

earth see **world**

elf see **goblin**

embassy/consulate/legation/high commission (official residence of the diplomatic representative in a foreign country)
An 'embassy' is the residence of the ambassador, a diplomatic agent of the highest rank. The 'consulate' is the residence of the consul, who though not officially a diplomat is a diplomatic agent carrying out particular administrative duties, such as issuing visas, renewing passports and the like, as well as – and chiefly – fostering the commercial interests of his country and aiding its citizens in a foreign city. Many countries thus have both an 'embassy' and a 'consulate', often in quite different buildings. A 'legation' is the residence of the legate, now an obsolete term for an ambassador, and in practice that of a diplomatic minister such as a chargé d'affaires (an ambassador's deputy) or an envoy (who ranks above a chargé d'affaires but below an ambassador). A 'high commission' is the residence of the High Commissioner, which is the title of the head of an 'embassy' from one Commonwealth country to another. 'Residence' here, of course, means not just dwelling place but central office.

emerald/jade (green stone, or its colour)
'Emerald' is a precious stone, bright green in colour and a variety of beryl. 'Jade' is a hard green stone (or a blue or white one), used as an ornament or for implements, and varying from bluish green to yellowish green in colour.

emergency/crisis (serious situation)
Both words are beloved by headline writers: ' "Emergency" union meeting', 'Oil tanker "emergency"', ' "Crisis" discussions',

'England face "crisis"' (they might lose the next test match at cricket). Distinguishing, however: an 'emergency' is a serious situation that has arisen and which has to be dealt with urgently, as a plane making an 'emergency' landing; a 'crisis' is not just a grave situation but properly the turning point in one, on which everything depends, as a financial 'crisis', personal or nationwide. 'Emergency' is misused slightly more often than 'crisis', perhaps, when it means 'sudden serious situation'. (Possibly, too, the word itself suggests 'urgent', which reinforces this misuse.)

enemy/opponent/foe (person or persons hostile to one, an adversary)
An 'enemy' is a hostile opposition, personal or general, domestic or military, literal or metaphorical. An 'opponent' is not necessarily hostile, but simply someone who is acceptably matched against you, as in a sport or a debate. A 'foe' is a rather rarefied 'enemy', especially a fearful or spiritual one. The word seems to imply, too, a consequent danger, as a deadly 'foe'. The word is related to 'feud', not 'fear', however.

England/Britain/Great Britain/British Isles/United Kingdom (native land of the English or British)
The various names present special difficulties to non-English-speaking people, in whose languages 'England', for example, tends to mean the whole of the 'British Isles', including Ireland. In spite of nebulous areas, it is possible, however, to make certain reasonably clear distinctions. 'England' is the southern and chief country of the island of 'Great Britain', as distinguished from Scotland to the north and Wales to the west. 'Britain' is a fairly informal name, and possibly a more emotive one, for either 'Great Britain' or, more commonly, the whole of the 'United Kingdom'. 'Great Britain', thus, comprises 'England', Scotland and Wales. It is 'Great' not so much for its age or authority but as opposed to 'Little' Britain, better known as Brittany, so named from the flight to this land of Celts from (historic) 'Britain' when the Angles and Saxons invaded their native country in the fifth and sixth centuries. The 'British Isles' is the name for the islands that comprise 'Great Britain' and Ireland (both Northern Ireland and the Irish Republic), including small islands such as the Orkney and Shetland Isles to the north and the Scilly Isles to the south-west. The Isle of Man and the Channel Islands, however, although not normally regarded as belonging to 'Great Britain', are often included in the 'British Isles'. The 'United Kingdom' is the most official of all the names, and its full version, the 'United Kingdom' of 'Great Britain' and Northern Ireland, is administratively self-explanatory.

engraving/etching (drawing or picture made by cutting into stone or metal)
An 'engraving' is done by cutting words, a pattern or a drawing in metal, stone, wood, glass, or other incisable substance. An 'etching' is a form of 'engraving' in which the cutting is done not with a cutting tool but with acids or corrosives, and moreover on metal only. The metal plate to be etched is first coated with a thin layer of gums, waxes and resins (the '"etching"-ground') through which the drawing or pattern is scratched. The plate is then placed in an acid bath and the acid bites or 'eats' (which is the origin of the word 'etch') into the lines traced. The actual etching has to be executed in mirror form, back to front, so that the positive print it produces is the right way round on paper. The 'etching' originated from the custom of etching designs on armour: those responsible for doing this, either enterprisingly or lazily, found it easier to etch this way instead of cutting.

envy/jealousy (feeling of resentment caused by someone else having something that one does not have oneself)
'Envy', one of the seven deadly sins, does not necessarily imply a feeling of ill will, but often simply a longing for something that someone else has, even if it is theirs by right. 'Jealousy' is a much more personal thing, a feeling that the other person's right to what he has is not as great as one's own, with a consequent sense of rivalry, as a tussle of love or a contest for promotion at work. *You* have the prior claim, you know you have!

épée see **foil**

epidemic/plague (widespread outbreak of disease)
An 'epidemic' is a fairly localised outbreak of a disease, especially of one that had not been known in the locality before, or of one that struck suddenly, as a flu 'epidemic' in a city or community. A 'plague' is not only more widespread – a 'pandemic' – but of a disease that is particularly severe or even fatal, as the Great 'Plague' of London in 1664–5, when 70,000 out of an estimated 460,000 died of bubonic 'plague'. The word looks French – possibly by false association with 'ague' (pronounced 'ay-gew', of course) – but very likely it derives ultimately from the Greek root for 'strike', as in 'paraplegic'.

ermine see **mink**

error see **mistake**

estuary see **mouth**

etching see **engraving**

eternity see **infinity**

Eton crop see **crew cut**

evacuee see **refugee**

evening dress see **morning dress**

evening star see **morning star**

Excellency see **Lordship**

exoneration see **acquittal**

exploit see **achievement**

extra time/overtime (time beyond that regarded as regular)
Both terms can have an official sense, as the 'extra time' in football, the additional playing time of (usually) fifteen minutes to achieve a decisive result, or the 'overtime' worked, which is usually paid for at higher rates. But 'extra time' can mean 'overtime' in a general sense, as 'I'm going to put in some "extra time" on my drawing this evening'.

fable see **legend**

faculties/senses (power inherent in a bodily organ)
'Faculties' can apply, loosely, to the bodily powers as a whole, or specifically to a particular organ. Usually, however, the word denotes mental power, such as will or reason. One's 'senses' are traditionally the five powers of sight, hearing, smell, taste and touch – together with the so-called 'sixth "sense"' which supposedly gives intuition or some kind of extra-sensory power. Otherwise the word can also denote mental power, but usually means 'mind' as the hallmark of sanity, as in the phrase 'to take leave of one's "senses"'.

faculty see **department**

falcon see **hawk**

familiarity/intimacy (close acquaintance)
'Familiarity' and 'intimacy' both denote a close acquaintance or knowledge of something or someone, with 'intimacy' implying, where 'familiarity' does not, a personal interest or sympathy or affection. The words are also used euphemistically for sexual behaviour, 'familiarity' (or 'familiarities') denoting caresses and the like, and 'intimacy' actual intercourse (itself a euphemism, even if one of longer standing). It is to be hoped that such coy usages will soon be mocked out of existence. '"Intimacy" took place on the top of a bus' conjures up an image that is more laughable than shocking.

farce see **comedy**

Far East see **Near East**

Far West see **Middle West**

fashion/style/vogue (current or popular method of doing something)
A 'fashion' is what distinguishes the habits

or dress or manners of a particular group of people, especially from a historical angle, as the 'fashions' of the 1930s. (Unless qualified, the word usually refers to dress.) A 'style' is close in meaning to a 'fashion', but can indicate a conformity to a general standard, as the Early English 'style' of architecture, or a Queen Anne 'style' chair, both attractively simple and elegant. A 'vogue' is more a passing 'fashion', a prevalent 'style': 'long scarves are the "vogue" this winter.' It is unfortunate that the word suggests 'vague'; it actually derives from Italian *voga*, 'rowing', the reference being to the capricious motion of a boat. In fact 'vogue' and 'vague' *are* related, however, since the latter means 'wandering', 'wavering'. Compare French *vague*, 'wave', which prompts one to recall that the *nouvelle vague* was a special 'vogue' or 'style' of French film-making in the 1950s.

fate/lot/destiny/doom (predictable, inevitable or predetermined future)
'Fate', which can be a loosely used word – 'what a "fate"!' – implies an inevitable outcome that is irrational and impersonal. 'Lot' is one's personal 'fate', fortune or 'destiny' – what has been apportioned or 'allotted' to one. 'Destiny' is similar to 'fate' or 'lot', but sometimes suggests a favourable outcome, whereas the other two can imply an unpropitious or burdensome future. 'Doom' always implies a final ending that is unhappy or terrible, however, and it is this finality that the word essentially denotes, with a connotation of ruin or death.

fatigue see **tiredness**

fault see **mistake**

faun/satyr (mythical woodland creature – half beast, half man)
A 'faun' has the ears, horns, tail and quite often the hind legs of a goat. He is not so called because he is fawn-coloured, but because he is identified with the god Pan, who was also called Faunus. (The first word of 'fauna and flora', meaning the animal and plant life of a region, derives from Faunus's sister, Fauna.) A 'satyr' is also part goat, but much more 'bestial' than a 'faun'. 'Satyrs' were the attendants of Bacchus, and made a reputation for themselves by their rioting

and lasciviousness. 'Satyrs' differed physiologically from 'fauns', too, in that they had no horns.

feast/banquet (large, sumptuous or formal meal)
A 'feast' is a grand or lavish meal, especially a public one for several guests. A 'banquet' is either an elaborate 'feast' or, more commonly, a formal dinner in celebration of something, often with speeches. 'Feast' is also used metaphorically, as a 'feast' for the eyes, but a 'banquet' is always a literal meal. (The actual word 'banquet' is not used extensively, 'dinner' often being preferred instead.)

feat see **achievement**

fellow see **don**

ferns/bracken (flowerless plants with feathery fronds found in woods)
There are literally thousands of species of 'fern', for example huge tree 'ferns' or ones that float on ponds. The most common British 'fern', however – a large, coarse variety growing abundantly on heaths and hillsides and in woods – is 'bracken', which although dying off in the autumn remains considerably standing, albeit dead, throughout winter, thus offering cover to game. Professor Alan Ross, of 'U and non-U' fame, claims in his book *Don't Say It* (Hamish Hamilton, 1973) that 'fern' is 'non-U Scots for "bracken"', as in 'Isn't the "fern" lovely?'

ferret/stoat/weasel (small animal with long slender body feeding on small rodents)
The 'ferret' is the domesticated albino variety of the polecat, when used for hunting in the burrows of rabbits and rats (and for the curious north-country sport of maximum time of concealment in trousers). A much rarer 'ferret' is the black-footed 'ferret' (*Mustela nigripes*). This is a wild variety found in the American prairies, especially the plains of Nebraska and Kansas, where it feeds largely on prairie dogs. It resembles the common 'ferret' in its general colouring but has a black mask across the eyes and brownish-black markings on its feet and tail tip. The 'stoat' and the 'weasel' are quite

closely related, although the 'weasel' is smaller, with a tail half the length (around two and a half inches) of that of the 'stoat'. The 'stoat' has a valuable fur, when it is known as the ermine (see **mink**).

fête/bazaar (function with stalls to raise money for some cause)
Broadly speaking, in a 'fête' the emphasis is on entertainment, and in a 'bazaar' the emphasis is on selling. But entertainment and selling are an essential feature of each, and both aim to raise money for charity or some particular cause. Both, too, are typically English functions, yet *fête* is a French word, meaning 'feast', and *bazaar* a Persian word, meaning 'market'!

feud/vendetta (lengthy period of hostility between two families)
A 'feud' – related not to 'feudal' but to 'foe' – is a wider term, denoting mutual hostility between not only families but tribes, with murderous attacks in revenge for previous injury or wrongs. A 'vendetta' is a more limited affair: a private or blood 'feud' in which the relatives of a murdered person seek to gain their revenge by killing the murderer or a member of his family. The 'vendetta', as the Italian word (related to 'vengeance' and 'vindictive') suggests, is specially associated with Corsica and particular regions of Italy.

fib see **lie**

field/course/court/rink/pitch/lawn (area of play for a game or sport)
A 'field' usually implies a sizeable area of grass, as for cricket, football or hockey. A 'pitch' normally applies to the 'business' area of a field, where the action really happens. This may be limited, as a cricket 'pitch', or occupy the whole playing area, as a 'football' pitch. A 'course' is a stretch of land set aside for a race, whether over land or water. A 'court' is usually an enclosed area, whether an actual building, as a squash 'court', or in the open air, as a tennis 'court'. A 'rink' normally means an area of ice for skating or curling, but is also the word for the strip of a bowling green that is used for a match. A 'lawn' implies an area of grass, especially a mown one. 'Lawn' tennis

is properly played, thus, on a grass 'court', not a hard one, although of course in practice it is played on both. 'Lawn' is also the word often used for the stretch of grass set aside for a game of croquet, although professionals talk of a croquet 'court'. (Possibly 'lawn' implies a kind of amateurishness?)

field/meadow (enclosed area of grass)
A 'field' is the wider in meaning but not necessarily in size. Apart from denoting an area of farmland set aside for a particular purpose ('hayfield', 'cornfield') it is the word for the region of a natural product, as a 'coalfield', oil-'field' or gas-'field'. A 'meadow' is a piece of grassland, especially one used for hay, or a stretch of low, well-watered ground, as by a river. Not all 'fields' and 'meadows' are enclosed. In some towns meadows are held as common land.

figure see **number**

filly see **colt**

fin/flipper (organ for swimming and propelling on aquatic creature)
'Fins' are usually found on fish, where they are used for propelling, steering and balance. Most fish have one 'fin' on their back – some have more – and all have a tail 'fin' and further 'fins' underneath their body. A 'flipper' is a limb used by a larger creature to swim with, as the 'flippers' of a turtle (its legs) or a penguin (its wings). Circus seals can be trained to clap with their 'flippers', but more conventionally they swim or progress over land with them.

fir see **pine**

firefly see **glow-worm**

firm/company/corporation (business or commercial or industrial organisation)
'Firm' tends to be used of a smaller, old-established commercial enterprise, as a printing 'firm' or a car hire 'firm'. Strictly speaking, a 'firm' is a partnership business, such as a 'firm' of solicitors. The word is generally used in a wider sense, however. 'Company' usually denotes a larger organisation, especially a business or trading undertaking or a manufacturing plant, as an

insurance 'company' or a road construction 'company'. The word very often forms part of the official title of a commercial organisation, especially in the form 'J. Bloggs & Co. Ltd' (meaning that Mr Bloggs's company has a limited liability: he is legally responsible for the company's debts only to the extent of his shareholding). A 'corporation' is technically a business company (in Britain) and likewise treated by law as though it was a single person. In the USA it is an organisation, large or small, chartered under law for doing business, and owned by individuals or institutions who have shares representing fractions of its holdings. It thus approaches the British 'company', and similarly occurs as part of the name of such organisations. Even when it doesn't, many American enterprises have a name ending in 'Inc.', indicating that they have been legally constituted or formed as a 'corporation', i.e. 'incorporated'.

flan see **tart**

fleece see **fur**

fleet/flotilla (number of ships or boats sailing together)
'Fleet' is a general word, with special reference to a naval force under one commander-in-chief, as the Pacific 'Fleet'. It can also mean a similar force of aircraft – not to be confused with 'flight', which is an RAF term for a group of about six aircraft. A 'flotilla', literally 'little fleet' in Spanish, is either a small 'fleet' or a 'fleet' of small ships or boats, as the 'flotilla' of 'little ships' used for the evacuation of Allied troops from Dunkirk in 1940.

fling see **reel**

flipper see **fin**

flock/herd/drove/pack (group or company of animals)
It largely depends on the animal in question. A 'flock' is usually of sheep or goats, or else a company of birds. A 'herd' usually consists of large animals, originally those that were under the charge of someone, as elephants, buffaloes or, in particular, cattle. Animals in a 'herd' are usually thought of as feeding or

moving together. A 'drove' – the word is related to 'drive' – is a group of oxen, sheep or pigs, especially when they are being driven. A 'pack' consists either of animals that are kept together, as a 'pack' of hounds, or of animals that hunt or defensively herd together, as a 'pack' of wolves. Some linguistic experts or eccentrics claim that virtually every animal has its special group word, as a watch of nightingales or a covey of partridges. For a whole bevy of these, see Eric Partridge's *Usage and Abusage* (Penguin, 1970) (under the surprising heading 'sports technicalities').

flotilla see **fleet**

flotsam/jetsam (type of wreckage)
'Flotsam', in legal terms, is the word for goods that have been lost from a wrecked ship and that are found floating. Such goods belong to the Crown if no owner appears to claim them within a year. 'Jetsam' is the word for goods that have been thrown overboard or jettisoned from a ship to lighten it, and that are usually subsequently discovered washed ashore. Figuratively, the words are used together as a term for vagrants, tramps and the like, the ' "flotsam" and "jetsam" of society'. The terms were also used as the stage names of a team of comic singers popular in the 1930s: 'Flotsam', a tenor, was B. C. Hilliam, and 'Jetsam' was Malcolm McEachern, an Australian bass singer.

flour/meal (sieved or ground grain product)
'Flour' is bolted (i.e. sieved) 'meal', from which the husks have been sifted out after grinding. 'Meal' is the ground product of any grain – of wheat it is familiar as 'wheatmeal' – or pulse (the edible seeds of peas, beans, lentils and the like). 'Wholemeal' bread is made of 'meal' that has not been bolted and thus deprived of some of its constituents. 'Meal' the word is not related to 'meal' meaning 'taking of food' but to 'mill'. (For what happens to the grains that get left behind in the bolting machine see **semolina**.)

fluid see **liquid**

flutter see **wow**

foal see **colt**

foe see **enemy**

fog/mist (effect caused by water vapour condensing onto particles of dust, soot, etc.) 'Fog' is thicker, of course, and 'mist' thinner. Meteorologically, 'fog' has a visibility of less than one kilometre and 'mist' a visibility greater than one kilometre (but less than two kilometres). 'Mist', too, often occurs in thin bands or layers, while 'fog' is cloud-like.

foil/épée/sabre (type of fencing weapon) The 'foil' is the basic weapon of fencing. It is light, with a small bell guard and a square, tapering blade. Hits with the 'foil' are valid only if they are made with the point on the body. The 'épée' is the duelling sword, heavier than the 'foil', with a fluted, triangular blade and a larger bell guard. Hits – with the point only – score when made on the opponent's body, head or limbs. The 'sabre' is the light Italian duelling sword. It has a half-circular guard and a flexible, flattened blade which can score hits with the whole of its front edge, the last third of its back edge, or its point. Such hits are valid on the head, arms, and body down to the waist. 'Épée' fencing is a more open, simpler and athletic game than 'foil', and hits tend to be concentrated on the sword-arm and wrist – as the nearest parts of the target – rather than elsewhere on the body.

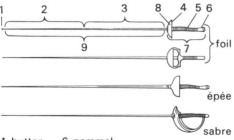

1 button	6 pommel
2 foible	7 mounting
3 forte	8 guard
4 cushion	9 blade
5 handle	

folio see **quarto**

foolscap see **quarto**

forceps/tweezers (instrument for holding something tightly) 'Forceps' are specialised surgical pincers, for anatomical repair work. 'Tweezers' are small, thin pincers for toiletry generally, and are used to pluck hairs, for example, or extract splinters – otherwise cosmetic repair work.

forest see **wood**

foreword/preface/introduction (material given at the front of a book) A 'foreword' is a 'word in advance' about what to expect in the book and is always written by someone other than the book's author. The word – sometimes confused with 'forward' and even misspelled as such – was devised in the nineteenth century as an English rendering of German *Vorwort*. A 'preface' is similar but is written by the author of the book. An 'introduction' is a more or less formal preliminary statement or guide to the book, and is often written by the author to explain what he is about. Some books have a sort of epilogue at the end called an 'afterword' or even some notes in the form of a 'postface'. An 'extroduction' is something that so far, mercifully, we seem to have been spared.

form see **class**

fort/fortress (fortified building) A 'fort' is any fortified building. A 'fortress' is essentially a military stronghold, especially a strongly fortified town where a large garrison is stationed. The nucleus of such a town was originally the 'fort', which is why many towns, especially in the USA and Canada, have a name that today has 'Fort' as the first element, as Fort Lauderdale, Fort Frances, Fort Wayne. For a similar reason the Scottish Fort Augustus, Fort George and Fort William are so named.

fortitude see **courage**

fortress see **fort**

foyer see **hall**

Frankenstein/Dracula (fearsome
humanoid monster of sinister central
European origin)
First, a popular misconception that must be
corrected: 'Frankenstein', in the original
Gothic novel by Mary Shelley, second wife
of the poet, was not actually the monster but
the student who created him – and who was
eventually killed by his own fiendish creation. So it was 'Frankenstein's' monster –
not 'Frankenstein', the monster – who was
brought to life from human bones in
charnel-houses and inspired loathing in all
who beheld it. 'Dracula' actually was a
human – that is, a vampire by night, but
Count 'Dracula' by day. The Count features
in the story by the Irish writer Bram Stoker,
and his activities begin – and end – in Tran-
sylvania, the traditional home of vampires
and werewolves. Both owe much of their
delectably gory image – or is it the other
way round? – to the Hammer horror films.
This dedicated company is said to make
several versions of its 'Frankenstein' and
'Dracula' films: the bloodiest for Japan, the
blandest for Britain.

freedom/liberty (absence of restrictions)
'Freedom' is the more common word, implying a positive free exercise of one's choice,
powers, rights, and so on. 'Liberty' is a more
stately or solemn word, and also a more
emotive one, since it normally suggests a
previous restriction or *lack* of 'liberty'. It
can, too, connote unwarranted 'freedom', as
when someone takes the 'liberty' of doing
something he should not do.

freehold see **leasehold**

free house/tied house (type of pub)
A 'free house' is not, alas, a pub that provides beer free, but one that sells liquor from
more than one brewery. A 'tied house', by
contrast, is a pub that is 'tied' to and often
owned by one brewery: it is bound to supply
that one brewer's liquor only.

freezer see **refrigerator**

freight/cargo (transported goods)
The difference is mainly in the means of transport used. 'Freight' is normally transported
in containers or by water – and in American
usage, also by land (hence the American
'"freight" train' which corresponds to the
British 'goods train'). 'Cargo' is usually
carried by ship or aircraft, although again in
the USA it can also go over land by motor
vehicle. 'Cargo' as a word is nothing to do
with cars, but is related to 'charge'.

fresco see **mural**

friar see **monk**

frock see **dress**

frog/toad (tailless amphibian found in
fields and gardens)
There are three main differences: 'frogs' like
water, are smooth-skinned, and leap; 'toads'
are not aquatic (except when breeding), are
dry or rough-skinned or warty (though, in
spite of superstitions, they do not actually
cause warts), and hop. This should be sufficient for the two to be distinguished, but if
not, look more closely: a 'frog' has teeth, a
'toad' has none.

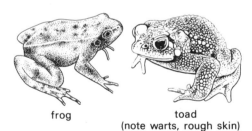

frog   toad
(note warts, rough skin)

frontier see **border**

fur/fleece (hair of animals used for
clothing)
'Fur' is the fine, soft, short hair of certain
animals (as such distinguished from longer
hair) used for coats, hats, wraps and the like,
as of the ermine, beaver, and so on. The
term usually applies to the skin of a dead
animal complete with such hair. 'Fleece' is
the woolly covering of the sheep – and, oc-

casionally, other animals – used for clothing materials. It is usually shorn from a live sheep rather than cut from the skin of a dead one.

further education/higher education
(education for those who have left school)
'Further education' is a blanket term usually referring to all post-school education outside the universities. 'Higher education' (postgraduate, first degree and similar level work) is provided at universities and on advanced courses at polytechnics (see **technical college**) and other establishments of 'further education'.

fury see **anger**

furze see **gorse**

Futurism/Surrealism (art movement still regarded by some as avant-garde)
Thanks to the rather vague use of the terms 'futuristic' and 'surrealistic' to apply to anything of weird and wonderful (or apparently incomprehensible) appearance or design – a futuristic curtain pattern or a surrealistic TV comedy – the original meanings have become rather blurred. 'Futurism', which evolved in Italy, had its heyday for about five years from 1910 to 1915, and aimed to depart violently from traditional forms in order to plan for a new, dynamic and revolutionary future. 'Surrealism' flourished rather later, at the end of the First World War, and was the conscious expression of an imagination uncontrolled by reason, 'more real than real'. Salvador Dali is one of the best known 'Surrealist' painters. The movements were not, however, restricted to art, but also embraced literature, music, and even, as the 'Futurists' envisaged in their movement, life itself.

galaxy see **constellation**

gale see **storm**

gallery see **balcony** (section of the auditorium of a theatre)

gallop see **trot**

gallows/gibbet (structure on which person used to be hanged)
A 'gallows' – the word is actually plural but treated as singular – normally had two uprights and a crosspiece, something like a goalpost. A 'gibbet' was usually a single upright post with an arm supported on an angle. It was, too, used more for hanging the dead body of a criminal than for actually executing him. It still features in the word-guessing pencil-and-paper game called 'Hangman' or 'Hanging', where the first three guesses are drawn as the upright, the arm and the support.

game/set/match/rubber (portion of play forming a scoring unit in tennis)
A 'game' of tennis can be won with a minimum of four points (with one side always winning and the other never winning a point), the scoring being 15-0, 30-0, 40-0, 'game'. A 'set' is a group of six 'games' won by one side, with a lead of at least two 'games'. A minimum score here would thus be 6-0. A straight 'set' is a result in which the winner does not lose a 'set'. This would be in a 'match', which usually consists of five 'sets' for men and three for women. A 'rubber' is a match of three 'games' in not only tennis, but other sports and games such as cricket, whist and bridge. If you win a 'rubber', you win two out of three 'games'. But in 'tennis', the exciting moment is when the winner eventually reaches his final point – 'match' point – so winning 'game', 'set' and 'match' simultaneously and becoming a triple victor.

game/sport (activity involving play and entertainment)
A 'game' is an individual contest of some kind, usually according to set rules, as a 'game' of football or of hide-and-seek. The word can also refer to the activity or pastime as a whole, so that football is a very popular 'game'. 'Sport' is a more professional word, and can likewise mean a 'game' that is particularly strenuous or tricky, as the 'sport' of boxing (one would hardly say game) or the 'sport' of fishing (which needs guile and patience). Many 'sports', too, are usually played out of doors. 'Games', however, can be played out of doors or in, and for this reason are often qualified as, for example, outdoor 'games', indoor 'games', ball 'games', team 'games', card 'games', board 'games', and the like. People who say that blood 'sports' are no 'sport' at all since they do not give the creatures a sporting chance may or may not be on the side of the gods. They are, however, overlooking the basic origin of 'sport' as a word: it does not mean an activity that gives the other side a sporting chance, i.e. a fair one, but a diversion. (It is actually a shortened form of 'disport'.)

gamma rays see **X-rays**

garret see **attic**

gasoline see **petrol**

gauze see **muslin**

GCE/CSE (school-leaving examination taken at about the age of sixteen)
'GCE' (General Certificate of Education) is run by eight examination boards, and held at 'O' or 'Ordinary' level for most pupils and at 'A' or 'Advanced' level for those who stay on at school for a further two years. It can also be taken by candidates at further education establishments as well as by private candidates. 'CSE' (Certificate of Secondary Education), organised by fourteen regional examination boards consisting mainly of teachers serving in the schools that provide the candidates, is designed for pupils at the end of their fifth year of secondary education and is more commonly held in comprehensive schools than in grammar-type schools (which tend to go for 'GCE'). 'CSE' is normally but not entirely correctly regarded as being of a lower standard than 'GCE', although the highest 'CSE' grade (1) is widely accepted as being the equivalent of at least grade C at 'GCE' 'O' level, both of these grades in turn being usually reckoned as qualifying for entry to a further education course of some kind.

gelignite see **dynamite**

gem see **jewel**

genus/species (scientific class or category of living things)
A 'genus' (plural 'genera') contains a number of 'species' (plural 'species'). The two are ranks in the hierarchy accepted by zoologists and botanists and based on the system devised by Linnaeus in the eighteenth century. They are the two lowest of the seven ranks, the others being (starting with the highest) kingdom, phylum, class, order and family. Thus man is 'species' *Homo sapiens* in 'genus' *Homo* in family *Hominidae* in order *Primates* in class *Mammalia* in phylum *Chordata* (comprising the vertebrates, or creatures with backbones, and some small groups of invertebrates) in kingdom *Animalia*. Members of a 'genus' have common structural characteristics distinct from those of all other groups, while members of a 'species' can interbreed and differ only in minor details.

German measles see **measles**

ghost/spectre/phantom (disembodied spirit or apparition)
A 'ghost' is the soul, spirit or image of a dead person as seen, or otherwise experienced or sensed, by a living person. A 'spectre' is usually the word for a terrifying or unearthly 'ghost', especially a visible one, otherwise a frightening apparition. A 'phantom' is a 'mere' apparition, one that appears in a dream, in the mind, or even in reality, but not normally a terrifying one. Put another way, from the point of view of 'spookiness' the 'spectre' is positive, the 'phantom' negative, and the 'ghost' neutral.

gibbet see **gallows**

giddiness see **dizziness**

gift see **present**

giggle/snigger/snicker/titter (suppressed laugh)
These suggestive words can be distinguished quite usefully. A 'giggle' (as of schoolgirls) is an affected or silly laugh, often at something trivial or 'catty'. A 'snigger' (as of schoolboys) is a secretive, usually 'smutty' laugh, often at something improper, or disrespectful in tone. A 'snicker' (as of fools) is similar to a 'snigger' but has a neighing or whinnying tone to it. A 'titter' (as of a church congregation) is a nervous or restrained or covert laugh, usually made when either one regards it as unseemly to laugh or because one is embarrassed.

ginger group see **pressure group**

gleam/ray/glimmer (dim or pale show of light)
A 'gleam' is a light that is not very bright, and which is often intermittent, as from a distant window or a remote star. A 'ray' is a single line of light narrower than a beam, often from a source that is small or, as with a 'gleam', distant. A 'glimmer' is a feeble or unsteady light, as of the moon or a glow-worm (who 'shows the matin to be near, And 'gins to pale his uneffectual fire', as Hamlet's ghostly father remarks before he exits). All three words are used figuratively, often with reference to a hope, a 'gleam' of which is brief or slight, a 'ray' slight but usually optimistic, and a 'glimmer' rather dim and not too promising, although clearly better than no hope at all.

glee see **madrigal**

glimmer see **gleam**

gloss/lustre/sheen (bright or shining appearance or quality)
A 'gloss' is a superficial 'lustre', and 'sheen' is a 'gloss' on the surface only. In other words, the two are much the same. A 'lustre', therefore, is more of a general term to mean the state or quality of shining by reflecting light, and comprehends a 'gloss' and a 'sheen'. The latter two, though, can be imparted by means other than reflection, as by polishing, say, or by brushing. A 'lustre' tends also to be more long-lasting, with a 'gloss' and a 'sheen' perhaps a temporary state, as of sleeked hair or highly polished shoes. A natural 'lustre', however, as on a butterfly's wings, is not a 'gloss' but a 'sheen'.

glow-worm/firefly (beetle emitting light after dark)
Both creatures emit phosphorescent light, although the 'glow-worm' gives a steady glow, while the 'firefly' produces flashes. The 'glow-worm' is normally the name of the wingless female beetle (not a worm at all) that emits such a light, although the term 'glow-worm' can also apply to the larvae of 'fireflies', especially ones in the Americas and the tropics. (Unlike 'glow-worms', 'fireflies' are beetles that do actually fly.) The light is usually greenish and at the rear end, although one so-called 'railroad worm' also thoughtfully has a red headlight. The idea behind this luminescence is to make signals to a likely mate. See also **gleam**.

gnat/midge/mosquito (small, annoying, biting insect)
'Gnat' is rather an imprecise word, since even 'mosquitoes', especially small or young ones, often get called this. At best it is a general word for any small annoying flying insect, as the black fly, fruit fly or, of course, the 'midge'. 'Midges' resemble 'mosquitoes' but their wings have no scales. There are two main kinds: those that bite, and those that don't. The latter are probably the more common ones, found around ponds or streams in late afternoon and evening in swarms. The biting 'midges', which are bloodsucking insects, are usually found along seashores, rivers and lakes. Occasionally they are known as 'no-see-ums', as the female, which is the one with the irritating bite, is difficult to find. The 'mosquito' is the most distinctive and maddening of the trio, with its ominous whining hum and often quite painful bite, but in this case it is fortunately rather easier to find (and catch).

gnome see **goblin**

goblin/dwarf/gnome/elf (small imaginary man-like creature)

A 'goblin' is a grotesque mischievous sprite, usually in human form although also appearing as an animal. A 'dwarf' is a creature from Scandinavian mythology, where he is specially associated with metal-working. In common with several other creatures, he was much popularised – and personalised – by Walt Disney, as one of the seven companions of Snow White. A 'gnome' is fabled to inhabit the interior of the earth and act as guardian of its treasures. He is usually thought of as a shrivelled malevolent little old man, but in spite of this has for some years now enjoyed popularity in Britain as a garden deity, where he can be seen perpetually angling or otherwise purposefully engaged. (His name looks Greek, and may in fact be related to Greek *gnome*, 'intelligence'; it was directly invented as a neo-Latin word, *gnomus*, however, by Paracelsus.) The 'elf' is closer to the German mountains than the Scandinavian mines. He has magical powers, which he enjoys using to interfere, in the nicest but also naughtiest way, in human affairs. All four, in fact, now that they have been resettled and domesticated, have lost much of their original evil influence on man. (Although if the love of money is the root of all evil, presumably the 'gnomes' of Zurich – those powerful Swiss financiers – must be regarded with more than a little awe and doubt by those who are wary of their great influence in the wicked world of capitalism.)

gorge see **ravine**

gorilla/orang-outang/baboon/mandrill (member of ape or monkey family)

The 'gorilla' is the largest of the man-like apes, living on the ground or in trees and a professed vegetarian. Its habitat is west equatorial Africa. The 'orang-outang' (or 'orang-utan') – whose name exotically although erroneously suggests 'orange glutton', but in fact is Malay for 'man of the woods' – is a now quite rare, alas, large, long-armed ape living in trees in Borneo. The 'baboon' is a monkey with a dog-like snout, large cheek pouches, and a short tail. It lives in Africa, south of the Sahara, and in parts of Asia. The 'mandrill' is a monkey that is actually a member of the 'baboon'

orang-utan

gorilla

baboon

mandrill

family, and possibly the most spectacular one, with its huge dog-like teeth, bright red buttocks, and gaudily striped blue and scarlet cheeks. It lives on the ground (but sensibly feeds and sleeps in trees) in west Africa.

gorse/furze/broom/whin (spiny shrub with yellow flowers growing on open land)

'Gorse' and 'furze' and 'whin' are three different names for one and the same plant, otherwise *Ulex europaeus*, with 'whin' more common in the east and north of Britain, and in some cases applied to other prickly or thorny shrubs such as rest-harrow or buckthorn. 'Broom' is a non-spiny shrub belonging to the pea family, with long slender branches (once used for making besoms, or brooms), having yellow flowers. The name can, however, also be applied to the prickly 'gorse' (or 'furze' or 'whin'), which is perhaps not very helpful.

go-slow see **sit-in**

goulash see **hash**

gown see **dress**

Grace see **Lordship**

grain see **corn**

grammar school see **comprehensive school**

grasshopper/locust/cricket (leaping, chirping insect)
All three are members of the order of insects called *Orthoptera* ('straight-winged'), although some insects of this order, such as the house 'cricket', have no wings. The 'grasshopper' is familiar on a hot summer's day for being the opposite of the proverbially well-behaved child: heard but not seen. It is not really a pest. The 'locust' certainly is, although not found in Britain. It is infamous in Africa, for example, where it can swarm in vast numbers and cause serious depredations to crops. The 'cricket' exists in around 900 species, of which two are found in Britain: the field 'cricket' and the house 'cricket', distinguished from the 'grasshopper' by their very long antennae and extra loud 'chirps'.

grave/tomb (burial place)
A 'grave' is primarily an excavation for a dead body, although the word can include, or even exclusively mean, the mound or monument above such an excavation. A 'tomb' is any hole or excavation made for a body, not necessarily below ground, but in rock, say. It also means the structure over a 'grave' or even a monument not over a 'grave' at all, as the many fine 'tombs' seen in some churches. The word 'tomb' generally differs from 'grave' in implying a resting place for the body, whereas 'grave' tends to mean just the place where someone is buried. The words are often used more or less interchangeably, though, and there is hardly any different shade of meaning between 'gravestone' and 'tombstone', for example. Compare both 'grave' and 'tomb' with **vault**.

Great Britain see **England**

greengrocer see **grocer**

Green Paper see **White Paper**

Gregorian calendar/Julian calendar
(type of reckoning for a calendar)
The 'Gregorian calendar' is the one prevailing in the vast majority of western countries today. It was devised by Pope Gregory XIII in 1582 in order to correct the 'Julian calendar' which was 'out' by thirteen days. He therefore aimed to restore the vernal equinox to the date (21 March) it had at the time of the Council of Nicaea in AD 325. So in the Italian states, Portugal and certain other countries 4 October 1582 was followed by 15 October. England followed suit in 1752, China in 1912, the USSR in 1918, Greece in 1923 and Egypt in 1928. The earlier 'Julian calendar' had been established by Julius Caesar in 45 BC as a reform of the confused Roman republican calendar. Unfortunately, Caesar's astronomer Sosigenes over-estimated the length of the year by eleven minutes – which by 1582 had accumulated to thirteen days. Hence Gregory's reform. The 'Gregorian calendar' itself differs from the 'Julian' only in that no century year is a leap year unless it is exactly divisible by 400. This means that 1900 was not a leap year, but 2000 will be. A relic of the 'Julian calendar' still survives in Britain in the date of 6 April as the start of the tax year. This date is the 'Gregorian' adjustment (by thirteen days) of the start of the New Year under the 'Julian calendar', which was on 25 March (in turn transferred from 25 December in the fourteenth century).

grocer/greengrocer (dealer in household provisions and foods)
A 'grocer' sells such things as tea, butter, flour, sugar, spices, canned foods, and miscellaneous household stores such as matches or soap. He originally was one who sold in the gross, that is, not net. A 'greengrocer' sells mainly fruit and vegetables, although these can also be sold by a fruiterer. Supermarkets, of course, sell all these things, but there are still, thank goodness, a number of high-class 'grocers' and 'greengrocers' left.

gross amount see **net amount**

grouse see **pheasant**

grove see **wood**

guarantee/warranty (pledge that something is genuine)
Both words are of identical origin, with 'guarantee' coming directly from French and 'warranty' via Middle English. As normally used commercially, a 'guarantee' is an undertaking to repair something free of charge or replace it within a specified period, while a 'warranty' is a pledge as to the reliability or good working order of something (often implying a previous thorough testing or servicing, especially with second-hand goods). A 'warranty' may also overlap to some extent with a 'guarantee' in that the vendor may undertake to repair any faults or to replace parts over a certain period after purchase. This especially applies to more substantial purchases, such as that of a second-hand car.

guerrilla/partisan (irregular or 'underground' fighter)
The chief difference between the two is that 'guerrillas' aim to harass the enemy (by surprise raids, sudden attacks and the like), while 'partisans' seek to form an armed resistance to an invading or conquering power, as the French Resistance in the Second World War. 'Guerrilla', sometimes spelt with one 'r', is Spanish for 'little war', and was introduced into English during the Peninsular War of 1801–14. 'Partisan' is French in origin.

guitar/banjo/ukelele (musical instrument played by plucking its strings)
The 'guitar' has now largely and popularly gone electric, but it still has its traditional six strings and is still played either with the fingers or a plectrum (a small pointed device for plucking the strings). The 'banjo' can have from four to nine strings, although the usual number is five or six. It has the neck and head of a 'guitar' but the body shaped like that of a tambourine. It is chiefly associated with Negro music and entertainment, especially of the seaside sort. The 'ukelele' (also spelt 'ukulele' and known as 'uke' to aficionados) is a small, four-stringed Hawaiian 'guitar' (in fact originally Portuguese) with a very short finger-board. The word is Hawaiian for 'jumping flea', prob-

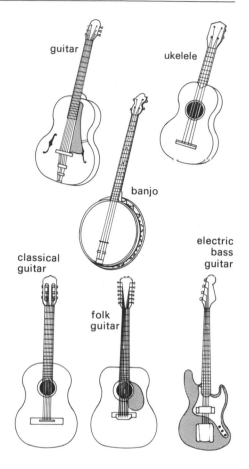

guitar
ukelele
banjo
electric bass guitar
classical guitar
folk guitar

ably from the native nickname of the nineteenth-century British army officer Edward Purvis, who was small and quick and who popularised the instrument. Another, more familiar name associated with it is of course that of George Formby, whose little 'ukelele' was sometimes called a 'banjolele', i.e. an instrument somewhere between a 'banjo' and a 'ukelele'.

gulf see **bay**

gun/cannon (firearm)
'Gun' is a very general word, so that it can apply to a small pistol on the one hand and a mighty howitzer on the other. In Britain 'gun' usually tends to mean a hand arm of the 'shotgun' type. In artillery, 'guns' are distinguished by having flat trajectories, while howitzers and mortars have arching

'hard' and 'soft' drinks, the former being powerful and possibly habit-forming, the latter inoffensive. A similar comparison is also popularly made between 'hard' pornography ('hard porn'), which is highly obscene and an offence in law, and 'soft porn' which is legally tolerated, as in 'X' films and many 'girlie' magazines.

hardware/software (computer or other technical components)
Both terms were originally computer operators' jargon. 'Hardware' is the actual computer equipment, the physical components, such as the keyboards and paper-tape punches. The 'software', contrasted with it, is the material necessary for operating the computers, that is, the written or printed programs and handbooks. (Instructions in these are followed by the 'liveware', the actual computer operators.) A similar distinction exists in the field of education, where the 'hardware' are devices such as tape recorders, closed-circuit television and other audiovisual equipment used for instruction, as compared with the materials (tapes, films, transparencies, etc.) used in such equipment and being the 'software'. A special type of (computer) 'software' is 'firmware', referring to programs and the like that are processed through a small special-purpose computer memory unit, as a 'read-only' memory.

hare see **rabbit**

harpsichord/spinet/clavichord/ virginals (early keyboard instrument)
The names for these precursors of the modern piano are sometimes used rather imprecisely, but the instruments are actually quite distinct. The 'harpsichord' has strings that are technically plucked, not struck (since 'harp-'), by leather or quill points connected with the keys. The 'spinet', possibly named after the Venetian inventor Giovanni Spinetti, is smaller than the 'harpsichord' and distinguished by its 'leg of mutton' outline. The 'clavichord' has strings that are struck, not plucked, by metal blades jutting from the rear end of the keys. Its name literally means 'key string'. Its tone is more brilliant than that of the 'harpsichord' and more expressive, since the force with which the keys are struck can be controlled by the player, as in a modern piano. The 'virginals' is, or was, the earliest and simplest form of 'harpsichord', with just one string to each note. The instrument, at its most basic, is really just a stringed box on a table. It is so named not because Queen Elizabeth, the Virgin Queen, particularly favoured it but, apparently, because it was regarded as a suitably 'maidenly' instrument for chaste young ladies.

hart see **stag**

hash/ragout/goulash (type of stew)
All three consist basically of a hot dish of small pieces of meat and vegetables cooked by simmering. A 'hash' is a dish in which the meat has been hashed, or cut up into small pieces beforehand. It will of course be eaten with vegetables, but these are not properly part of the 'hash'. A 'ragout', from the French *ragoût*, meaning a dish that 'regusts' you or revives your appetite, is usually a highly seasoned affair: a stew of poultry or meat and vegetables flavoured with mushrooms, tomatoes, port wine and the like. It must not be confused – the two foreign words look rather alike – with a 'goulash'. This is also a meaty seasoned stew, but the meat is usually beef or veal and the seasoning paprika. The dish is perhaps the most exotic of the three, as its name suggests: it is derived from the Hungarian for 'herdsman's meat'.

hat/cap (item of headwear)
A 'hat' usually has a brim and a fairly roomy crown, and is normally worn out-of-doors, as a bowler 'hat', top 'hat' or panama 'hat'. A 'cap' is normally brimless, soft, close-fitting, and frequently has a peak, as a cricket 'cap', school 'cap', peaked 'cap' or forage 'cap'. 'Caps' are mainly intended for outdoor wear, but some have specific indoor uses, as a 'nightcap', smoking 'cap' or awesome black 'cap' worn by a judge when pronouncing a death sentence. But such 'caps' are today either obsolete or obsolescent, and even the outdoor ones have only limited uses, notably in the worlds of sport and military life.

trajectories. A 'cannon' is a large 'gun', howitzer or mortar, as against a musket, rifle or other small arm. Modern 'cannon' usually have rifled bores. From the seventeenth century, the word came to apply to every 'gun' that was fired from a fixed carriage or fixed mount, usually with a bore greater than one inch. In the twentieth century, 'automatic cannon' came to be rapid-firing 'guns' in aircraft, with a calibre of 20 mm or more. In 1952 the United States Army introduced the 'atomic cannon', a 280 mm 'gun' that fired atomic shells. (Subsequently, however, atomic explosives came to be fired from standard artillery.)

gun/rifle (portable firearm)
'Gun' is a general word that covers most kinds of firearms, such as pistols, revolvers, muskets, machine 'guns', cannon, artillery 'guns' and the like. For most people, though, who read or hear a sentence such as 'He had a "gun"', the word denotes either a pistol of some kind or perhaps a 'shotgun'. At any rate it means a portable (hand-held) weapon, although not a 'rifle', which is a firearm with a rifled barrel (that is, a barrel with spiral grooves that make the bullet rotate and thus attain the target with greater accuracy), since the term 'gun' is almost always applied to firearms with no rifling. Those who do, however, call a 'rifle' a 'gun' may like to know that in a sense they are not far short of the mark, since a 'rifle' was originally called a 'rifle gun'. See also previous entry.

gynaecologist/obstetrician (doctor specialising in women's diseases and disorders)
A 'gynaecologist' – a title impressively hard to say and spell correctly – deals with diseases that in women differ from the equivalent in men, i.e. diseases of the urinary and genital organs, and thus subsumes diseases of childbirth – which is precisely what an 'obstetrician' deals with, since he cares for women in, before, and after labour, especially when there may be complications. The terms are respectively of Greek and Latin origin and mean 'one skilled in the study of women' and 'one standing facing' (i.e. like a midwife).

haberdasher/milliner (dealer in minor or ornamental items of dress)
A 'haberdasher' formerly dealt in a variety of items, in particular hats, caps and the like. Today he specialises in accessories for clothing and dressmaking, as ribbon, lace and thread. The word suggests 'hatter' but is of uncertain origin. The derivation may be in the name of some fabric. A 'milliner' is usually a woman who makes or sells women's hats or trimmings. She was originally a dealer from Milan. (The male equivalent, less originally, is a hatter.)

halibut see **cod**

hall/lobby/foyer (entrance or other passage in a building)
A 'hall' is usually an entrance passage although in American English can be a passage or corridor. A 'lobby' is a ra vague word meaning either an entr 'hall' or any passage, especially one s as some kind of ante-room. A 'foyer' is the large entrance 'hall' of a hotel. large room or 'hall' in a cinema o set aside for use of the audience in val. (The word is French, meanin 'fireside'; originally it was the theatre in which audiences we themselves in between acts.)

halter see **rein**

hamlet see **village**

handball see **netball**

harbour see **port** (place dock)

hard drugs/soft dru
As popularly divide
potent, addictive
heroin and LSD, w
not likely to caus
juana and cann

hawk/falcon/kestrel (bird of prey)
'Hawk' is a word applied fairly generally to all diurnal (daytime) birds of prey except the vulture and eagle. The 'hawks' proper, in Britain, are the 'sparrowhawk' (*Accipiter nisus*, which preys extensively on sparrows and other small birds) and the 'goshawk' (*Accipiter gentilis*, formerly used in falconry, and one of the larger or 'goose-sized' 'hawks'). In general, 'hawks' have short wings. 'Falcons', by contrast, have long wings. The name is applied to about sixty species of 'hawks' that are thus long-winged, and that formerly were trained – and are still, by a few dedicated enthusiasts – to hunt game-birds for sport. In a restricted sense the name 'falcon' applies to the genus *Falco* which has over 35 species, one of them being the small 'falcon' known as a 'kestrel' (*Falco tinnunculus*), the only 'kestrel' in Britain, where it is also known by the name

a falcon hooded, cast off and lured back by the falconer

'windhover' from its distinctive habit of hovering in the air with its head into the wind.

hawks/doves (political group advocating a specific policy)
'Hawks' advocate a hardline policy, even a militant one, while 'doves' prefer negotiation to violence, especially to terminate or prevent a military conflict. In the Cuban Crisis of 1962, the 'hawks' favoured an air strike to eliminate the Cuban missile bases, but the 'doves' opposed this policy and favoured a blockade. In the event it was the 'doves' who won the day when a blockade – tactfully called a 'quarantine' – was mounted on Cuba and Khrushchev subsequently backed down. It was this incident, in fact, that introduced the terms to the language at large, in the account of the crisis by the American journalist Charles Bartlett, President Kennedy's confidant.

haws see **hips**

health resort/spa (place visited for the benefit of one's health)
A 'health resort', or just 'resort', is often a place that has naturally beneficial amenities, as one by the sea, in the mountains, or with mineral waters. A 'spa' is specifically the latter of these, named after Spa, in Belgium, which has such a spring. In England Cheltenham was formerly a 'spa' and Bath still is, an association that is still officially recognised in the names of the railway stations of these towns, Cheltenham 'Spa' and Bath 'Spa'. Many visitors to 'spas' today perhaps derive as much benefit from the agreeable surroundings of the resort as directly from the mineral waters themselves.

heart attack see **stroke**

heath/moor (extent of open, flat, uncultivated land covered with shrubs)
A 'heath' properly has the shrub called heath, or heather, growing on it, especially in Scotland. A 'moor' is virtually the same, but the reference is more to the peaty land rather than the shrubs that grow on it. 'Moors' are characteristically found in high altitudes where the drainage is poor, as 'Dartmoor', 'Exmoor' and Bodmin 'Moor',

61

all in the West Country. The former existence of a 'heath' is often indicated (in disguised form sometimes) in place-names such as Heathcote, Hadley and Hatfield, while 'moors' can be similarly detected in places called Morton, Morden, and the two Leicestershire (late lamented Rutland) villages of Morcott and Cottesmore.

heathen/pagan (person who does not belong to an established religion)
The words have certain overtones. A 'heathen' is by implication a barbaric or unenlightened or – at the least – primitive person, who does not believe because he does not understand the prevailing religion, or who *will* not understand it. A 'pagan' is perhaps a more civilised person, especially a Greek or Roman in classical times who was not a Christian. Both words have interesting origins. A 'heathen' is so called because he was, most likely, a heath-dweller, that is, a kind of savage. A 'pagan' was so called because he was a 'civilian' – Latin *paganus* (originally 'country-dweller'): he was called this because he was not a 'soldier of Christ'. (The Roman Christians called themselves *milites*, 'soldiers'.)

Hebrew see **Jew**

heifer see **calf**

height/depth (measurement to the top – or to the bottom)
The 'height' of something is the distance from its base, where you are standing, to its top, as with a house, tree, cupboard, person or mountain. But it is also the distance of an elevated object above sea-level, such as a cliff-top, where you might be standing, in which case the measurement is in a sense downwards, or from below upwards. In measuring 'height', therefore, you yourself may be at the bottom or top. And if you are on that cliff-top, you could also measure the 'depth' of the rocks below you, since 'depth' is defined as 'measurement from top down' (*Concise Oxford Dictionary*). Normally, however, the 'height' of something is the measurement of a thing that is regularly above you, and the 'depth' the measurement of a thing that is regularly below you, as the bottom of the sea or a pot-hole. 'Depth', too,

is the measurement of a thing from its front to its back, as a shelf with a 'depth' of two feet, or from the surface inwards, as (try this for size) a gash in the plaster of the ceiling two inches in 'depth'. Tricky words, therefore – in their spelling, too, since 'height' has gained an 'e' (from 'high') and 'depth' has lost an 'e' (from 'deep'). And those who say – or even write – 'heighth', or an analogy with 'depth' and 'width' and 'length' and 'breadth', are unfortunately wrong.

helicopter/autogyro (type of aircraft propelled by rotating blades)
A 'helicopter' has one or more overhead rotors that turn horizontally around a vertical (or nearly vertical) axis, and it is these rotors that propel it and enable it to take off and land vertically and hover. An 'autogyro' is a form of 'helicopter', not so common now as formerly, whose overhead rotors are, however, non-powered, so that it is propelled by a propeller in front, like a conventional aeroplane. Because of its different type of propulsion it cannot take off vertically like a 'helicopter', although it can land vertically. The word is also spelt 'autogiro' and was originally a trade name meaning 'self-rotating'.

helm see **rudder**

herd see **flock**

herring/bloater/kipper (edible sea fish)
The 'herring' is a versatile fish from the North Atlantic. It can be sold fresh, salted, pickled, smoked, or canned (tinned). When cured and smoked – that is, split open, cleaned, rubbed with salt, and dried in smoke – it is called a 'kipper'. A special 'herring' is a 'bloater' which is one cured by bloating, that is, salted and smoked, but only slightly. (The word is related to 'bloat' meaning 'inflate', 'swell', although the obsolete word 'bloat' meaning 'soft and wet' gives the direct derivation.)

high commission see **embassy**

higher education see **further education**

high frequency/VHF/UHF (radio and television frequency band)

A 'high frequency' is one in the range 3 to 30 megacycles a second, i.e. 3 to 30 megahertz, or 10 to 100 metres. (A megahertz is the same as one million hertz, so that one hertz equals one cycle per second. The basic unit is named after the German physicist H. R. Hertz, who died in 1894.) 'VHF' (very high frequency) is a frequency between 30 megahertz and 300 megahertz (1 to 10 metres), while 'UHF' (ultra high frequency) is between 300 megahertz and 3000 megahertz (10 centimetres to 1 metre). (Above this there also exist super high frequency and extra high frequency, which are mainly used for satellite broadcasting.) Below 'high frequency' there is medium frequency, better known as medium wave, with a range of 300 kilohertz to 3 megahertz (100 to 1000 metres), and below this, low frequency (long wave), ranging from 30 kilohertz to 300 kilohertz (1000 to 10,000 metres). Most radio broadcasts in Britain go out on both medium frequency and 'VHF', with the 'high frequency' (short wave) used for broadcasting to Europe and overseas. Television broadcasts are made on both 'VHF' (or 405 lines) and 'UHF' (625 lines) by BBC 1 and ITV, and 'UHF' only by BBC 2. Eventually all three channels will broadcast on 'UHF' only. For more about cycles and frequency, see **alternating current**.

highway see **motorway**

hill/mountain (elevation of the Earth's surface)
When is a hill high enough to become a mountain? In Britain, the traditional definition of a 'mountain' is that it must be over 1000 feet high. However, any large or steep 'hill' can be called a 'mountain', and conversely, many 'hills' are over 1000 feet high: the Cheviot 'Hills', for example, rise to 2676 feet. In other parts of the world there are 'hills' higher than Britain's highest 'mountain'. The Chagai 'Hills' bordering Afghanistan and Pakistan, for example, rise to 2462 metres (8077 feet), while Britain's top peak, Ben Nevis, manages only 1343 metres (4406 feet). So it's all rather relative.

hind see **stag**

hippopotamus/rhinoceros (large, ungainly, thick-skinned animal)
The scientific names of the animals – more like those of prehistoric creatures – mean respectively 'river horse' and 'horny nose', and this brings out the immediate difference between them: the 'hippopotamus' lives in rivers in Africa, the 'rhinoceros' lives in both Asia and Africa but not in rivers, and moreover has one or two upright horns on its snout. The wretched rhino is, alas, a declining species, since its horn is valued as an aphrodisiac and worth almost half its weight in gold.

hips/haws (wild berries)
'Hips' are the red, fleshy, edible, berry-like fruit – not actually a true fruit – of the wild rose, and in particular the dog-rose. When there was a shortage of citrus fruits in the Second World War they were collected in large numbers by schoolchildren to make vitamin-packed rose-hip syrup. 'Haws' are the deep red inedible berries of the hawthorn – inedible to humans that is, for birds love them, especially finches.

hobby/pastime (leisure pursuit)
A 'hobby' is a favourite subject or occupation that is not one's main business, as gardening, 'do-it-yourself', or the rather vague 'reading' entered against 'hobbies' by some job applicants in the hope that it will impress as a cultural interest (although it may involve little more than a daily scan of the tabloid press). A 'pastime' is a recreation, something that makes the time pass agreeably, as playing cards, watching television or dining out.

hog see **pig**

Holland/Netherlands/Low Countries
(kingdom in western Europe famous for canals, tulips and windmills)
'Holland' is the popular but not official name of the country – which does, however, have two provinces named North 'Holland' (Noord-Holland) and South 'Holland' (Zuid-Holland). The official name is thus The 'Netherlands', which formerly included Belgium and Luxembourg as well. The 'Low Countries', which obviously means the same, is more a historic name, in turn once

63

applying to a wider region divided into a number of small states. Opinions seem to be divided about the actual meaning of the name 'Holland': possibly 'hollow' land, i.e. low-lying land, or 'wooded' land (related to 'holt'). One thing is clear: the district of 'Holland' in Lincolnshire (called officially the Parts of 'Holland' until 1974, when most counties in England were reorganised administratively) is, in spite of its tulips, nothing to do with its Dutch cousin. The name means 'heel' land, that is, land by the spur of a hill – which admittedly is surprising as the district is notoriously flat and fenny.

Holy Land see **Israel**

home see **house**

homicide/manslaughter (killing that may be justifiable or excusable)
'Homicide' is usually divided into justifiable, excusable and criminal. Justifiable 'homicide' is carried out: as a legal sentence of death, by an officer of justice as a means of taking a person who assaults or resists him and cannot be taken otherwise, or as a means of dispersing a riot or 'rebellious assembly' or preventing an atrocious crime such as murder or rape. It is excusable when committed by misadventure or in self-defence (when it virtually is the same as justifiable 'homicide' in the third instance mentioned above). Criminal 'homicide' embraces all other forms of killing, and is subdivided into 'manslaughter', murder, and infanticide. 'Manslaughter', as distinct from murder (see **murderer**), is unlawful killing without express or implied malice, especially where a person was provoked to lose his self-control or there was a high degree of negligence (as in a fatal motor accident). The difference between 'manslaughter' and murder is often, in fact, one of degree.

homonym/synonym (word closely associated with another)
A 'homonym' is a word identical in spelling to another, but having a different meaning, as 'bark', 'fair', 'like', and 'till'. (Some people also distinguish 'homophones', which are words pronounced alike but having a dif-

ferent meaning *and* spelling, as 'air' and 'heir', 'right' and 'write'.) A 'synonym' is a word that means approximately the same as another, as 'tired' and 'weary', 'tepid' and 'lukewarm', 'bit' and 'piece'. Not many synonyms have *exactly* the same meaning: there is usually a discernible difference or shade of meaning, if only a very fine one, or at any rate a difference of usage, as in 'little' and 'small', and 'begin', 'start' and 'commence'. The opposite of a 'synonym' is an antonym. Some apparent antonyms are in fact 'synonyms', as 'flammable' and 'inflammable', 'loose' and 'unloose', 'bend' and 'unbend'.

hornet see **wasp**

horsebox see **stall**

hotel/inn/pub (place where guests or customers can eat, drink, be merry, and often stay overnight)
The main purpose of a 'hotel' is to offer overnight accommodation. It therefore also offers, and usually to resident and casual guests alike, meals in a restaurant and drinks in one or more bars. An 'inn', broadly, seems to have two meanings: either a small 'hotel', which in turn may have developed or grown from a 'pub', or a 'pub' itself, especially an 'olde worlde', well-appointed, or simply pretentious one – or just an ordinary 'mine host' 'pub' which happens to have 'Inn' as part of its name, as the New 'Inn' or the London 'Inn'. This leaves us with the 'pub', the Englishman's local, social, club and serious drinking establishment. Many 'pubs' do, however, offer, if on a more modest scale, the services basically provided by 'hotels', since in a number you can eat as well as drink and also stay the night. Tourists in Britain seeking to eat, drink or stay overnight somewhere should not, though, seek the place of their choice through the telephone directory Yellow Pages, where all three categories are listed without any clear form of distinction, but should be guided by personal recommendation or a specialist publication!

house/home (place to live in)
The distinction was once more clear-cut than it now is. A 'house' was a building for

living in. A 'home' was a 'house' (or flat or any family residence) seen as not just a place to live in but a place of domestic comfort and family happiness. Today the two words are – at any rate in the jargon of estate agents – one and the same thing: 'new show "homes" for sale'. (Not that estate agents do not use the word 'house', they do – extensively. But when they say 'home' they simply mean 'house'.) In senses other than 'house', however, 'home' remains a highly emotive word, as in 'homeland', 'homesick', '"home" town' and even the 'Home' Guard. (For yet another example, see **longing**.)

humidity see **damp**

humiliation see **shame**

humour/wit (expression of the clever or amusing)
'Humour' usually depends on incongruities of some kind for its effect, whether verbally or visually. 'Wit' is a more intellectual affair, with carefully chosen words or ideas. This is not to say that it depends on careful or lengthy preparation: 'wit' can be spontaneous, and indeed the quickness of a witty response adds to its effectiveness. 'Wit' frequently uses analogy, especially between unlike things, for its impact, especially when such an analogy is expressed vividly or entertainingly. By implication, 'wit' is sharper than 'humour', 'humour' more kindly than 'wit'. 'Humour' can be unintentional; 'wit' rarely is. Furthermore, 'wit' is not necessarily amusing, of course – it can be perfectly serious.

hurdy-gurdy see **barrel-organ**

hurling/curling (Gaelic team game)
'Hurling' is a Gaelic game like Highland shinty, played with a team of fifteen on a field. The game, played in Ireland, resembles hockey, because the hurley, used for hitting the ball, suggests a heavy hockey stick. However, when 'hurling' you can catch the ball, kick it, hit it with your hurley *and* with your hands – a licence not permitted in the relatively more genteel hockey. 'Curling' is a Scottish game with four players on each side. It is played on an ice rink with two 'stones' – rock blocks shaped

like a squashed ball with a curved handle on top – as a kind of 'bowls on ice'.

hurricane see **storm**

hydrogen bomb see **atomic bomb**

hypothesis see **theory**

Ice Age see **Stone Age**

idiot/moron/cretin/imbecile (stupid or mentally subnormal person)
'Moron', 'imbecile' and 'idiot' are terms still sometimes officially used in Britain, in this order, for increasing degrees of mental subnormality, with a 'moron' having an IQ of 50 to 69 (the average is 100) and the mental age of a child of eight to eleven, an 'imbecile' having an IQ of 20 to 49, or a mental age below eight, and an 'idiot' having an IQ of 20 or under. A 'cretin' is specifically a person with a deformity and mental retardation caused by a thyroid deficiency. (Cretinism, this condition, is now usually called hypothyroidism.) The words have interesting origins: 'idiot' comes from the Greek meaning 'private person' (as in 'idiosyncrasy'); 'moron' (perhaps more predictably) is Greek 'foolish'; 'cretin' derives, via French, from 'Christian' (that is, a simple, holy person, 'God's fool'); 'imbecile', from Latin, literally means 'without a stick', that is, for support (the same Latin word, *baculus*, gives 'bacillus' as a term for a rod-shaped bacterium). All four words, of course, are used, viciously or playfully, as terms of abuse for a stupid or foolish person. It is a hard linguistic fact of life that words denoting mental or physical abnormalities or deficiencies often become insults: compare 'spastic', for example.

illness/disease (disorder of the body or a bodily organ)
An 'illness' is often a general disorder, usually not severe, but occasionally grave. A 'disease' is a more specific disorder, especially an active, lengthy or serious one. An 'illness' is a relatively vague word, too, so that it is often qualified, as a slight 'illness', serious 'illness', short 'illness' or long 'illness'. It relates, moreover, to the whole body or state of health, whereas a 'disease' may be in a particular organ *or* the whole body.

imbecile see **idiot**

impetus see **momentum**

incentive see **motive**

Indian elephant see **African elephant**

indignation see **anger**

infant see **child**

infant school see **nursery school**

infinity/eternity (state of continuing for ever)
The two words are rather mind-bending. 'Infinity' is a space, time or quantity that is boundless: no end or limit to it is known or can be envisaged. 'Eternity' relates to time only, where it is not quite the same as 'infinity', since it not only has no end, but – even more awesomely – had no beginning. Something that is thus eternal will exist, and has existed, for ever.

infra-red rays see **X-rays**

inlet see **bay**

inn see **hotel**

inoculation/vaccination (medical process of producing immunity against disease)
An 'inoculation', in general, induces a milder form of the disease and so safeguards against attacks from it. The word is not related to 'innocuous' but derives from Latin *inoculare*, 'to engraft'. A 'vaccination' is an 'inoculation' given specifically against smallpox, when the virus inoculated – the vaccine

– is that of cowpox. The word comes from the Latin for 'cow', *vacca*.

insecticide/pesticide (preparation for destroying unwanted creatures)
An 'insecticide' is designed to kill harmful insects. A 'pesticide' kills pests – which are not only harmful insects but animals and plants that are a threat to man or his interests. Some pests need specialised 'pesticides' such as a *herbicide* for weeds, a *fungicide* for fungus or a *vermicide* for worms. Take your pest, translate him into Latin, add '-cide' to denote the killing agent, and you have a particular 'pesticide'. (Ants? Formicide. Foxes? Vulpicide. Rats? Raticide.) Although take this too far and you tend to get a form of verbicide ('deliberate distortion or destruction of the sense of a word', as *Webster* defines it).

insignia/regalia (badges of honour or of office)
'Insignia' is a general term for distinguishing badges of any kind, as the ebony wand carried by the House of Lords official known as Black Rod, or the crown and three stripes that are the 'insignia' of a staff sergeant in the army. 'Regalia', as the term implies, are the 'insignia' of royalty, especially the 'regalia' used at coronations, such as the crown, orb and sceptre. The word also applies, however, to the 'insignia' of civic dignitaries, as a mayor (his chain of office, for example), or of an order of Freemasons.

insolvency/bankruptcy/liquidation (state of being unable to pay one's debts)
'Insolvency' is the inability to settle one's debts when they fall due. It is not the same as 'bankruptcy' since a very rich man can be insolvent if he cannot actually realise his assets at the time he needs the cash. 'Bankruptcy', which may follow 'insolvency', is the state of a person who declares that he is unable to pay his debts, or who by his conduct makes this obvious, and whose property is accordingly distributed by law among his creditors. Such a person will remain bankrupt officially until he has been discharged. He will have certain so called disabilities (such as not being able to be a company director or become an MP or JP) but he can continue in business. 'Liqui-

dation' is, in effect, the 'bankruptcy' of a company, with two sorts: voluntary and compulsory (which terms are self-explanatory).

institute of education see **teacher training college**

intellect see **mind**

intimacy see **familiarity**

introduction see **foreword**

invention/discovery (making or revealing of something previously unknown)
An 'invention' usually implies the creation of a new device or mechanism by thought, planning and the deliberate application of one's knowledge. A 'discovery' may well result from a planned course of action, but equally it can follow as a pure chance, with no idea of a deliberate search for something new. A 'discovery', too, is often simply the finding or establishing of something that was already in existence, whereas an 'invention' is always something that is new. Hydrogen was thus 'discovered' by Henry Cavendish in 1766; the hydrometer was 'invented' by Hypatia of Alexandria in 400.

inventory see **list**

invoice see **account**

iron/steel (tough, heavy metal)
Iron is an element with the atomic number 26 and is a white, magnetic metal. It is rarely found in a pure condition but in its impure form it is used for making a variety of tools, implements, machinery and the like. Pig-'iron' is the impure form of 'iron' obtained from 'iron' ores, wrought 'iron' is the purest commercial form of 'iron' ('iron' nearly free from carbon). 'Steel' is 'iron' containing a small percentage of carbon in the form of cementite. The properties of different 'steels' vary according to their percentage of carbon and other metals and to the method of preparation. 'Steel' with very little carbon, so called 'mild' or 'dead mild', is used for sheets, pipes and plates. Ultra-high-carbon 'steel' is used for the manufacture of chisels, files, razors and other turning and cutting tools. 'Steel' itself is now often blended with alloying elements such as nickel and chromium, and thus 'alloy steel' is used, for example, for tyres and widely for table knives.

irony see **sarcasm**

Israel/Palestine/Holy Land (country on shores of eastern Mediterranean)
'Israel' is the modern republic formed as a Jewish state in May 1948 out of the former British mandated territory of 'Palestine'. 'Israel' originally extended over approximately eight-tenths of this territory, the remainder being occupied after the Six Day War in June 1967, together with the Sinai Peninsula and Golan Heights in Syria. (In October 1973 these two latter regions became the scene of a new conflict between Arab forces, led by Egypt and Syria, and 'Israel'.) In biblical times 'Israel' was the northern kingdom of the Hebrews, with capital Samaria, the southern kingdom being Judah (Judaea), with capital Hebron. 'Palestine', now a historic region, was an ancient country that for centuries was closely linked to the Jewish people and to Syria. In biblical times it was occupied by these same two kingdoms of 'Israel' and Judah – and in the twentieth century has remained the scene of conflicts between Jews and Arabs. Its age-long religious associations have caused it to be known as the 'Holy Land' and a world centre of pilgrimage. It is a land sacred not only to Christians but, of course, to Jews, for whom it was the 'Promised Land', and to Muslims also, since certain sites are associated with Mohammed. The latter tie has resulted in the keen desire of Arabs, especially members of the Arab nationalist movement, to claim 'Palestine' (as they call 'Israel') as the homeland of the Arab people, who have lived there since the Muslim conquest of the seventh century. Meanwhile, in spite of the initiative of President Carter in bringing about the peace treaty between 'Israel' and Egypt, signed in Washington on 26 March 1979, unrest remains, and rival claims to the territory continue to be made with continuing loss of life.

Israeli see **Jew**

Israelite see **Jew**

jacket see **coat**

jade see **emerald**

jaguar see **leopard**

jam/marmalade (kind of fruit preserve)
'Marmalade' is not simply orange 'jam' eaten at breakfast. It is properly a jelly in which small pieces of citrus fruit (as oranges, lemons, or limes), including the rind, have been suspended. The citrus fruit ensures that the taste of 'marmalade' is thus normally sharp and tangy. Jam, on the other hand, is made from whole fruit (not usually citrus) that has been slightly crushed or pulped to make a preserve, as typically (and tastily) from strawberries, raspberries, apricots, plums, blackcurrants and the like. Depending on the kind of fruit, the taste of 'jam' is thus usually sweet and sugary. In spite of its close association with the English (and American) breakfast table, 'marmalade' in fact derives from the Portuguese for 'quince', since this was the fruit that the preserve was originally made from.

janitor see **caretaker**

jargon see **slang**

javelin see **lance**

jealousy see **envy**

jeans/denims (type of clothing popular with younger people)
'Jeans', characteristically a faded or blotchy blue in colour, are properly made of a twilled cotton cloth called 'jean' or 'denim'. When 'denim' is used for the fabric of overalls or work clothing, however, the garment is usually actually called 'denims'. As such, they are familiar to an older generation as a type of military working trousers, although they are toughish, loose-fitting and khaki-coloured in contrast to the thinnish, tight-fitting blue 'jeans' of today. Both are imports, as materials and words, since 'jeans' – or the fabric called 'jean' – originally came from Genoa in Italy, while 'denim' was once, in French, *serge de Nîmes*, or 'serge from Nîmes', a town in the south of France.

jelly/blancmange (sweet or flavoured gelatinous dessert)
A 'jelly' is clearish in consistency, a 'blancmange' opaque, as every child knows. But how does a milk 'jelly' differ from a 'blancmange', since both are opaque? The answer is in the ingredients. A 'blancmange' contains cornflour as a thickening agent, a 'jelly' does not. (What makes a milk 'jelly' opaque is its milk alone, even though milk, too, is present in the 'blancmange'.) Otherwise both contain gelatine or some similar substance, both are sweet or fruit-flavoured, both are made in a mould and both are attractively wobbly. They come in different colours, but originally, because of its cornflour, the 'blancmange' was white only, as its French name indicates.

jersey see **pullover**

jetsam see **flotsam**

jetty see **quay**

Jew/Israelite/Israeli/Hebrew (person whose religion is Judaism)
The word 'Jew' has essentially religious connotations, and applies especially to a descendant of the ancient nation of Palestine (called 'Hebrews' in the Bible) whose present-day representatives have found homes in many countries of the world apart from Israel, the 'true' Jewish homeland. 'Jew' as an appellation has lost most of its former derogatory associations, and is frequently used today as a contrast to 'Christian'. An 'Israelite' was a member of the ancient kingdom of Israel, just as an 'Israeli' is a native or inhabitant of the modern state of Israel. The 'Hebrews' were a Semitic people in ancient Palestine, familiar in Old Testament stories. (The 'Hebrews' to whom an Epistle in the New Testament is addressed were probably Hebrew Christians, that is, 'converted' 'Hebrews' from either Palestine or Rome.)

'Hebrew' is also the word for the ancient language of the 'Hebrews', revived as the official language of 'Jews' in Israel. In Europe, and elsewhere in the world as emigrants, 'Jews' speak a vernacular language, Yiddish. This is usually written in the 'Hebrew' alphabet and historically is a dialect of High German, with words from other languages.

jewel/gem (precious stone)
A 'jewel' can be three things: an ornament containing a precious stone; a precious (or semi-precious) stone itself, especially a cut and polished one; a special precious stone, or its substitute, used in a watch or some other delicate instrument. A 'gem' coincides with the second of these two definitions (a cut and polished precious stone), but the word is also used of a precious or semi-precious stone that has an engraved design – in other words a cameo.

jig see **reel**

jobber see **stockbroker**

joiner see **carpenter**

journal see **magazine**

journey see **trip**

judge/magistrate (public officer appointed to hear and try cases in court)
'Judge' is an all-embracing term but as normally used applies to 'judges' of the House of Lords, the Court of Appeal, the High Court, the Crown Court, and county courts. In England and Wales, a 'magistrate' is a minor judicial officer, such as a JP, or a stipendiary 'magistrate' (i.e., a paid one, usually in a large provincial town). In Scotland he is a provost or bailie of a burgh. More basically, 'judges' are major judicial officers, while 'magistrates' deal with less serious or weighty matters – and at the same time are 'judges' in their own right. 'Magistrates' also, however, conduct preliminary investigations into more serious offences. Judging which 'judge' does what is a rather complex business.

Julian calendar see **Gregorian calendar**

jumper see **pullover**

kerosine see **petrol**

kestrel see **hawk**

kindergarten see **nursery school**

kingdom/monarchy/sovereignty/realm
(state ruled by a king or queen)
A 'kingdom' is ruled by a king – or queen, as of course is the case with the United 'Kingdom'. (There *is* a word 'queendom' but it is rarely used.) A 'monarchy' is a state in which the absolute power is vested in a monarch, who is a hereditary sovereign ruler as a king, queen, emperor, tsar, etc. In an *absolute* 'monarchy' the monarch's powers are not limited by laws or constitution; in a *constitutional* 'monarchy', as in Britain, his or her powers are so limited. A 'sovereignty', or sovereign state, is one ruled by a sovereign – a title which more or less equals that of 'monarch' but which implies a recognised supreme head (which is what the word means) of a state, especially from the point of view of authority and overall supervision. ('Monarch', which literally means 'ruling alone', can sometimes virtually mean 'autocrat', especially in an *absolute* 'monarchy'.) A 'realm' is the domain of a king or queen, by implication including his or her subjects. The word is related more directly to 'regal' than to 'rule'.

kipper see **herring**

knave see **rascal**

knight see **lord**

knot see **mile**

labyrinth see **maze**

lacquer see **varnish**

lager see **ale**

lair see **den**

lake/pool/pond (enclosed body of water)
A 'lake' is the largest of the three, as the 'Lake' District with its fine mountain scenery and fifteen 'lakes', or the Great 'Lakes' of North America. A 'pool' has water that is usually still and often deep. It may not be surrounded entirely by land, but be a still or deep place in a river, as the 'Pool' of London, or reach of the Thames below London Bridge. A 'pond' is a relatively small body of still water normally formed naturally or by hollowing or banking, and an essential feature of rural or village life, still often viewed as picturesque or romantic ('Four ducks on a pond, A grass-bank beyond,' and that sort of thing). A 'lake' is called 'loch' in Scotland and 'lough' in Ireland, although these words can also denote an arm of the sea, as Loch Fyne and Lough Foyle.

lance/javelin (type of spear)
A 'lance' has a long wooden shaft and a pointed steel head and was used in war by soldiers on horseback (lancers) in charging. The word is also used for a spear for spearing fish or killing a harpooned whale. The 'lance' is thus an instrument of death and destruction. The 'javelin' is used for more peaceful purposes. It is the light spear thrown in an athletics contest. In the original Greek Olympics throwing the 'javelin' was one of the five events of the pentathlon, so it has an honourable history. It also, however, was originally used for hunting or in battle, in the days when man was beginning to discover the lethal potential of guided (more or less) missiles.

larboard see **port** (side of a ship)

larceny see **theft**

laudanum see **opium**

laurel/myrtle (evergreen plant with dark green shiny leaves)
The most straightforward distinction is that the 'myrtle' has white scented flowers and black berries, both quite conspicuous; the 'laurel' has small, inconspicuous yellowish or greenish white flowers and a rather insignificant green, purple or blackish berry. (The laurel is also known as the bay tree.) There is also a difference in height: the 'laurel' grows 20 to 60 feet tall, the 'myrtle' rarely reaches 20 feet.

lawn see **field** (area of play)

lawyer/barrister/attorney (professional person practising in court of law)
'Lawyer' is a general term for the person who conducts suits in court or gives legal advice and aid. He is usually a solicitor or a barrister. The latter acts for his clients in court, pleading a case or defending it. He does not deal directly with his clients but through a solicitor. Collectively, 'barristers' are called the 'Bar', and individually are known as 'counsel'. An 'attorney' – more correctly, 'attorney-at-law' – is a member of the legal profession who represents a client in court when pleading or defending a case, that is, in his client's absence he takes his place or 'turn'. In the USA 'attorney' applies to any 'lawyer'. Most of us are familiar with the American 'district attorney', or 'DA', who is the prosecuting officer of a district.

leasehold/freehold (type of basis for house purchase)
'Leasehold' gives the purchaser ownership for a limited number of years, traditionally 99. Today most houses, however, are sold 'freehold', so that the purchaser has full ownership for all time.

legation see **embassy**

legend/fable/tale/myth (fictitious, traditional or non-historical story)
A 'legend' was originally a collection of lives

of the saints, or something similar, such as the Golden 'Legend' of the thirteenth century. Later the word came to be used of a traditional story popularly regarded as historical or mythical, such as the stories about King Arthur. A 'fable' is a fictitious story often involving animals or inanimate things, and one that is designed to teach a moral, as the famous ones by Aesop. A 'myth' usually has an element of the supernatural, with fanciful ideas often based on natural or social phenomena, as the ancient Greek 'myths' (which attempted to explain such phenomena). A 'tale' is any narrative story treated imaginatively, as the *Canterbury Tales* by Chaucer, or the 'tales' of the Crusades, or Dickens's *Tale of Two Cities*.

leopard/panther/puma/jaguar/cheetah
(member of the lion or tiger family)
The 'leopard', found in Africa and southern Asia, regrettably in decreasing numbers, is closely related to both lions and tigers and has a pale brown or yellow coat with black spots or 'rosettes'. (It was once thought to be a cross between a lion and a pard, or 'panther' – hence its name.) The 'jaguar', found in Central and South America, rather resembles it but is more thick-set, although on the whole a little shorter. 'Panther' is another name in India for the 'leopard', especially the black variety (the black panther). The 'puma', called, confusingly, 'panther' by early settlers in Peru, where it lives also as the mountain lion, is related to the 'jaguar' but differs from it by its lack of spots. Another distinction between the two is that the 'puma' is timid in the presence of man, but the 'jaguar' is more likely to attack. The 'cheetah', also known as the 'hunting leopard', is found widely in Africa and India – although also in rapidly decreasing numbers – and is distinguished by its long limbs, non-retracting, blunt claws, and its extreme speed when in full chase, even as fast as 60 miles an hour.

libel/slander
(defamation of another in spoken or written form)
Roughly – 'libel' is defamation in written or printed form, and 'slander' is oral defamation only. The scope of 'libel' – the word derives from Latin *libellus*, 'little book' – is more extensive than that of 'slander', however, and

can be punished as a criminal offence, whereas 'slander' can be proceeded against only civilly. 'Libel' must in fact consist of matter published in permanent form, and since 1952 this also includes broadcast statements. It seems wiser to steer clear of either, though.

liberty see freedom

lie/untruth/fib
(false or incorrect statement)
A 'lie' is a fairly serious falsehood, usually a deliberate one that is told with the intention of deceiving. An 'untruth' may be deliberate or unintentional, and it is not so grave as a 'lie'. A 'fib' is the least serious type of falsehood – a trivial 'lie', or just a partial 'untruth'. It's almost a pleasant, homely word: 'What a "fib"!' you say in secret admiration of such daring. It's also a rather curious word, in origin an abbreviation of 'fibble-fabble', itself a reduplication of 'fable'. Such an explanation sounds itself like a 'fib' – but it's no 'lie'.

lift-off/blast-off
(stage in the launch of a spacecraft)
'Blast-off' is the initial firing of the rocket's motors. This gives the thrust for 'lift-off', the actual launch, when the rocket leaves the ground. The well-known countdown ('Ten, nine, eight, . . .') is actually to 'lift-off', with 'blast-off', or 'ignition', occurring a few seconds before 'zero' or 'launch'.

limerick/clerihew
(short, witty, biographical verse)
A 'limerick', which can range from the epigrammatic through the ribald to the downright indecent, has five lines, with the first and second rhyming with the last and the shorter third and fourth lines rhyming. It was popularised by Edward Lear's nursery rhymes (many of which are still very effective, but spoilt by repetitiveness in the last line). The 'limerick' traditionally starts, 'There *was* a blank blanket of blank . . .', as Lear's:

> There was an old person of Ealing,
> Who was wholly devoid of good feeling;
> He drove a small gig,
> With three Owls and a Pig,
> Which distressed all the people of Ealing.

71

The name is said to derive from the chorus, 'Will you come up to Limerick?' sung after each verse as a refrain, Limerick being the town in Ireland. A 'clerihew' is in four lines, with the first two rhyming and the last two, and is a 'potted biography' of some kind, usually with a dig at the subject's reputation or characteristic behaviour. It was devised by the English journalist Edmund Clerihew Bentley, who died in 1956. Some of his classic 'clerihews' are still quite cruel, as the famous:

George the Third
Ought never to have occurred.
One can only wonder
At so grotesque a blunder.

The 'clerihew' obviously offers considerable scope for development, but has never acquired the general popularity enjoyed by the 'limerick'.

liqueur see **liquor**

liquid/fluid (non-solid substance)
A 'liquid' is a substance such as water, oil or alcohol that is not solid or gaseous. Very often it is wet. A 'fluid' is anything that *flows* (which is what the word means), either a 'liquid' or a gas, 'liquids' being technically incompletely elastic, and gases completely so. Substances can change, of course, so that water, for example, can be a 'liquid', or a 'fluid' (as steam), or solid (as ice), and oxygen, say, can be reduced from a gaseous state to a 'liquid' by intense cold.

liquidation see **insolvency**

liquor/liqueur (strong alcoholic drink)
'Liquor' usually means spirits, as whisky and brandy, as distinct from wines and beer. In the USA, however, 'liquor' can mean any alcoholic drink, although often the reference is specifically to spirits. A 'liqueur', in Britain often pronounced 'likyure', is a class of 'liquors', especially the strong, sweet, highly-flavoured, after-dinner ones such as chartreuse, curaçao and cherry brandy. The two words are close in spelling and meaning, and are sometimes confused.

list/catalogue/inventory (written record or list)

A 'list' is a series of things in order or not, as a shopping 'list' or a laundry 'list' (possibly in no special order) or a price 'list' or school 'list' (presumably in some kind of order). A 'catalogue' is a special 'list' of things, such as books for sale, that are arranged according to some principle, as alphabetically or by subjects. A 'catalogue', too, will often have particulars of the things listed. An 'inventory' is a descriptive 'list' of property, stock, goods or the like. Military 'inventories' are noted for their distinctive, and sometimes curious, word order, as 'Chair, arm, officer's, one' or 'Polish, boot, other ranks, for the use of'. This sort of thing is used by some writers in order to produce laughs, cheap, readers, for the delectation of.

load/burden (something carried)
Originally, both words meant the same: something carried by a person or animal or conveyed in or on a vehicle. 'Burden' – except in the phrase 'beast of "burden"', where the word is still used neutrally – now means an unwelcome or unduly heavy load. In a figurative sense, however, both words imply an unreasonable amount of duties, cares, and the like, as in the 'real "load" on my mind' that is a constant worry. To say that 'children can be a "burden"', though, suggests something of a pun, since 'burden' is related to 'bear', 'born' (and 'borne') and 'birth'.

lobby see **hall**

locust see **grasshopper**

loft see **attic**

Londoner/cockney (native of London)
A 'Londoner' is any native of London, or someone who has lived there a long time. A 'cockney' is a 'Londoner' who comes from the East End, especially with his distinctive accent and 'rhyming slang' dialect. A true cockney is held to have been born within the sound of Bow Bells – the bells of the church of St Mary-le-Bow in Cheapside. The name might be supposed to derive from 'cocky', which is also fitting, but in fact comes from 'cock's egg' which, although obviously a biological impossibility, was a slang term, a nickname given by country folk, for a small,

misshapen egg, and subsequently a towns-man. To country people, a townsman, and especially such a blatant one as a 'Londoner', would be regarded as a queer fish, and a strange species of the human race.

longing/craving/yearning (strong desire for something)
A 'longing' is a keen wish for something, especially a thing that is remote but which may one day be attainable, as a 'longing' for peace or for a meeting with a loved one. A 'craving' is a sense of need in spite of oneself, usually implying a kind of hunger, as a 'craving' for a drink or for affection. A 'yearning' is often a wistful or romantic 'longing', as a 'yearning' for home when one is away from it. It's not for nothing 'yearn-ing' turns up in romantic or nostalgic songs to rhyme with 'burning', 'turning', 'spurn-ing' and the like. Perhaps the *locus classicus* is the First World War song, 'Keep the home fires burning'. (The word 'yen' is apparently not related to 'yearn', in spite of the close-ness in meaning.)

loosebox see **stall**

loot/booty (stolen goods or possessions)
'Loot' and 'booty' are both some kind of spoil or plunder, as from an enemy, but 'booty' nearly always implies a common acquisition, a plunder that is to be divided. In addition, 'loot' is also the word for a burglar's haul, and a slang term for money. The term 'booty' suggests a haul of old boots, as in the stock cartoons of incom-petent anglers, but actually derives from the French *butin*, with the same meaning, itself apparently coming from a German word meaning 'share'.

lord/peer/knight (high-ranking title of the nobility)
'Lord', as a rank or title, has several appli-cations. It is used for any 'peer', for certain high officials as a 'Lord' Mayor, 'Lord' Com-missioner or 'Lord' Lieutenant, for a bishop or archbishop, less formally for a marquis, earl, viscount or baron, as a courtesy title for the younger sons of a duke or marquis (before his Christian name), and for a legal official or dignitary as a 'Lord' of Appeal in Ordinary or the 'Lord' Chief Justice. 'Peer' is the title for the member of any of the five degrees of nobility: duke, marquis, earl, viscount and baron. A 'peer' of the realm is one entitled to sit in the House of 'Lords'. A 'knight' is a man on whom a special honour or 'dignity' has been conferred by the sovereign for personal merit or services to the country. In Britain he holds a rank next below that of a baronet, with 'Sir' before his Christian name. The title is not hereditary, and not so high-ranking as many suppose.

Lordship/Excellency/Grace/Worship (title or form of address for member of the nobility or other high-ranking person, preceded by 'Your', 'His', etc.)
'Lordship' is used of any holder of the title Lord, as well as of a judge or woman sheriff; 'Excellency' is the title of a governor or am-bassador; 'Grace' applies to a duke, duchess or archbishop; 'Worship' is the word for a mayor and for most magistrates. Both 'Lord-ship' and 'Worship' can be used ironically for any 'superior' person, especially one who fancies himself: 'I'll have a word with His "Lordship"', 'Oh yes, Your "Worship"', three bags full, Your "Worship"!'

lot see **fate**

loudspeaker/amplifier (instrument for increasing the volume of sound)
A 'loudspeaker', or simply 'speaker', is either an individual instrument, as one for boosting the volume of speech, music, and so on in a hall or the open air, or an instrument that is an integral part of a record player, music centre, radio, TV set or the like. It will be actuated by an 'amplifier', which is a device that accepts a small input signal which it 'converts' to a large output signal by means of a circuit containing transistors or valves. An 'amplifier' thus amplifies the electrical charge, not the sound. 'Loud-speaker' is a word which in several lan-guages has been literally translated from the English, as French *haut-parleur*, German *Lautsprecher*, Italian *altoparlante* and Russian *gromkogovoritel'*.

Low Countries see **Holland**

loyalty/allegiance (devoted or dedicated attachment to a person or thing)
'Loyalty' is a lofty but usually personally motivated sense of dedication, as to one's country, family or friends. 'Allegiance' is more an impersonal sense of duty, as that of a citizen to his country or ruler, or a party member to a cause.

lumbago see **sciatica**

lunch/dinner (one of regular meals of the day)
Most people have a meal at or shortly after midday. What they call it depends rather on their eating habits and social (and even regional) background. Those who call it 'lunch' may regard it as the main cooked meal of the day, in which case they will have a lightish supper (or tea) in the evening. Those who take a light 'lunch' may do so because their main meal of the day will be in the evening, when it will be called 'dinner'. (A formal 'lunch' is called a 'luncheon'. This rather strange word probably derives from the equally strange 'nuncheon', which originally meant a 'noon drink'.) But for many people, in particular manual workers and children, the main midday meal is called 'dinner', and the evening meal will be either tea or, perhaps less often, supper. Such manual workers, especially those active out of doors, may additionally have a mid-morning snack which they call 'lunch', which more or less corresponds to other people's 'elevenses'. So depending how they regard their midday meal, people have either a 'lunch' break or a 'dinner' break half-way through their working day. Household pets, incidentally, always have 'dinner' as their main meal. Exactly when they have it depends on their boss.

lustre see **gloss**

mackintosh see **raincoat**

madrigal/glee (musical composition for unaccompanied voices)
These charmingly dated yet often romantic forms of music originated two or three hundred years ago and still have a small but loyal and enthusiastic following. A 'madrigal' is a part-song for several voices sung properly with elaborate contrapuntal imitation and without instrumental accompaniment. It originated in Italy and came to England in the sixteenth century, where such composers as Byrd, Orlando Gibbons, Weelkes, Wilbye, Morley and Tomkins brought it to a fine and popular art. A 'glee' is a composition for three or more voices – strictly, adult male ones – with one voice to each part and words grave or gay and, as the 'madrigal', without instrumental accompaniment. The heyday of the 'glee' was the eighteenth century with its 'glee' clubs, such as the famous Noblemen and Gentlemen's Catch Club founded in 1761 and still in existence. The chief difference between the two is in the words: 'madrigals' are mostly musical love poems; 'glees', which may be gleeful (the latter word comes from the former), have as their themes a range of more or less poetic or fanciful subjects. They are also a purely English form, whereas, as mentioned, the 'madrigal' was an import.

magazine/journal/periodical (publication appearing regularly)
A 'magazine' is a general term for a popular publication of some kind, often a weekly or monthly one, usually thought of by contrast with a newspaper, published daily. A 'journal', in spite of its name, which means 'daily', is normally a monthly or even quarterly publication on a specialised or learned topic, especially a scientific one. (As a specific example of the difference, compare the *Geographical Journal*, the learned quarterly of the Royal Geographical Society, and the *Geographical Magazine*, the popular

monthly.) A 'periodical' is a general but rather formal word, usually seen in public reading rooms, for any regular publication, including newspapers.

magenta see **violet**

magician see **conjuror**

Maginot Line/Siegfried Line (line of fortifications in Europe built before the Second World War)
The 'Maginot Line', named after the French minister of war, André Maginot, was built in the 1930s on the north-east border of France, along the French-German frontier (but not the French-Belgian frontier, which the Germans broke through in 1940). The 'Siegfried Line' was constructed, also in the 1930s, as the German answer to the 'Maginot Line', and in fact faced the latter along the German western frontier. The Germans used it when retreating from France in 1944. The name was also used in the First World War of a fortified line occupied by German troops in France, although the Allies knew this as the Hindenburg Line. The Second World War 'Siegfried Line', named after the legendary German hero (whose own name, perhaps ironically, means 'victory-peace'), became well known from the British song of the late 1930s, 'We're gonna hang out the washing on the Siegfried Line'. When the Canadians broke through it in the spring of 1945 they hung a number of sheets on it with a large notice, 'The Washing'.

magistrate see **judge**

malice see **spite**

mandarin see **tangerine**

mandrill see **gorilla**

manslaughter see **homicide**

map/chart (representation of surface of earth or of the sky)
A 'map' is a graphic or pictorial representation of a particular area, with conventional symbols. A 'chart' can be an outline 'map' or a special 'map' for navigators in water or air. Distinguishing another way, a 'map' is

more for passive use (fact-finding, study), while a 'chart' is for active use (calculating one's route, estimating distances, exploring territory).

marchioness see **marquis**

margarine see **butter**

marijuana see **cannabis**

marionette see **puppet**

marmalade see **jam**

maroon see **violet**

marquess see **marquis**

marquis/marquess/marchioness
(high-ranking member of the peerage)
A 'marquis' ranks between a duke and an earl in Britain; in other countries between a duke and a count. A 'marquess' is not the wife of a 'marquis' – this is a 'marchioness' – but a form of 'marquis' used by some peers who hold this rank. The spelling 'marquess' is an official one, as used in the Roll of the House of Lords and as favoured by *The Times*. Some Scottish 'marquesses', however, prefer the spelling 'marquis', since this is the French spelling, which reminds many Scots of their particular French connection – the 'Auld Alliance' between Scotland and France that dates back to the thirteenth century. See also **lord**.

marriage see **wedding**

marsh/swamp/bog/slough (tract of wet or soggy land)
A 'marsh' is a tract of low, wet land in general. A 'swamp' is wet ground that is also soft and unfit for cultivation even though certain trees may be growing in it. A 'bog' is wet, spongy ground with soil mainly composed of decayed vegetable matter (see **turf**). A 'slough' is a piece of soft, muddy ground in Britain; in Canada and the USA it is a marshy or reedy pool, pond or other stretch of water. The word is not now commonly used in Britain, but still exists in the place name Slough, the industrial town in Berkshire, of which John Betjeman wrote, in

jaunty but characteristically jaundiced vein, 'Come friendly bombs and fall on Slough, It isn't fit for humans now.'

martin see **swallow**

mascot see **charm**

mason see **builder**

mass see **weight**

mast/spar/yard (pole on a ship to which sails are attached)
The 'mast' is the general pole set up vertically to support the sails. The 'spar' is the word for the actual pole that serves either for the 'mast' or for a 'yard', which is a cylindrical 'spar' slung horizontally (a so called square 'yard') or slantwise (a lateen 'yard') across the 'mast' to hold the sails. The word derives from 'yard' – 'branch', 'stick', not 'yard' – 'enclosed piece of ground'.

match see **game** (portion of play forming a scoring unit)

mate see **check**

mauve see **violet**

maze/labyrinth (confusing pattern of paths or routes)
The two words are more or less completely synonymous, with 'maze' perhaps being the commoner word, as the famous one at Hampton Court. Possibly a 'maze' is a less convoluted thing, such as one cut out of the turf, or merely with low hedges, while a 'labyrinth' applies more to a mass of confusing passages, a 'rabbit-warren', as in a large building. The original 'labyrinth' was the one in Crete, where the mythological Minotaur was confined. A 'maze' is designed to amaze, or bewilder, confuse and confound. 'Mazes' may well have been originally built as defences, designed to baffle the enemy.

meadow see **field** (enclosed area of grass)

meal see **flour**

meaning/sense (what is expressed, indicated or intended)
'Meaning' denotes what is – or is intended to be – actually expressed, as the 'meaning' of a word or the 'meaning' of a pictorial sign. 'Sense' tends to mean a particular 'meaning', as 'knave', which used to mean 'boy', but has become obsolete in this 'sense'. 'Sense' is used rather more loosely to mean 'intelligible "meaning"', as 'I don't see the "sense" of it'. This dictionary is concerned not only with the 'meanings' of words but their differing 'senses'.

measles/German measles (infectious disease with red spots)
The popular names for the two diseases are as alike as their medical names, respectively *rubeola* and *rubella*. 'Measles' is the contagious virus disease with fever and a blotchy rash commonly contracted by children. 'German measles' is shorter and milder, although it has a longer incubation period. It is more common in older children and young adults, for whom it is a minor inconvenience. It is a more serious thing for a pregnant woman, however, since it may lead to a defect of the foetus. One attack of 'German measles' gives lasting immunity. Oddly enough, there is no cross-immunity between 'measles' and 'German measles', so that many supposed second attacks of 'measles' are in fact of 'German measles'. Why 'German'? The name derives from the close study of epidemics of the disease made in Germany in the nineteenth century.

medicine man see **witch doctor**

melody see **tune**

metaphor see **simile**

meteor see **comet**

meteorite see **comet**

middle/centre (location of something furthest from the edges or sides)
The difference is in precision: the 'middle' is somewhere *near* the 'centre' – which is the exact 'middle'. Thus the 'middle' of the night is at some time during it, and if you find yourself in the 'middle' of an argument

you are simply engaged in one. The 'centre' of a square, however, is right in the 'middle', and a person who is the 'centre' of attraction is the focus of everyone's attention.

Middle East see **Near East**

Middle West/Far West/Wild West (area of the USA)
The 'Middle West', or Midwest, is the northern portion of the central USA covering the states of Ohio, Indiana, Illinois, Missouri, Michigan, Wisconsin, Iowa, Minnesota and parts of Kansas, Nebraska and North and South Dakota, which is one of the world's most fertile farm regions. The term 'Middle West' came into use with the settlement of the 'Far West' – the area of the Rocky Mountains and Pacific Coast – in the late eighteenth and early nineteenth centuries. The 'Middle West' is sometimes also known as the Heartland of America. The 'Far West', however, is not the same as the rootin', tootin' 'Wild West', home of cowboys and westerns, which was the western frontier region of the USA before the establishment of a stable government.

midge see **gnat**

midget/dwarf/pygmy (very small person)
Thinking here of real human beings: a 'midget' is a perfectly formed, normally functioning person, but very small; a 'dwarf' is a person whose growth has been checked and who is of stunted appearance, perhaps with a large head or improperly formed in some way; a 'pygmy' is a member of one of the naturally small-sized peoples of Africa and Asia, as some of the Bushmen of the Kalahari Desert. (The latter word wrongly suggests 'piggy'; it actually derives from Greek *pugme*, the name of a measurement – the length from a person's elbow to his knuckles.) For mythical 'dwarfs' see **goblin**.

mild see **ale**

mile/knot (unit of distance or speed)
There are 'miles' and 'miles'. The statute 'mile' is 1,760 yards in length, or about 1.609 kilometres, and the standard unit of distance in both Britain and the USA. In Britain there is also an admiralty, air, geographical,

nautical, and sea 'mile'. These are all different names for the 'mile' that is approximately 2,025 yards in length, or more precisely, one minute of the great circle of the earth. A 'knot' can also be this (the nautical 'mile' especially), but properly it is a unit of speed equal to one nautical 'mile' per hour. This speed was originally measured by knots on a log-line that ran out from a moving ship: the number of knots that ran out in a certain time, measured by a running sandglass, was the 'rate of "knots"'. Thus 'knots', because of the difference in length between a statute and a nautical 'mile', seem slower to the landlubber than his customary m.p.h.

milliner see **haberdasher**

mind/intellect/brain/brains (mental faculties)
'Mind' is that which thinks, feels and wills, and is usually contrasted with 'body' and occasionally with 'soul' or 'spirit'. Part of one's 'mind' is the 'intellect', which thinks or reasons, as distinct from feeling or willing. It is often contrasted with emotions, 'head not heart'. 'Brain' – other than the bodily organ – is virtually synonymous with 'intellectual capacity' or simply 'intellect', so that one can talk of a fertile 'brain' or a lively 'brain'. 'Brains' tends to mean shrewd or practical intelligence, so that you can pick someone's 'brains' – if he has the 'brains', that is. 'Brain' also, of course, means 'brainy person', as in 'brain' drain and the brains trust.

minister/priest/pastor (person authorised to conduct religious worship)
'Minister' is normally the title assumed by a Nonconformist clergyman, as a Methodist 'minister'. Strictly speaking, the title can apply to any clergyman, even an Anglican one. (See various rubrics in the Book of Common Prayer, where, for example, 'the Minister shall read with a loud voice', or 'Then shall the Minister kneel'.) In practice, in the Church of England, a 'minister' is normally regarded as the conductor of a religious service – whether a 'priest' or not – with a 'priest' in turn often being regarded as one appointed, and ordained, to represent the people before God. According to the

OED, the word minister was used 'at first chiefly by those who objected to the terms "priest" and "clergyman" as implying erroneous views of the nature of the sacred office'. A 'pastor' – the word deliberately evokes a shepherd – is used in some churches (non-Anglican ones) as an alternative to 'minister'.

mink/sable/ermine (precious fur)
'Mink' is a brown fur from the mink, a small animal like a stoat. 'Sable' is not a black fur, as might be supposed, but a dark brown one. It comes from the Arctic or Subarctic marten, an animal like a weasel. Weasel-like too is the 'ermine', an animal that has brown fur in summer, and white, except for a black-tipped tail, in winter. It's the white, winter fur that is used for the robes of judges, peers and other dignitaries. The name is said to derive from Latin *mus armenius*, 'Armenian mouse', which is a reminder that the richest and best 'ermine' still comes from Russia. For the distinction between stoats and weasels see **ferret**.

minnow/tiddler/stickleback (small fish traditionally caught in streams by small boys with jam-jars)
The 'minnow' can rise to the scientific name of *Phoxinus phoxinus*. It is a small fish up to three inches long found in streams and rivers. The 'tiddler' is the name of any small fish, in fact, but especially the 'stickleback', which is distinguished by the sharp spines on its back. In length it is from two to four inches, and it is found in both fresh and salt water. All three small fry have names that suggest their diminutiveness: the 'minnow' seems to be related to 'minute', the 'tiddler' is probably a combination of 'tiddly' and 'tittlebat', a childish name for the 'stickleback', while the 'stickleback' itself has the little spines ('stickles') on its back in front of its dorsal fin.

minor see **child**

minster see **cathedral**

minstrel/troubadour (medieval musician who sang or recited to the accompaniment of a musical instrument)
A 'minstrel' was rather more than just a singer or reciter; he was really a professional itinerant entertainer, who could tell stories, juggle and do acrobatics, much welcomed in castle households in the winter months, when hunting was not possible and there was a dearth of distractions. A 'troubadour' was more of a specialist; he sang songs of chivalry and courtly love, and he notably sang them in southern France. (The word comes from Provençal *trobador*, meaning 'one who finds', that is, seeks out, invents and composes.)

minute/moment (short period of time)
Apart from the exact sense of 'minute' (60 seconds), which denotes the briefer time? If I say 'Wait a "minute"', am I likely to be longer than if I say 'Wait a "moment"'? On the whole, the answer is yes. Compare such expressions as 'in a "minute"', meaning you must wait while I complete what I am doing (which may even take more than the 60-second 'minute'), or 'just a "minute"', meaning I want to object and wish you to pause while I do so. However, the difference is certainly a fine one, and many people use the words interchangeably. The *Concise Oxford Dictionary* does in fact define 'minute' as 'short time', though, and 'moment' as 'very brief portion of time' as well as 'short period of time'.

mist see **fog**

mistake/error/fault (incorrect or wrong act)
A 'mistake' is usually caused either by bad judgment or by disregard of some rule – in which case, of course, it is deliberate. An 'error', by contrast, although an infringement of a similar nature, is unintentional, as an 'error' of judgment or an 'error' in calculating. A 'fault' is a 'mistake' made because of some kind of defect or imperfection or moral shortcoming. The word often implies an offence, as a 'fault' at tennis.

module see **probe**

moisture see **damp**

molasses see **treacle**

mollusc/crustacean (class of shellfish)
These are the two broad categories of shell-fish, of which altogether there are more than 90,000 varieties. Among 'molluscs' are oysters, mussels, clams, scallops, whelks and snails; among 'crustaceans' are lobsters, crabs, crayfish, shrimps, prawns and barnacles. Neither category – technically a phylum – has a backbone. 'Molluscs' have a soft body (Latin *mollis*, 'soft') inside a shell that builds up in layers and becomes hardened with calcium carbonate from the water; 'crustaceans' have a crusty shell that they periodically shed as they grow.

moment see **minute**

momentum/impetus (moving force)
Two rather technical words, or at any rate imposing ones. The simplest distinction is: 'momentum' is the force *of* something moving; 'impetus' is the force *with which* something moves. Otherwise, 'momentum' is the 'impetus' of something that is gained by movement.

monarchy see **kingdom**

monastery/abbey/priory (residence of a religious community)
A 'monastery' is usually a community of monks – as a nunnery is of nuns. An 'abbey', which is or was centred on an 'abbey' church or cathedral, is a community of monks or nuns under an abbot or abbess. Many 'abbeys' disappeared with the dissolution of the 'monasteries' under Henry VIII, and all that was left was the 'abbey' church. This is what happened with Westminster 'Abbey' in London. The status of an 'abbey' is that of an important 'monastery'. A 'priory', thus, is normally a smaller 'monastery' or nunnery governed by a prior or prioress respectively, and may also be subordinate to an abbey. (A prior belongs to a mendicant or 'begging' order, as does a prioress. Apart from being the head of a priory or nunnery, a prioress may be the title of a 'second-in-command' in an 'abbey', where her superior will be the abbess.)

money order see **postal order**

monk/friar (member of male religious order)
A 'monk' is properly a member of a monastery, where under a superior he is bound by vows of poverty, chastity and obedience. The female equivalent is 'nun'. A 'friar', strictly, is not attached to a monastery, but a member of a so-called mendicant order (who originally worked or begged for a living), such as the Franciscans, Augustinians, Dominicans and Carmelites. If he lives, as he probably does, in a religious house, it will be a friary. He will, however, be bound by the same vows as a 'monk'. There are female equivalents, as the Poor Clares who form the Second Order of Franciscans. They are simply called 'sister'. The title 'friar' originates from Latin *frater*, 'brother'.

monologue/soliloquy (scene in a play in which one person alone speaks)
In origin, the words are exact doublets: Greek 'monologue' and Latin 'soliloquy' both meaning 'single speech'. They are now carefully distinguished, however. A 'monologue' is a speech made by one person in the company of others; a 'soliloquy' is spoken by one person on his own. Dramatically, Hamlet's 'To be or not to be' speech is thus a 'soliloquy', since no one else is on the stage. (For definition purposes, the audience doesn't count!) Henry V's 'Once more unto the breach, dear friends' is a 'monologue', therefore.

moor see **heath**

moped see **motorcycle**

morning dress/ evening dress (formal clothes worn on a special occasion)
'Dress' here is used in the sense 'men's costume', not 'garment worn by women'. 'Morning dress', worn typically at weddings, consists of black morning coat with grey or lavender waistcoat and striped trousers. Accessories are: white shirt, white stiff collar (wing or turned down), grey tie and grey top hat. 'Evening dress', as worn at an official dinner or special theatre performance, comprises a black tail coat with silk lapels, black trousers, white waistcoat, stiff-fronted white shirt, white wing collar and white bow tie. In place of the tail coat the

more popular alternative today is the dinner jacket (the American tuxedo), which is a black (occasionally, white) jacket with silk lapels and without tails. This is worn with black trousers and with a waistcoat or cummerbund, a plain or pleated white or coloured shirt and a black bow tie. On like occasions women can also wear 'evening dress', and this is usually in the form of an evening gown, especially a long, floor-length one. A form of 'evening dress' with tails is still worn traditionally by pianists, waiters – especially wine waiters and head waiters – and, where they exist, butlers.

morning star/evening star (heavenly body brightly visible in the morning or evening)
These two names are poetic but misleading – they are both used as names of Venus, which is a planet, not a star! At certain times of the year, Venus can be seen in the east before sunrise or in the west after sunset. (For the characteristics of Venus, see **star**.) The name 'morning star', the political press apart, is sometimes also given to other planets, such as Mercury, or even to a real star, so long as it is one prominent in the morning. The name is also sometimes used figuratively for the precursor of the dawn of a new age of some kind: Wycliffe was thus the 'morning star' of the Reformation. The 'evening star' is a name also sometimes extended to other planets or stars, but not so readily to people.

moron see **idiot**

morphine see **opium**

mortification see **shame**

mosquito see **gnat**

moth see **butterfly**

motion see **resolution**

motive/incentive (inducement to action)
A 'motive' is what actually 'moves' you to take some action, as an inner urge or the desire to see a satisfactory completed result. An 'incentive' is what stimulates you to action, as the prospect of a bonus, a prize, or a promotion. A 'motive' is thus more from within, and an 'incentive' from without.

motorcycle/moped (two-wheeled motor-driven road vehicle)
A 'moped' is not simply a small or low-powered 'motorcycle', but specifically one that has pedals (which a 'motorcycle', even a low-powered one, never has). Basically the 'moped' is a form of motorised bicycle, usually one with a cubic capacity of 50 c.c. or less. It was extensively developed in Germany in the 1950s, although the word 'moped' is itself, rather unexpectedly, of Swedish origin: the abbreviation of *tramp-cykel med motor och pedaler*, 'pedal cycle with engine and pedals'.

motorway/trunk road/highway/clearway (type of main traffic road)
A 'motorway' is a specially constructed road designed for fast motor traffic and mainly running between large cities, as the M1 London to Yorkshire 'motorway' or the M6 from Birmingham to Carlisle. Distinctive features of a 'motorway' are its lanes (as a dual carriageway), its special signals and signs, and its service stations. It cannot be used by pedestrians, learner drivers, cyclists, and riders of small motorcycles. The world of 'motorways' is one that has attracted its own jargon of 'slip roads', 'hard shoulders' and 'central reservations'. A 'trunk road' is the first of three categories of road in Britain (the other two are 'classified' and 'unclassified' roads) and caters for long-distance traffic. It includes most 'motorways'. A 'highway' is a semi-legal or technical term for a main road in general – in full, the 'Queen's highway', which is regarded as protected by the power of the monarch. In its strictest sense, a 'highway' is a public road which all the subjects of the realm have a right to use (as distinct from a private road). It is also maintained and improved at public expense. A 'clearway' is a British term for a stretch of road on which vehicles must not stop, the aim being to keep the road *clear* for moving traffic. A special sort is an 'urban "clearway"', on the main roads into a large town or city, where stopping *is* allowed but only on certain days or between certain times.

mountain see **hill**

mouth/estuary (place where river enters the sea)
'Mouth' is a rather vague word for the 'sea end' of a river, thought of as the opposite to its source. An 'estuary' is the 'tidal mouth' of a river, or any part of the lower reaches of a river where its current meets the tides of the sea and is affected by them. This means, for example, that the 'estuary' of the Thames is strictly speaking 92 miles long, and extends not just from below London Bridge to the sea but upstream to Teddington Lock, a further 19 miles, where the first lock from the sea (apart from the one at Richmond) is situated. An 'estuary' is generally regarded as the seaward rather than the landward stretch of a river, however, so that at high tide the 'estuary' virtually *is* the sea.

mucus see **phlegm**

muffin see **crumpet**

mule see **donkey**

multiple store see **chain store**

mural/fresco (type of wall painting)
A 'mural' is any painting executed on a wall, whether inside a building or out. A 'fresco' – sometimes thought, by association with 'fresh air' or 'al fresco', to be an exclusively external painting, which it is not – is a wall painting (or ceiling painting) done before the plaster is dry, that is, while it is fresh (so called 'true fresco', or *buon fresco*), or when the plaster is partly dry ('dry fresco', or *fresco secco*). The technique is a complex and ancient one: many famous Greek 'frescoes' were executed several hundred years BC. The Italian word indicates, however, that some of the finest 'frescoes' since the Middle Ages are to be found in Italian churches, such as the ones by Michelangelo in the Sistine Chapel.

murderer/assassin (killer)
A 'murderer' is one who kills unlawfully, legally known as 'with malice aforethought', i.e. express malice (where the person intends to kill or cause grievous bodily harm), or implied (where he does not intend to do either, yet intentionally does an act which he knows will lead to death). An 'assassin' is one who kills treacherously, often for political motives. The unusual word comes from the Arabic for 'hashish-eater'; in Muslim history the 'assassin' was a fanatic sent by the founder of his sect, the so-named Old Man of the Mountain, to murder either Crusaders or the leaders of rival Muslim sects. He did this in a hashish-drugged state.

**musical/revue/music hall/cabaret/
vaudeville** (light dramatic entertainment with music)
The 'musical' – properly 'musical comedy' – is a development of the operetta (see **opera**) and today is a fairly general word for a light play or film with songs, dialogue and dancing and a rather insubstantial plot. The songs and dialogue are not necessarily comical, but are almost invariably light-hearted and reasonably undemanding. Two well-known traditional 'musicals', both box office hits, are *West Side Story* and *My Fair Lady*, and two rock 'musicals', a development of the 1970s, *Hair* and *Jesus Christ Superstar*. A 'revue' is composed of a rapid series of short items, such as songs, dances and sketches, with a vaguely topical or satirical basis. *Beyond the Fringe* was a 'revue' of the early 1960s that has since been emulated but rarely equalled. 'Music hall' was a variety entertainment, mainly of songs and comic turns, at which the audience could buy drinks. It flourished in Britain from roughly 1880 to the First World War, and developed out of the earlier tavern entertainments. The keynote of the 'music hall' was precisely its variety, with a succession of artistes – unlike a 'revue', where the same artistes perform in different items – and even with interludes of ballet dancing, for example. Licensing laws banned drinking in the auditorium from 1902 and the popularity of the 'music hall' began to fade with the increasing competition of films and, later, radio. (Some might say, though, that a number of radio variety shows are in fact an extension of 'music hall'. Certainly television, with such programmes as 'Sunday Night at the London Palladium', has proved that the genre of 'music hall', when transferred to this particular medium, is as popular as ever.) 'Cabaret', an offshoot of the traditional 'music hall', is an intimate entertainment – 'intimate', so that individual performers can establish a close relationship with the audi-

81

ence – in a club, bar or restaurant, usually while patrons are wining and dining. 'Cabaret' in pre-war Germany was linked with political and artistic groups, and the film *Cabaret* (1972) was one of the Broadway 'musicals' so named which was based on the play *I am a Camera* by John Van Druten that in turn was based on Christopher Isherwood's sketches of Berlin life in the 1930s (including the role of 'cabaret'), *Goodbye to Berlin*. 'Vaudeville' is variety entertainment, approximately the American equivalent of the British 'music hall', with the same heyday (1880s to 1920s) and the same fate – ousted by the cinema.

music hall see **musical**

muslin/gauze/cheesecloth (thin cotton fabric)
'Muslin', originally from Mosul, a city in Iraq, is a fine cotton fabric of plain weave used for curtains and the like. It is frequently printed or embroidered in patterns. The word has a much more specific meaning than 'gauze' – originally from Gaza, in the Middle East – which is the name for any thin transparent fabric made from any fibre (for example, cotton or silk) in a plain or so-called leno weave (in which the warp threads are arranged in pairs). Cotton 'gauze' is used for surgical dressings, for example, and silk 'gauze' for dress trimmings. Similar to it is 'cheesecloth', which is made of cotton – originally as a wrapping for pressed cheese – and used commercially for book bindings, dustcloths and the like. The actual difference between 'gauze' and 'cheesecloth' is in the finishing: 'cheesecloth' may be bleached and stiffened, when it is called 'scrim'; 'gauze' is usually very fine on account of its use for delicate applications.

mussel see **cockle**

mutiny see **revolt**

myrtle see **laurel**

myth see **legend**

narcissus see **daffodil**

Near East/Middle East/Far East (region to the east of Europe)
The regions are rather imprecise and in some cases their names are used interchangeably. The 'Near East', now more often called the 'Middle East', is thus an indefinite term for the countries from Egypt to Iran, that is, from the eastern shores of the Mediterranean and Aegean to (but not including) India. Formerly the 'Middle East' included not only Iran but also Afghanistan, India, Tibet and even Burma, while the 'Near East' was restricted to Turkey and the Balkan countries. The 'Far East' is a similarly wide-ranging term which embraces 'the Orient', that is, the countries of east and south-east Asia, such as China, Japan, Korea and Thailand. For the occidental opposite, see **Middle West**.

nebula see **constellation**

neigh/whinny (characteristic cry of a horse)
A 'neigh' is the word for any 'speech' by any horse. By a 'whinny' is usually meant a pleasant-sounding or happy 'neigh', especially a low, gentle or joyful one (or any combination of these). Both words are ultimately imitative in origin, with 'whinny' related to 'whine'.

net amount/gross amount (measure of a financial quantity)
The 'net (or "nett") amount' is the amount after deductions or expenses have been paid, so that a 'net' profit is an actual gain, a 'net' price has no discount, and 'net' pay is 'take-home' pay, after tax and other deductions. 'Gross' is thus the opposite – before deductions, so that to 'gross up' is to increase the 'net amount' to its value before tax, or whatever, was deducted. People who complain that they earn 'only £80 a week' may tactfully neglect to add that this is the 'net amount' they receive, whereas normally a

pay or salary figure is quoted in 'gross' terms since the deductions will to a large extent depend on the individual and will vary. (The £80-a-week man may, too, be in receipt of certain benefits, which he also overlooks when making his claim for a pay increase.) The term 'net' relates not to 'net' as in fishing – as if the deductions had slipped through and were not 'caught' – but to 'neat', that is, not liable to (further) deduction, 'clear'.

netball/volleyball/basketball/handball (team game in which a ball is struck by the hand)
Perhaps 'basketball' is the best known. This is essentially an American game played usually indoors by two teams of five men or women. Points are scored by throwing the ball through baskets located high on a stand at the end of each court. 'Netball' is similar to it, but mainly played by (English) women or girls, with seven players in each team. The game is played with the ball entirely in the air, whereas in 'basketball' it frequently rebounds against the floor. 'Volleyball' is really a sort of hand tennis played with a football. The game is played outside or in a gym, with six players a side, and has the object of preventing the ball from touching the ground by banging it from one side to the other over a net. 'Handball', with eleven players a side, is also played with a football. In fact, the rules are similar to those of football, so that the ball can be caught, thrown, passed back or forward or 'dribbled' (by being 'caressed'). It can be struck not only with the hand but with any part of the body except below the knee (although the goalkeeper can kick it). The game is popular on the continent, especially in Germany.

Netherlands see **Holland**

neurotic see **psychopath**

ninepins see **bowls**

noise see **sound** (thing heard)

Nosy Parker/Paul Pry/Peeping Tom (unduly inquisitive or prying person)
A 'Nosy (or Nosey) Parker' is one who pries or meddles, a real busybody who minds everyone's business except his own and who

sticks his nose in everywhere. A 'Paul Pry' is similar, but perhaps more of an interferer than a busybody, and less of an active meddler than a 'Nosy Parker'. A 'Peeping Tom' is a furtive observer, especially a voyeur, who gets a kick out of the naughty things he sees. Did this unholy trinity actually exist? Was there actually a prying Mr Parker? In his *Words and Names* (John Murray, 1932), Ernest Weekley quotes an 'amateur philologist' who boldly states that the original 'Nosy Parker' was Matthew Parker, Queen Elizabeth's first archbishop of Canterbury, who was a 'human ferret' and, moreover, had a long nose. Perhaps. (The female equivalent, incidentally, is sometimes called Rosa Dartle.) 'Paul Pry' is of surer origin: he was the hero of a play of this name written in 1825 by the English dramatist John Poole. (He is said to have been based on a real person, one Thomas Hill.) 'Peeping Tom' was, according to the story, the man who took a sneaking look at Lady Godiva as she rode naked through the streets of Coventry.

notary see **solicitor**

number/figure/numeral (word or sign used for counting)
A 'number', the commonest word of the three, is a symbol or 'figure' that stands for a count or sum or total, especially when identifying one of a series, as a telephone 'number', house 'number', or car 'number' (which also includes letters as well as 'figures'). A 'figure' is a numerical symbol, especially one of the Arabic notation (1, 2, 3, 4, 5, etc.), so that one talks of a 'figure' of eight, double 'figures' (10 to 99) or a three-'figure number'. The term 'numeral' is used for a word expressing a 'number', as a cardinal 'numeral', or a letter or 'figure', or group of letters or 'figures', that expresses a 'number', as a Roman 'numeral', which is expressed as a letter or letters.

numeral see **number**

nursery school/play school/ kindergarten/day nursery/play group/ infant school (school or centre for young children)
A 'nursery school' provides a combination of

informal, simple teaching and play activities for children aged two to five. It exists independently or as part of a primary school. A 'play school' and a 'play group' are the same thing, in effect. They are the paying equivalent of the (free, state-run) 'nursery school' and are run by a voluntary organisation or a group of parents. They differ from a 'nursery school', however, in that – as the name suggests – the emphasis is on play rather than any kind of formal education. A private school corresponding to the state 'nursery school' where education *is* provided on a formal or informal basis is a 'kindergarten', which may also exist separately or be part of a preparatory school or a pre-preparatory school (which would take over at the age of five). This latter school has a state equivalent, too: the 'infant school', which, as before, may also be a department of a primary or 'first' school. This leaves the 'day nursery', which partly corresponds to a 'nursery school' or 'play group'. It is not really, though, an educational establishment proper, but more a place where parents can park their children while they are at work. For this reason the 'day nursery' does not operate in 'terms' but is open virtually throughout the year. The odd name out of all these, 'kindergarten', owes its German origin (literally, 'children's garden') to the deviser of schools of this type, the nineteenth-century educator Friedrich Froebel.

nursing home/convalescent home/rest home (special type of hospital)
A 'nursing home' is not a home for nurses but a private hospital where both medical and surgical treatment are obtainable (for payment). A 'convalescent home' is a rehabilitation centre, either a state one (National Health, non-paying) or a private one. A 'rest home' is a residential centre for old and/or frail people, usually one run by a voluntary organisation or privately. A number of 'rest homes' are, however, also provided by local authorities, and are non-paying.

obstacle/obstruction (hindrance or impediment)
An 'obstacle', whether material or not, is something that stands in the way of literal or figurative progress. It usually can be overcome with an effort, ingenuity, or patience. An 'obstruction' is something that more or less completely blocks a passage of some kind, making progress difficult or even quite impossible. The word is not used so frequently in a figurative sense, although in Parliament an 'obstruction' is the use by an MP of his right to speak and move motions for the purpose of delaying or preventing the passing of some measure to which he objects – usually strongly.

obstetrician see **gynaecologist**

obstruction see **obstacle**

occupation/business/profession/trade
(one's regular work or employment)
'Occupation' is the general word, usually a more or less formal word for 'job'. 'Business' usually implies a commercial 'occupation', especially one that renders an essential or useful service, as a car sales 'business'. 'Profession' denotes a specialist or highly qualified 'occupation', as the legal 'profession' or the nursing 'profession'. 'Trade' generally suggests an 'occupation' that involves craftsmanship or manual skills, as the building (or, as it is now more often called, construction) 'trade'.

ocean see **sea**

octavo see **quarto**

octopus/squid/cuttlefish (mollusc noted for its ability to eject a type of inky substance)
All are mutually related. The 'octopus' has eight arms (literally, 'eight feet') and lives on the seabed, where it ejects an inky substance when threatened. The 'squid', whose name

is not a Lewis Carroll-type portmanteau blend of 'squirt' and 'fluid' but is of obscure origin, has ten arms and ejects ink as a characteristic cigar-shaped object as long as itself, the aim being to leave a 'dummy' so that it can escape. The 'cuttlefish' is actually used as a source of ink called sepia, which is brownish in colour and can serve for drawing with brush or pen. Both the 'octopus' and the 'squid' are edible, but not the 'cuttlefish'. The latter's shell, however, is popular when dried with budgerigars, who peck it and so 'manicure' their beaks.

offence see **crime**

ohms see **volts**

opera/operetta (musical dramatic composition)
In general, an 'operetta' is a short, light 'opera', usually with a considerable proportion of spoken dialogue. More specifically, it is either a light 'opera', such as one by Johann Strauss or Suppé (but not, say, Mozart's *Così fan tutte*, which is a comic 'opera'), or a musical comedy, that is, a comedy with plenty of music in it. (This is more familiar today as a musical.) Whether the much-loved Gilbert and Sullivan 'operas' are really 'operettas' is rather a subjective matter: they are certainly quite far removed from 'grand' 'opera', yet not slight enough, or consistently comic or light-hearted enough, to be called 'operettas'.

operetta see **opera**

opium/morphine/laudanum (soporific drug)
'Opium' is made from the juice of the poppy (*Papaver somniferum*). It may (usually illegally) be smoked or eaten as a stimulant, intoxicant or narcotic, or (normally legally) be used in medicine as a sedative, when it is called 'laudanum' – a tincture of 'opium'. (The name 'laudanum' was invented by that mostly unappreciated genius, the Swiss alchemist and physician Paracelsus.) 'Morphine' is the name of the principal alkaloid in 'opium', used in medicine to deaden pain or as a hypnotic. The highly addictive narcotic heroin is derived from it.

opponent see **enemy**

orang-outang see **gorilla**

oratorio/cantata (dramatic musical composition for chorus, soloists and orchestra)
The 'oratorio' has its origin in the musical services held in the church of the Oratory of St Philip Neri, in Rome. It has come to be the term for a rather 'grand' or extended musical composition, with a more or less dramatic text, based on a religious theme – although with no action, costume or scenery, as in an opera, say. Handel's *Messiah* is one of the best-known examples of an 'oratorio'. A 'cantata' (Italian for 'something sung') is a form of short 'oratorio', either sacred or secular, especially a lyric work. Bach's *Christmas Oratorio* is in reality a series of 'cantatas' designed to be performed on six days successively at Christmas-tide.

orchid/orchis (rare, exotic plant and its flowers)
The 'orchid' is a member of the large family *Orchidaceae*, and typically (and familiarly) the exotic plant with brilliant flowers, with one petal usually larger than the other two, that traditionally is born to blush unseen in an inaccessible wood somewhere. The 'orchis' is an 'orchid' that is wild (as distinct from the hothouse variety) or that, more narrowly, belongs to the genus *Orchis*, which has a tuberous root and an upright fleshy stem with a spike of purple or red flowers. The names are often used interchangeably, however, since all 'orchises' are 'orchids'. Both words derive from Greek *orkhis*, 'testicle', from the appearance of the root tubers in some of the genus *Orchis*. One wonders whose fertile imagination invented the name. (Compare 'porcelain' under **china**.)

orchis see **orchid**

order/command/direction (instruction)
An 'order' is usually an instruction given by a superior to an inferior, with the relationship between the two marked by rank, standing or age, for example. A 'command' is similar, but is a more formal word – and possibly a less specific one – and emphasises the authority of the one who commands. A

85

'direction' is simply a general instruction what to do in order to carry out some task, as the 'directions' for use that accompany several commercial products.

ordinary shares/preference shares (types of shares on the stock market)
'Ordinary shares' are ones which have no special right to a dividend but entitle their holder to all the profits after prior demands, such as loan interest or 'preference' dividends. By implication, therefore, 'preference shares' have a preferential right to dividends, that is, the holder is entitled to his profits before anything is paid to the holders of 'ordinary shares'. On a more technical level, holders of 'ordinary shares' are regarded as the true owners of the company, while the voting rights of the holders of 'preference shares' are strictly limited.

oven/stove/cooker (apparatus for cooking, usually in the kitchen)
An 'oven' is an enclosed heated compartment for baking or roasting, as for example in a gas 'stove' or electric 'stove'. A 'stove' itself is a wider term to mean an apparatus that provides heat for any purpose, as heating (oil 'stove') or cooking (gas 'stove' – complete with 'oven') or some mechanical process. Loosely, 'stove' can mean 'cooker' – 'Put the saucepan on the "stove" would you?' – but 'cooker' is the general purpose cooking appliance, portable or fixed, and usually heated by gas or electricity, that contains an 'oven', cooking rings and often a grill, and stands in most kitchens.

overtime see **extra time**

ox/bull/bullock/steer (male bovine animal found on farms)
An 'ox' is a fully-grown castrated 'bull', used either as a draught animal or for its beef. More generally, it is any bovine animal. A 'bull' is an *un*castrated 'ox', used in particular for breeding. A 'bullock' is either a young bull or an 'ox', especially one that has never been used for breeding. A 'steer' is a young 'ox', although in the USA the word is used of male beef cattle of any age. The word seems to be related to 'steer' meaning 'guide the course of' rather than be derived from Latin *taurus*, 'bull'.

pack see **flock**

package see **packet**

packet/package/parcel (something packed and wrapped)
A 'packet' is basically a small 'package', a 'pack-ette', while a 'package' is a bundle or collection of things that are packed, but not necessarily wrapped. A 'parcel' is the word for goods that are normally wrapped in a single 'package', and especially such a 'package' wrapped in paper and designed to be sent through the post. The British Post Office regards its mail as consisting of letters and 'postal "packets"', with the latter including 'parcels'.

pagan see **heathen**

pain see **ache**

palate see **tongue**

Palestine see **Israel**

pamphlet see **brochure**

pan see **track**

panama/boater (type of straw hat)
A 'panama' hat is a soft one, made by hand-plaiting strips of leaves from a South American plant, the screw-pine. The hats were not made in Panama but widely marketed and distributed there: their country of origin is in fact Ecuador. The 'boater', correctly worn in boating, especially at the turn of the century and also between the wars, has a hard, stiff brim. It is still worn in some sections of society for certain occasions, and also regularly, as part of the uniform, at some boys' and girls' public schools, such as Harrow and the Godolphin School.

panorama see **view**

panther see leopard

pants see trousers

paraffin see petrol

parcel see packet

parka see anorak

parody/pastiche/skit/burlesque (literary or theatrical composition mocking an author or his work)
A 'parody' is a humorous imitation, designed to make the author's work or words seem ridiculous. A classic example is Stella Gibbons's *Cold Comfort Farm* (1932), which is a 'parody' on the novels of Mary Webb. A 'pastiche' is a medley or patchwork of words, sentences or complete passages from one or several authors, so is also a type of imitation. If this is intentional, it will also be a 'parody'. A 'skit' comes close to both a 'parody' and a 'burlesque'. It aims to caricature a person or his style of writing by a kind of 'guying'. As such it is common in musical revues, where famous people are 'taken off' by humorous impersonation. A 'burlesque' is a derisive imitation, an exaggerated 'send-up' of a person or his work, and usually stronger and broader in style than a 'parody'. It chiefly occurs in stage plays. An example of 'burlesque' is the rendering of the play 'Pyramus and Thisbe' performed by Bottom and company in Shakespeare's *Midsummer Night's Dream*. (The word is not related to 'burly' or 'hurly-burly' but comes from Italian, through French, meaning 'mockery'.)

parsnip see turnip

parson see vicar

part/piece/portion (section of the whole)
A 'part' is a general word to mean any division or section or bit of something, as 'part' of the road or a spare 'part'. 'Piece' suggests a 'part' that is a complete unit on its own, as a 'piece' of cake or a 'piece' of advice. 'Portion' is the word for something given or allotted to a person, as a 'portion' of ice cream or the 'portion' of an estate.

partisan see guerrilla

partridge see pheasant

passage/corridor (way through)
In a building, a 'passage' is any way, not necessarily particularly narrow or lengthy, that gives access to another room or area. The word does imply, however, an intermediate or linking part through or along which one must pass to get from A to B. A 'corridor', thus, is a main passage in a large building, giving access to several rooms and usually fairly narrow and straight, as the 'corridors' in a hotel that lead to various bedrooms. The word came to English from Italian, via French: Italian *correre* means 'to run'. Schoolchildren forbidden from running in the 'corridor' must feel the word to be rather a misnomer.

pastiche see parody

pastime see hobby

pastor see minister

pasty see tart

Paul Pry see Nosy Parker

peach/apricot (soft luscious fruit)
The 'peach' is a large, round fruit, with a downy white or yellow skin flushed with red – the model of a 'peaches and cream' complexion – a sweet, juicy flesh, and a rough stone. Its name rather unexpectedly comes from Latin *persicum malum*, 'Persian apple', but then the best 'peaches' came from Persia, and 'apple' can be used of fruit other than apples (as the pineapple, which is neither an apple nor grows on pine trees). The 'apricot', which is smaller, is related to both the 'peach' and the plum. Its skin when ripe is orange-pink and not 'flushed' in quite the same way as a 'peach', which otherwise it resembles. It, too, has something of an exotic name, which comes from Arabic *al barquq*, 'the early-ripe', in turn from Latin *praecox* (which gives 'precocious') under the influence of Latin *apricus*, 'ripe', via several other languages. (Dictionaries get quite excited about the origin of 'apricot': in the 'big' dictionaries, such as the *Oxford English* and Wyld's *Universal Dictionary of the English Language*, the etymology of the word takes up

considerably more space than the actual definition of the fruit.)

peal/chime (ring of bells)
A 'peal' is normally the word for a series of changes rung on a set of bells. A 'chime' describes the melodious or tuneful sound produced by bells rung harmoniously, as the carillon played on church bells in Belgium, for example. It is the method for ringing, in fact, that signifies the real difference between the words: bells that 'chime' are usually struck with an external hammer (as in many striking clocks) or by the mechanical movement of a clapper (as in the carillon); bells that 'peal' are swung by means of ropes, as church bells – although church bells can in fact be sounded both ways.

peat see **turf**

**pedestrian crossing/zebra crossing/
pelican crossing** (place where pedestrians have the right to cross the road)
A 'pedestrian crossing' is a general term for a place where the road can be crossed. A 'zebra crossing' is a common form of crossing where the black and white stripes, compared to those of a zebra, indicate that pedestrians, once on the crossing, have right of way over vehicles. Points where such crossings are located are indicated by flashing Belisha beacons. 'Pelican crossings' are the ones where pedestrians have their own lights, which they can control – the 'green man' – to tell them when it is safe to cross (many 'pelicans' also have a bleeper as an audible signal), and motorists have a conventional set of traffic lights with, however, a flashing amber light following the red to indicate that they must give way to any pedestrians who may be on the crossing. 'Pelican crossings' bear little resemblance to the ungainly bird that stores fish in its pouch: the name comes from (near enough) the first letters of '*pe*destrian *li*ght *con*trolled crossing'. Such crossings were introduced in 1966.

Peeping Tom see **Nosy Parker**

peer see **lord**

pelican crossing see **pedestrian crossing**

perfume/scent (fragrant cosmetic product)
In common usage, the words are hardly differentiated. However, 'perfume' is basically the substance – either natural, as the oil from leaves, trees or flowers, or artificial – from which 'scent' is made, 'scent' being the commercial product. But 'perfume' is the term also used for a natural substance used commercially outside cosmetics, as for example in toothpaste, tobacco, plastic wrappings and so on. Thus 'perfume' is more wide-ranging, and 'scent' is almost always, too, a liquid product.

periodical see **magazine**

perry see **cider**

pesticide see **insecticide**

**petrol/paraffin/petroleum/gasoline/
kerosine/diesel oil** (type of liquid fuel)
'Petrol' is refined 'petroleum' and the most familiar to the man in the car on the street. So what is 'petroleum'? It is the hydrocarbon oil found in the upper strata of the earth, known also as crude oil. This is the 'oil' found in the North Sea. 'Paraffin' – more fully, paraffin oil – is also got from 'petroleum', by distillation, and is commonly used for lamps, domestic heaters, and as a fuel for jet aircraft. 'Gasoline' is the American equivalent word for 'petrol' (hence 'step on the gas' and similar phrases), while 'kerosine' is American parlance for 'paraffin', as it also is in Australia and New Zealand. (The spelling is the commercial one; formerly it was 'kerosene'.) This leaves 'diesel oil', or diesel fuel, which is a heavy 'petroleum' fraction used in diesel engines. A special form of this is derv, used in heavy road vehicles such as buses and lorries. The word is made up of the initial letters of '*d*iesel-*e*ngined *r*oad *v*ehicle' – rather oddly, since one would expect the name to be based on the fuel rather than the type of vehicle it is intended for.

petroleum see **petrol**

phantom see **ghost**

pharmacist see **chemist**

pheasant/partridge/grouse/ptarmigan
(game bird found in fields or on moors)
The male 'pheasant' is rather a striking bird, both in colouring and often literally, alas, in its inability to avoid speeding cars as it is crossing the road. The bird has a long tail, lives mainly in open fields and woodlands, and is larger than the 'partridge', by an average of three feet in length to one. The 'partridge' is thus rather a squat bird, often living on farmland (and seasonally in pear trees). The 'grouse' is sometimes wrongly called by the name of 'partridge', especially in the USA. The 'grouse', about twice the length of the 'partridge', often has a heather habitat, in particular on the Scottish moors. Among the special kinds of 'grouse' are the capercaillie (or capercailzie), also called the wood 'grouse', and the 'ptarmigan', the fourth of this game bag. This is a bird that has black or grey plumage in summer and white in winter and is decidedly small rather than large. In Britain it is confined to northern Scotland. It differs from other members of the 'grouse' family in having toes covered with stiff feathers, a distinguishing feature almost as original as its Greek-looking name. This is actually derived from Gaelic *tarmachan*, with an initial classy 'p' added by association with such scientific zoological names as 'pterodactyl' or Greek words in general beginning 'pt-'.

phlegm/mucus (viscous substance secreted by a mucous membrane)
'Mucus' is the general word for the viscid secretion, acting as a lubricative or to moisten the passages, found in the digestive system, nose, windpipe, bladder and other organs. 'Phlegm' is the thick, morbid form of this, especially in the lungs and throat passages, which is normally discharged by a cough or nose-blowing. 'Phlegm', ultimately from the Greek for 'flame', was originally one of the four so-called humours or bodily fluids, the others being blood, choler (yellow bile) and melancholy (black bile). 'Phlegm' was regarded as the clammy humour that caused sluggishness or apathy.

physician see **doctor**

pianola/piano-player/player-piano (type of mechanical piano)
The 'pianola', originally a trade name apparently intended to be a kind of diminutive of 'piano', was an American invention of the end of the nineteenth century and to begin with was just a contrivance pushed up to an ordinary piano, on whose keys it played with felted fingers. Later it was physically incorporated in the body of the piano. The piano music produced by it came about by air from a 'tracker-bar' passing through the little perforations of an unrolling paper roll and striking the necessary hammers against the strings. Such music was mostly of the tea-time variety, and essentially Victorian. The 'pianola' was generically a 'piano-player', otherwise a 'player-piano', the first of these being a device that plays the piano, and the second a piano that can be played automatically, i.e. one and the same instrument. 'Pianolas', like certain other Victoriana, had a revival in the 1950s, with even several new instruments being built.

piano-player see **pianola**

pickle/chutney (type of pungent relish)
'Pickle' basically consists of vegetables, such as cucumbers, onions, cauliflowers and the like, that have been preserved in vinegar or brine or something similar. 'Chutney' is a condiment of Indian origin, and normally contains both sweet and sour ingredients, especially fruit – as mangoes, chillies or even, as a more homely substitute, apples – together with vinegar, sugar, spices and other seasoning. It is perhaps a matter of taste which is 'stronger', but possibly 'chutney' has the slight edge. (The name comes from a Hindi word meaning 'to lick'.)

pie see **tart**

piece see **part**

pier see **quay**

pig/hog/boar (animal noted for its bacon, bristles and boorishness)
'Pig' is the generic word, of which the feminine is 'sow'. A 'hog' – the word is used more widely and generally in the USA – is a domesticated 'pig', and especially a castrated

male raised for slaughter. By contrast a 'boar' is an *un*castrated male, especially one used for food. ('Boar''s head – traditionally served up with an apple in its mouth – was long a Christmas dish, as witness pubs and inns so named.)

pigeon/dove (wild or tame bird associated with pies or peace)
All 'doves' are 'pigeons', and all 'pigeons' are 'doves', since these names are used for any member of the family *Columbidae*. However, 'pigeon' usually means a larger bird, either those found in squares and railway stations, or the ones bred by fanciers or for racing. This means that 'dove' normally applies to the smaller bird, especially a particular variety, as the turtle-'dove', stock-'dove', ring-'dove' (otherwise wood 'pigeon', which is a menace to crops) and rock-'dove', from which many breeds of domestic 'pigeon' are derived. The 'dove', too, is the more poetic or symbolic bird, in particular representing peace (in politics) or innocence, gentleness and tenderness (in literature). In this connection see **hawks**.

pilchard see **sardine**.

pill/tablet (small piece of prepared medical substance for swallowing whole)
A 'pill' is usually round or flat and normally regarded as a capsule containing a drug or medicinal substance. A specific type is 'the pill', the colloquial term for an oral contraceptive. A 'tablet' is normally flat and round, and usually homogeneous, and with no outer casing, so that it consists of a solid or compressed substance, such as aspirin.

pillar/column (upright support)
The general word is 'pillar'. A 'column' is an individual or special kind of 'pillar', in particular one that is architecturally interesting or otherwise noteworthy, as Nelson's 'Column' in Trafalgar Square. A 'column', too, is often thought of as consisting of three parts: base, shaft and capital.

pillory see **stocks** (old instrument of punishment)

pinafore see **apron**

pine/fir (evergreen tree with needle-like leaves)
The difference is in the leaves and their arrangement: on a 'pine', leaves grow in clusters of two or more, on a 'fir' the needles are placed singly on the shoots. To complicate matters, however, a Scots 'pine' is the same as a Scotch (*sic*) 'fir', otherwise *Pinus silvestris*, the only British native 'pine' grown for its valuable timber.

pink see **carnation**

pip see **stone**

pistol/revolver/automatic (firearm fired from the hand)
'Pistols' are divided into single-shot 'pistols', 'revolvers' and 'automatics'. 'Revolvers', as the name indicates, have an element that revolves, in modern 'revolvers' a multi-chambered cylinder, turned by pulling the trigger. This is the weapon for playing Russian roulette: insert one cartridge, spin the cylinder, and you may or may not have a round to fire when you pull the trigger. 'Automatics' have a magazine in the butt, and a mechanism that is actuated by the energy of the recoil when the bullet is fired. The US police force is armed with 'revolvers', although the police in many other countries are issued with 'automatics'.

pitch see (1) **field** (area of play), (2) **tar**

pitfall see **trap**

plague see **epidemic**

plaice/sole (edible flatfish)
The 'plaice', or *Pleuronectes platessa*, is a European flatfish around fifteen inches long, with red or orange spots on a brownish skin, found in the North Atlantic and around British coasts and popular for its equally palatable partner – chips. The 'sole' can be one of a number of flatfish, but especially the genus *Solea* which gives the well-known Dover 'sole', *Solea solea*. It is under two feet in length, of a more or less uniform brown colour (no orange spots), and found chiefly in the eastern Atlantic and Mediterranean. The lemon 'sole' is not a 'sole' at all but a kind of 'plaice' that resembles one. More-

over, it may be eaten with a slice of lemon, but its name has nothing to do with lemons in origin: it is a corruption of French *limande*, of unknown origin.

plaid see **tartan**

plan/project/scheme/design (proposed method of doing something)
'Plan' is the general word to denote something thought out in advance with the aim of putting it into effect. A 'project' is a more complex or tentative 'plan', which may perhaps not be realised. A 'scheme' is also speculative, or even dishonest, although commonly it is closer to a large-scale 'project', as a 'scheme' to build a new estate or to increase production in a factory. A 'design' is a cunning 'plan' – in the good or bad sense of the word – and usually hints at the actual objective, which is why literally it is often a drawing or sketch of some kind, as in the design for a new theatre.

planet see **star**

platitude see **commonplace**

platoon see **corps**

player-piano see **pianola**

play group see **nursery school**

play school see **nursery school**

playwright see **dramatist**

plutocrat see **autocrat**

poetry/verse (metrical compositions)
'She writes "poetry", you know.' 'Yes, and he writes "verse".' What is the difference? The trouble is, that 'poetry' actually *is* 'verse', often as not. The word implies lofty feelings, though, and an inspired passion. 'Verse', on the other hand, is usually contrasted with prose, and is the expression of something in words which conform to accepted metrical rules and structure as a literary form. As an art form, 'verse' is more lowly than 'poetry', which is why one has light 'verse', not light 'poetry'.

politeness/courtesy (observance of considerate behaviour)
'Politeness' is the general word, implying a habitual 'courtesy' as a result of one's upbringing – otherwise 'good manners'. 'Courtesy' is a positive show, possibly a rather old-fashioned one, of consideration for others, especially on a specific occasion, such as 'an act of courtesy'.

politician/statesman (one skilled in politics or diplomacy)
The difference perhaps lies in the connotations of the words. 'Politician' can be used disparagingly to imply the scheming of small politics for party ends or one's own advantage, although more usually the word means someone who is professionally engaged in politics, such as an MP. 'Statesman', on the other hand, can never be used disparagingly. Indeed, it suggests a wise, far-sighted 'politician', one who is unselfishly devoted to the interests of his party or country. In the everyday sense, however, the words are almost equal – with 'statesman' nevertheless always having the edge as an important or senior or experienced 'politician'.

polytechnic see **technical college**

pond see **lake**

pool see (1) **billiards**, (2) **lake**

porcelain see **china**

porpoise see **dolphin**

port/harbour (place where ships can dock or shelter)
Up to a point the two words are synonymous. A 'port', however, is normally thought of as a seaside or riverside town with a busy or extensive 'harbour' and very likely docks as well. A 'harbour' itself was originally a place of shelter for ships, as its relationship with the word 'haven' suggests. More generally, it is a naturally or artificially protected stretch of water which, while providing a safe and secure anchorage, also has facilities for the loading and unloading of ships, landing and boarding of passengers, and the like. Strangely, this second but wider sense of the word – that is, as more than just a place of

shelter – is not given in many standard dictionaries. Yet surely the general definition is the way most people regard it?

port/starboard/larboard (side of a ship or other craft)
When facing forwards, 'port' is the left side of a ship or aircraft, and 'starboard' the right side. Why these strange terms, and what is 'larboard'? 'Port', perhaps, because this side was usually next to the shore when the ship was in port. 'Starboard' since this is the 'steering side': boats were originally steered by a paddle over the right-hand side. 'Larboard' was formerly – and still is, in the USA – a term for 'port'. It was replaced by 'port' to avoid confusion, especially in shouted orders. ('Larboard' itself may have derived from 'loading side', with the word assimilated to 'starboard'.) 'Port' exists as a verb in the phrase '"port" the helm'. This originally meant 'turn the tiller to "port"', so that the ship turns to "starboard"'. Since 1933, however, the meaning has nautically been redefined as 'turn the ship to "port"'. The slang word 'posh' ('elegant', 'upper-class') is popularly supposed to derive from the acronym of '"port" out, "starboard" home', these being the desirable sides of the ship for cabins when sailing to and from the East in the days before air-conditioning, but no evidence has been found to support this. (Perhaps a slang word 'posh' meaning 'money' or 'dandy' is the origin.)

portion see **part**

postal order/money order (Post Office order to pay money)
'Postal orders' provide a way of transmitting reasonably small sums of money safely through the post. They are currently (1980) issued in values from 20p up to £10, on which a fee ('poundage') is extra. 'Money orders' were similar but for larger amounts (up to £50). They ceased to exist in 1974, although inland telegraph 'money orders' – now called inland telegraph payment orders – can still be made.

pottery see **china**

prawn see **shrimp**

précis see **summary**

predicament/dilemma (difficult or awkward situation)
A 'predicament' is an unpleasant or even crucial situation which one is faced with. If you run out of petrol or break down on the M1, you are in a 'predicament', you have a difficult situation that you must somehow cope with. A 'dilemma' is a situation in which you are faced with two equally awkward or undesirable alternatives. Wedding presents often cause a 'dilemma': your second favourite aunt gives you a tea-making machine, but you have one already – do you accept it (and wonder what to do with it), or tell her (and run the risk of offending her)? It's a 'dilemma'. The alternatives are the 'horns' of a 'dilemma' on which you, the victim, are likely to be impaled, as a matador on the horns of a bull.

preface see **foreword**

preference shares see **ordinary shares**

prejudice/bias (strong inclination for or against something)
A 'prejudice' is often an unfavourable view or opinion of a thing, as seen in racial 'prejudice' or a 'prejudice' against democracy. Where sides can be taken, however, over a specific issue, a 'prejudice' can be favourable or unfavourable, for or against, as a 'prejudice' in favour of younger applicants for a job. Either way, the word implies a literal 'prejudging' of a case, with a consequent lack of fairness or impartiality. A 'bias' can be favourable or unfavourable, perhaps rather more subjectively, resulting in a tendency to lean the wrong way, as a political 'bias' (a lack of objectivity) or a 'bias' against a new proposal (not giving it fair consideration). The word suggests a 'two-way' idea, and derives from Latin *bifax*, 'two-faced'.

prerogative see **privilege**

present/gift (something given freely, usually to mark an occasion)
A 'present' is a less formal, more personal thing, as a birthday 'present' or a Christmas 'present'. A 'gift' is more formal, and is often

given with a degree of ceremony. It is more impersonal, too, as a free 'gift' (so-called) given with the purchase of a particular merchandise – from a remote firm to an anonymous individual. Similarly, 'gift' vouchers or 'gift' tokens are frequently used as prizes or for some kind of presentation. Perhaps rather surprisingly, the Old English word 'gift' has come to be used for the more formal thing, while the Norman 'present' is the homely, everyday object. Usually when there are Anglo-Saxon and French doublets like these, the 'homely/formal' sense is the other way round (as 'freedom' and 'liberty', 'holiday' and 'vacation', 'fire' and 'conflagration').

president/chairman/secretary/director
(head or important official of a company or body of some kind)
A 'president', who presides, or literally 'sits in front', is the head of a permanent or temporary body of people, especially an academic, literary or scientific one, as the 'President' of the Royal Society. As such, the word is in effect a title, as it also is for the heads of some colleges in Britain, as at Queens' College, Cambridge, or most universities in the USA, as at Harvard. A 'president', too, is the title of the presiding officer of a legislative body, especially a government one, as the 'President' of the Board of Trade, and, in an honorary capacity, of a retired member of a board of 'directors', when he acts as their head. At the same time the 'president' of a board of 'directors' in the USA is not retired, since the title corresponds to the British 'chairman'. (Thus an American vice-'president' in a company virtually corresponds to a British 'director'.) Also, of course, the word is used for the head of a republican state, as notably the USA and France. (In 1977 Mr Brezhnev, already General 'Secretary' of the Communist Party of the Soviet Union, and therefore fairly and squarely in the driving seat, was also elected 'President' of the USSR, otherwise 'Chairman' of the Presidium of the Supreme Soviet.) A 'chairman' is therefore a person chosen to 'chair' or preside over a meeting, but not a regular body, although here again the word is used for the permanent head of a committee, company or board of 'directors', and may indeed preside over the meetings of the latter

but otherwise be little but a figurehead. (An active company chairman is often both 'chairman' and managing 'director' of his firm.) A 'secretary' in the world of companies – apart, of course, from the essential lady stenographer and typist – is the man who generally keeps the books and supervises the administration of affairs. It is a responsible position and regarded in most companies as a senior post. 'Secretaries' exist, too, in politics as the title of the principal assistant of a government minister, while the 'Secretary' of State in Britain is the head of a major government department, as the 'Secretary' of State for Trade. (In America this title is the equivalent of Foreign 'Secretary'.) Finally, a 'director' is a member of the managing board of a commercial company, the head of this board being the Managing 'Director', and is elected to control or govern its affairs. In many cases he has a special field of responsibility, as Sales 'Director'.

pressure group/ginger group (group aiming to stir others to action)
A 'pressure group' has the aim of persuading others, especially politicians or the authorities ('them'), to implement certain policies, and does this by lobbying and other forms of 'pressure'. A 'ginger group' has the aim of persuading others to take action rather than remain inactive. They thus strive to 'ginger things up' by a form of harassment, usually directed at any body that could have a tendency to be passive rather than active, as a political party, a local authority, or even an individual, such as their MP.

priest see **minister**

priory see **monastery**

privilege/prerogative (special right or advantage)
A 'privilege' is a benefit or advantage that has been conferred or attained, whether justly or not – the latter being an unfair 'privilege'. A 'prerogative' is a particular or official 'privilege' that has been granted as a right and that is regarded as fitting for a certain rank, status or position, as a royal 'prerogative' (the rights of a sovereign, which in theory are unrestricted).

93

probe/module/capsule (type of spacecraft)
A 'probe', as a lunar 'probe', is a (complete) spacecraft designed to make preliminary investigations, for example into the atmosphere of a planet. A 'module' is the detachable section of a spacecraft which can be used independently, as is the case with a lunar 'module' which lands on the Moon and later rejoins the parent craft which is still orbiting. A 'capsule' is similar, but is specifically the detachable nose-cone of a spacecraft which can carry an astronaut or astronauts, scientific instruments and the like. It may be manned or unmanned, recoverable or non-recoverable. In early usage, and still loosely, 'module' and 'capsule' are used without distinction, and 'capsule' on occasions means simply 'rocket' or 'spacecraft', without any idea of a detachable section.

producer/director(person responsible for the realisation of a play, film or radio or television programme)
The two carry out complementary and often overlapping work, with the 'producer' basically responsible for the overall production and the 'director' specifically for the direction of the acting. But, to complicate things, in Britain 'producer' is the term often used for the 'director', especially on the stage (and in a radio or television production), where he personally manipulates the actors and 'runs the show', and whose authority is therefore respected. In the film world this person is actually called the 'director', and moreover, according to his authority, also supervises the script, casting and editing as well as overseeing the shooting of scenes in the studio. This means that for films the 'producer' has another role to play, and this is usually a financial one, since he is the man in charge of the budget and the person ultimately responsible for the film's commercial success or failure. He thus is responsible for all personnel involved in the making of the film, including the 'director', as the film itself will probably have been his personal brainchild. He normally, however, delegates his various responsibilities, although remaining in overall charge. The distinction is therefore largely between the jargon of stage, radio and television on the one hand, and the film world on the other.

profession see **occupation**

project see **plan**

prorogation see **abolition**

protectorate see **colony**

proverb see **saying**

psychopath/schizophrenic/psychotic/ neurotic (mentally or emotionally deranged person)
A 'psychopath' is a person afflicted with a personality disorder characterised by a tendency to commit antisocial and sometimes violent acts and a failure to feel guilt for these acts. A 'schizophrenic' is a person who suffers from psychotic disorders characterised by progressive deterioration of the personality which include withdrawal from reality, hallucinations, delusions, social apathy, emotional instability, etc. A 'psychotic' is a person who suffers from psychosis which is any form of severe mental disorder in which the individual's contact with reality becomes highly distorted. The cause of a 'psychotic's' derangement may be a physical one, such as brain damage, and in this respect he differs from a 'neurotic', whose neurosis, a mental discord that is also milder than that of a 'psychotic', has an emotional cause, not a physical one. A 'neurotic' will therefore display such symptoms as anxiety, hysteria or obsessive behaviour and will often be aware of his condition. A 'psychotic's' derangement is total, and the sufferer will not appreciate that his behaviour is abnormal.

psychotic see **psychopath**

ptarmigan see **pheasant**

pub see **hotel**

pullover/jersey/sweater/jumper (woollen outer garment for top half of body)
A 'pullover' – 'pulled over' the head, as indeed are the others – has long or short sleeves or none at all. It is normally regarded as a male garment. A 'jersey' is a type of 'pullover' that is close-fitting and warm, typically as worn by sailors and fishermen. It, too, is usually a male item of

clothing, quite often thought of as giving a 'rugged' air to the appearance of the wearer. A 'sweater' is a 'jersey' (thick, close-fitting) chiefly associated with games and sports, either for wear before or after exercise to prevent chills – or even during exercise to induce sweating – or as part of a traditional costume, as worn by cricketers. In general use it often has a V-neck and is normally designed for informal wear. The garment can be worn by males or females – indeed, a 'sweater' girl, now something of a rare breed, is one who wears it to emphasise her bust. A 'jumper' is essentially a woman's garment, usually of soft wool and quite light. All four can be knitted by machine or hand, and many are not made of wool at all but of some artificial fibre such as acrylic.

puma see **leopard**

pun/riddle/conundrum (verbal joke or puzzle)
A 'pun' is a play on words. Shakespeare has dozens of them, and *Romeo and Juliet* kicks off with three:

Sampson Gregory, o' my word, we'll not carry coals.
Gregory No, for then we should be colliers.
Sampson I mean, an we be in choler, we'll draw.
Gregory Ay, while you live, draw your neck out o' the collar.

(Ones more bawdy than this follow.) They are also favourites with journalists ('Smashing trip' the staid *Times* once headed a news item describing a particularly rough crossing of the Atlantic on board a passenger liner, when all the crockery was shattered) and with children ('Opened the window and influenza', and many more, to a greater or lesser degree ribald or ghoulish). A 'riddle' is a question, or sometimes a statement, that expects an ingenious reply or response. It may itself involve a 'pun' ('What are cows in the Arctic called? Eskimoos'), and this, specifically, is called a 'conundrum' – a strange, learned-looking word, whose origin is unknown (and therefore a 'riddle').

puppet/marionette (small figure of person or animal manipulated to provide dramatic entertainment)

The difference between the two is mainly one of manipulation or motive power. 'Puppet' is the general word for a figure that can be operated by wires, rods, strings, or directly by hand (as a 'glove puppet'). Punch and Judy are among the best known. 'Marionettes' are 'puppets' worked by strings (only). The name is a French one, ultimately from holy figures of biblical personages and in particular the Virgin Mary. A blend of 'marionette' and 'puppet' gave the name of those famous (or infamous) television stars of the 1970s, the Muppets.

purple see **violet**

pygmy see **midget**

python/boa constrictor (large snake that crushes its prey)
Both are tropical snakes, with the 'python' found from West Africa to China, Australia and the Pacific Islands, but the 'boa constrictor' chiefly in South and Central America. There is also an anatomical difference: 'boas' have teeth in their premaxillae (the bones in the front of the upper jaw) and no bones supra-orbitally (above the eye); 'pythons' do not have premaxillary teeth, and do have supra-orbital bones.

quarto/octavo/folio/foolscap (book and paper sizes)
The first three are sizes of bound books, the names deriving from the number of times a sheet of paper is folded to give the finished size. Traditionally three finished sizes – crown, demy and royal – obtain for each division, though other sizes also exist.
For 'folio' the sheet is folded once (giving

two leaves, thus four pages), crown folio measuring 15 by 10 inches, demy folio 17½ by 11¼ inches and royal folio 20 by 12½ inches. For 'quarto' the sheet is folded twice (giving four leaves, thus eight pages), crown quarto measuring 10 by 7½ inches, demy quarto 11¾ by 8¾ inches and royal quarto 12½ by 10 inches. For octavo the sheet is folded three times (giving eight leaves, thus sixteen pages), crown octavo measuring 7½ by 5 inches, demy octavo 8⅜ by 5⅝ inches and royal octavo 10 by 6¼ inches. These imperial measurements have now been superseded by metric equivalents but the names and principles remain the same.

'Foolscap' is a standard size of paper, originally measuring 17 inches by 13½ inches, a useful size to twist into a dunce's cap in schools and also called after the old watermark of a fool's cap-and-bells. This and other paper sizes have again been largely superseded by new metric paper sizes, of which the most common in general use are A4 (210mm by 297mm) and A5 (148mm by 210mm).

quay/jetty/pier (projecting landing-place or loading-place for ships)
A 'quay' may not in fact always project into the sea but be part of a harbour, where the 'quayside' is the area where passengers embark and disembark or where ships load and unload. A 'jetty' does run out to sea, and although it can double up as a landing pier, it is usually there to protect the harbour or coast, and so is fairly stoutly made for this purpose. 'Quay' was originally spelled 'key' (ultimately from a Celtic word), meaning a low reef or sandbank. Later it was respelled after the French word for this sandbank, but retained its 'key' pronunciation. 'Jetty' is direct French, however: literally something 'thrown out'. For more about the functions of seaside structures, see **port** (place where ships can dock). A 'pier' is a raised and fairly spacious structure built out over water, traditionally at a seaside resort, where it serves not only as a landing place for boats and ships but as a promenade for holidaymakers, with a variety of entertainments ranging from coin-operated amusement machines to a theatre.

quire see **ream**

rabbit/hare (brown-furred animal with longish ears)
Both animals are members of the same family, *Leporidae*, with 'hare' in the USA often used to designate a 'rabbit'. The general differences are these: 'rabbits' are naked, blind and helpless at birth and are usually gregarious. They are also smaller than 'hares', with shorter head, ears, hind legs and feet, are greyer in colour, and lack the black tips to the ears that 'hares' have. They live in burrows. 'Hares' at birth are (there is no other word for it) well-haired, and soon able to hop, and are normally solitary. They have long ears and hind legs, short upturned tails, and a characteristic divided lip. They live in 'forms' – that is, they do not burrow like 'rabbits' but make shallow nests on the surface of the earth in the grass.

very similar, but note stance of hare and relatively larger size

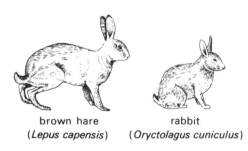

brown hare   rabbit
(*Lepus capensis*)   (*Oryctolagus cuniculus*)

radar/sonar/Asdic (direction-finding navigation system for ships or aircraft)
All are acronyms, respectively: *ra*dio *de*tection *a*nd *r*anging, *so*und *na*vigation and *r*anging, *A*nti-*S*ubmarine *D*etection *I*nvestigation *C*ommittee. 'Radar' is the best known. Basically, the system involves sending out short radio waves and detecting them or measuring them when they have been reflected by some object. 'Sonar' (the word is analogous to 'radar') is a similar system, but used under water, mainly by

ships and submarines, but also by aircraft who can 'dunk' a device in the water for example, when flying over it. 'Asdic' was the early form of 'sonar', officially superseded by the latter name in 1963 to conform with NATO practice. All three systems were widely used in the Second World War.

radial tyres/cross-ply tyres (types of vehicle tyre)
'Radial' – really, radial-ply – tyres have a number of inner cord layers running at right angles to the crown of the tyre, that is, running in a direction that is 'radial' to the centre of the wheel. These are braced together below the tread by a band of additional cords, called breaker cords, that are set at different angles, usually diagonally. 'Cross-ply' tyres have inner cord layers that run crosswise or diagonally, that is, they criss cross one another. 'Cross-ply' tyres are the conven-

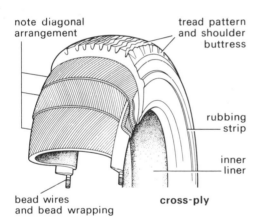

note diagonal arrangement

tread pattern and shoulder buttress

rubbing strip

inner liner

bead wires and bead wrapping

cross-ply

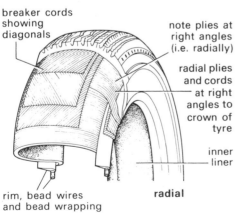

breaker cords showing diagonals

note plies at right angles (i.e. radially)

radial plies and cords at right angles to crown of tyre

inner liner

rim, bead wires and bead wrapping

radial

tional kind, with 'radial' tyres more suitable for high speeds. As more and more cars are designed for fast travel, so 'radial' tyres are rapidly superseding 'cross-ply' ones. (An alternative American name for 'cross-ply' tyres is 'bias-ply' tyres.)

radius/diameter (straight line on a circle or its length)
The 'radius' of a circle runs from its centre to any point on the edge. The 'diameter' runs right across a circle, passing through its centre, thus in length being the same as two 'radii'. In fact any figure can have a 'diameter', so long as the line passes through the figure's centre.

rage see **anger**

ragout see **hash**

raincoat/mackintosh/burberry
(waterproof coat)
A 'raincoat' is the general word for the light overcoat that is normally proof against moderate rain only, or even just shower-proof. A 'mackintosh', or 'mac' (or 'mack'), is either an alternative word for any 'rain-coat' or, more accurately, a rather heavier waterproof overcoat (or sometimes not so heavy) made of impervious material such as the rubberised cotton invented by the Scottish chemist Charles Macintosh. A 'burberry' – properly Burberry, since it is a trade name – is also occasionally used loosely as a word for any type of 'raincoat', although strictly it is one manufactured by Burberrys Ltd. This English firm, founded in the late nineteenth century, aimed to 'substitute overcoats made of self-ventilating materials for "macintoshes" proofed with rubber, which for nearly a hundred years were regarded as the only possible safe-guards against getting wet' (*The Royal Warrant Holders Who's Who*, 1921).

raisin/sultana/currant (small sweet fruit used in the making of puddings and cakes)
A 'raisin' is a partially dried grape (compare French *raisin*, 'grape', and *raisin sec*, 'raisin'). It is usually dark brown and larger than a 'currant'. Most 'raisins' are exported from the shores of the Mediterranean, or from France or California. A 'sultana' is a light

golden brown seedless 'raisin', which can be eaten raw or cooked. 'Sultanas' originally came from Smyrna, now Izmir, in Turkey, which was ruled over by a sultan. A 'currant' – the dried sort, not the fresh, which is an entirely unrelated fruit – is a small dried grape, also seedless – a small seedless 'raisin', in fact – coming from the same regions as the 'raisin' itself. Originally the 'currant' came from Corinth, in Greece – hence its name.

rascal/rogue/scoundrel/knave (dishonest or 'naughty' person)
Most of these words are now used facetiously or even affectionately. In their proper senses, however, they can be distinguished. A 'rascal' is a dishonest person who is also shrewd or sly. (The word 'rapscallion' is related to it.) A 'rogue' is basically a cheat or a fraud. The term seems to be a blend of 'roamer' and 'beggar'. A 'scoundrel' – the word is of unknown origin – is a particularly nasty or selfish 'rogue'. A 'knave', more a historic term, on something of a par with 'villain' or 'varmint', is essentially a constantly dishonest person and a worthless one. Originally the word simply meant 'boy' or 'servant': compare modern German *Knabe*, 'boy'. For the 'Knave' of Hearts to steal the tarts was absolutely in character. In cards, too, the 'knave' may be a courtier but he is the lowest of his kind – a jumped-up jack, in fact.

raven see **crow**

ravine/gorge/canyon (deep cleft or cutting in rocks)
A 'ravine' is a long, deep, narrow valley, a mountain cleft worn by fast-flowing water. A 'gorge' is narrow above all else, and usually has a stream at the bottom and steep, rocky walls. A 'canyon', by contrast, is deep first and foremost, although it, too, has steep sides and usually a stream at the bottom. All three are technically valleys, and all three, whether actually containing a stream or not, are the result of a fast flow of water over resistant rock.

ray see **gleam**

realm see **kingdom**

ream/quire (large quantity of paper)
A 'ream' equals twenty 'quires' and contains 480 sheets (or more, to allow for waste). (A printer's ream contains 516 sheets.) A 'quire' thus contains 24 sheets. 'Quire' has the original sense of 'four sheets of paper folded to form eight pages', deriving from Latin *quaterni*, 'set of four'. 'Ream' is also used in a general way to express a large quantity of something, especially on paper: 'reams and reams of writing'. There is no connection between 'quire' here and 'quire' the affected spelling of 'choir'.

rear see **back**

rebellion see **revolt**

recital see **concert**

rector see **vicar**

reed/rush (type of grass growing in marshy places)
The 'reed' is the name of a number of tall grasses, especially the genus *Phragmites*, growing in marshy places. More precisely, it is the stem of such a grass. The 'rush' is properly the leaf of a grasslike herb, especially the genus *Juncus*, whose stems, more commonly called 'rushes', as is the plant itself, are pithy and hollow and used for making chair-bottoms, mats and the like. A particular type of 'rush' is the bulrush, which has as little to do with bulls as cowslips have to do with cow's lips: 'bull' probably means 'coarse', 'large', as in 'bullfrog'. The biblical bulrushes that hid the infant Moses, incidentally, were not this sort but stems and leaves of the papyrus plant, or paper 'reed'.

reel/jig/fling (lively Scottish or Irish dance)
The 'reel', with music in 2-4 or 4-4 time, is traditionally and chiefly a Scottish dance performed by two or more couples in line and basically consists of the execution of circular figures – which will indeed make your head reel. There are also Irish and English 'reels', but in these the music is usually smoother and the action more 'flowing'. A 'jig' has music in 6-8, or sometimes 3-8, 9-8 or 12-8 time, and is found in Ireland

and England as well as in Scotland. It originated as a dance for one or more people, with the English morris-dancing 'jig' being a solo dance executed with raised arms. The 'fling', or 'Highland fling', is a Scottish dance that is a vigorous 'reel', performed with 'flinging' movements of the arms and legs – hence its name.

referee/umpire (judge or arbitrator in a game, sport, or dispute)
The most straightforward distinction is by the particular sport. 'Referees' officiate in football, boxing, ice hockey (two of them), tennis and rugby football, among others, while 'umpires' operate in cricket (two), hockey (two), tennis, lacrosse (three), and baseball (one or more – four in major league games). Tennis, it will be noted, has both: the 'referee' is in charge of the tournament; the 'umpire', who is the one in the public eye, especially on the Centre Court at Wimbledon, is in charge of a match. In an industrial dispute, according to the provisions of the Arbitration Act, 1950, a 'referee' is a person to whose judgment the disputed matter is referred, with all matters in the dispute being submitted to arbitrators. When two such arbitrators cannot agree, the 'referee' who is called in to decide the matter is often known as an 'umpire'. 'Umpire' as a word falls into the category of 'adder' and 'apron': 'an umpire' should really be 'a numpire', since he is a 'non-peer', that is, a person not equal with the others.

refrigerator/freezer/deep-freeze
(appliance for cooling and storing food and drink products)
The 'refrigerator' or 'fridge' is the general word, of course. The temperature in the main compartment of a 'refrigerator' is usually a few degrees above freezing. 'Freezer' has three meanings: a refrigerated room, a compartment for freezing in a 'refrigerator', or a 'deep-freeze', which itself is an appliance for storing a reasonable quantity of food for a long time at a very low temperature, approximately o degrees F (−18 degrees C). The word was originally an American trade name (DeepFreeze), with 'deep' referring to the temperature, not the actual depth of the container.

refugee/evacuee (person leaving home country or region in a time of threat or danger)
A 'refugee' is a person who has chosen to leave his native land, or been obliged to leave it, as a result of war, religious persecution, a hostile regime, or a natural disaster such as an earthquake. An 'evacuee' is a person removed from a dangerous place to one of safety. In Britain 'evacuees' are chiefly thought of as the London children who were sent to live in country areas in the Second World War.

regalia see **insignia**

regiment see **corps**

regret/remorse (sense of sorrow or guilt)
'Regret' is distress or sorrow for a wrong-doing – not necessarily one's own. 'Remorse' is a more complex thing, and deeper altogether. It implies qualms of conscience, guilt, repentance – and 'regret', and is usually experienced for a grave wrong that one has oneself committed. In origin the word means 'bite' (as in 'morsel'), since the feeling of deep regret seems to bite into one. (Compare the modern slang phrase 'What's eating you?')

rein/bridle/halter (part of a horse's harness, usually made of leather)
The 'rein' is a long strap fastened to the 'bridle' or bit, usually one of two, designed for restraining or guiding the horse. The 'bridle' is that part of the harness that goes round the horse's head, usually consisting of a head-stall, the bit, and the 'reins'. The 'halter' is a rope or strap, with a noose or headstall, used for leading a horse or tying him up to something.

remand home/borstal/detention centre
(centre for young offenders)
A 'remand home' is now an obsolescent term for what is called a 'community home', where child offenders under the age of seventeen are committed to the care of the local authority. A 'borstal', named after the original of its kind at the village of Borstal just south of Rochester in Kent, is a residential centre for somewhat older offenders, between the ages of fifteen and twenty. A 'detention centre' is

99

designed for young male offenders aged between seventeen and twenty – ones for younger boys being called 'remand centres' – where life is officially planned to be 'brisk and formal', with one hour's physical training a day, for example. None of these is a prison in the proper sense of the word, and no offender under the age of seventeen would be sent to prison anyway.

remorse see regret

Republican/Democrat (member of one of the two major American political parties)
The divisions are not clear-cut, and there is no obvious 'right' and 'left' as there is in Britain. The 'Republican' party is in fact regarded as 'right of centre' and the party of 'big business', but it is really a coalition of changing interests and sectional groups, as indeed is the 'Democratic' party. The latter, however, tends to be the party of the 'small man' and has its stronghold in the Southern states, the 'solid south'. Broadly speaking, also, the 'Democratic' party – which came to be caricatured in the form of a donkey in the late nineteenth century – is now identified with social welfare, economic regulation, and civil rights, while the 'Republicans' are largely associated with state rights. The 'Democrats' have thus won the support of a number of industrial workers and, because of their initiative on the racial question, have gained the support of most black voters. Over recent years the 'Democratic' party has become more liberal than the 'Republican'. The 'Republican' party arose in 1854 to combat slavery. Among noted 'Republican' US presidents have been Theodore Roosevelt, Eisenhower, Nixon and Ford. The 'Democratic' party originated in 1792 as a group of voters who supported Jefferson to defend the rights of the individual states against the centralising policy of the Federalists. (It was originally called the 'Democratic-Republican' party, and adopted its present name in 1830.) Well known 'Democratic' presidents have been Jackson, Woodrow Wilson, F. D. Roosevelt, Truman, Kennedy, Lyndon B. Johnson and Jimmy Carter.

resolution/motion (proposition at an assembly passed, or to be passed, by voting)
The two words overlap, but strictly: a 'resolution' is the expression of an opinion on which it is proposed to take action – which may in the event, however, not be taken, even if the 'resolution' is passed. A 'motion' is the same – except that passing it *will* result in action being taken.

rest home see **nursing home**

retinue see **suite**

revolt/revolution/uprising/rebellion/ mutiny (form of active resistance against authority)
A 'revolt' normally takes the form of a vigorous outbreak against authority that arises either from general turbulence or from opposition to tyranny or oppression. A 'revolution' is a successful 'rebellion', especially one that having overthrown a government or political system establishes another. Two famous 'revolutions' in this respect were the ones in France (1789) and Russia (1917), which both overthrew the monarchy and replaced it with a radically different type of government by the people. An 'uprising' is really the same as a 'revolt', denoting perhaps more the actual insurrection than the violent outcome that results as a protest against authority. A 'rebellion', thus, is a large-scale 'revolt' that aims to secure independence or bring down the government. A 'mutiny' is normally thought of as a 'revolt' or 'rebellion' by soldiers or seamen (as the famous 'mutiny' on the *Bounty*). When in 1789 news was brought to Louis XVI of France that the Bastille had fallen, he asked, 'C'est une révolte?' 'Non, Sire,' replied the Duc de la Rochefoucauld-Liancourt, 'c'est une révolution.'

revolution see **revolt**

revolver see **pistol**

revue see **musical**

rheumatism/arthritis (disease with pain and inflammation in the joints)
'Rheumatism' ('rheumaticks') is a popular word for vague or ill-defined aches and pains in various parts of the body, whether the joints or not. 'Arthritis' is a more precise term

for the inflammation specifically of a joint. It has the three forms 'septic arthritis', which results from infection via the bloodstream, 'rheumatoid arthritis', whose cause is unknown, and 'osteoarthritis', which is a degenerative disease of the joints (and not so widespread as 'rheumatoid arthritis', notorious as a chronic disease that affects the whole body).

rhinoceros see **hippopotamus**

rice/sago (starchy foodstuff)
'Rice' consists of the starchy seeds or grain of the grass botanically known as *Oryza sativa*. 'Sago' is not from a grass at all, but a starchy food from the soft interior or the trunk of various palms, but especially the attractively named *Metroxylon rumphii* and *Metroxylon sago*, that are native to Indonesia.

rick see **stack**

riddle see **pun**

rifle see **gun** (portable firearm)

rim/brim (edge or boundary of a circular or curved area)
'Rim' is the word for the edge or border of a hollow vessel, as the 'rim' of a cup or a glass. 'Brim' is usually the word for the inside of the 'rim', especially at the top of a full vessel, as a glass that is filled to the 'brim'. The 'brim' of a hat, though, is its projecting edge, while the 'rim' of a wheel is the outer ring of its framework (not including the tyre). The words are related respectively to 'ridge' and 'border'.

ring road see **by-pass**

rink see **field** (area of play)

rite/ritual (ceremonial act or series of acts)
A 'rite' is very often a religious ceremony, as the 'rites' of baptism or the last 'rites'. A 'ritual' is an established procedure for a religious or any ceremony, or simply a social custom – letting the dog out into the garden before breakfast could be a daily 'ritual'. The word does have religious connotations, however, if only because of its use to mean a

book containing a prescribed order of service – a book of 'rites', in fact.

ritual see **rite**

road/street (public way for vehicles)
A 'road' usually runs between two distant points, such as two towns. 'Roads' (and 'streets') leading out of a town are often named after the town to which they lead, as the Bath 'Road' out of Bristol, the London 'Road' out of Leicester (and numerous other towns), and the Woodstock 'Road' out of Oxford. The word is a general one, too, and can apply to a 'street', which is thus a 'road' in a village, town, city or other populated area, especially one lined with houses, shops, and other buildings and having a pavement. The implication here is that if a 'street' does not have these things, it will probably be a 'road'. For this reason, when a town expands, what was formerly a 'road' will become a 'street'. This happened with Oxford 'Street' in London, which was the Oxford 'Road' before – if one can imagine it – it acquired its present wealth of shops. But, again, many 'streets' (by the above definition) are actually named 'road', often because of their importance as a recognised through route for traffic, as London's Bayswater 'Road', Vauxhall Bridge 'Road', and North Circular 'Road'.

road fund licence see **driving licence**

robbery see **theft**

roedeer see **stag**

rogue see **rascal**

roll see **bun**

roller see **billow**

rook see **crow**

rostrum/dais (raised platform)
A 'rostrum' is a platform primarily intended for public speakers, although the word is also applied to an orchestral conductor's podium. The word is actually Latin for 'beak', the explanation being that the platform or elevated place for speeches in the

ancient Roman forum was decorated with the beaks of captured galleys or warships. A 'dais' – also (via French) from Latin, *discus* meaning 'table' as well as 'disc' – is more of a lecturer's desk, or a platform at the end of a hall for a high table.

round/volley/salvo (firing of a shot or shots)
A 'round' is a single shot by one or each of a number of guns, rifles or the like. A 'volley', directly related to French *voler*, 'to fly', is in the narrow sense the flight of a number of missiles together; of shots it is a simultaneous discharge. A 'salvo', often fired as a salute (to which word it is related), implies a firing of shots in regular succession, although applied to bombs dropped from an aircraft it means much the same as a 'volley', that is, a simultaneous (and single) release. All three words are used of applause, with 'round' thought of as a plural, since several people are clapping at once. (This is in fact the correct or original sense, since 'round' implies the distribution of something – everybody or everything has or does something, it 'goes round'; 'round' meaning 'single shot' is thus a secondary and strictly speaking inaccurate sense.)

rubber see **game** (portion of play forming a scoring unit)

rudder/tiller/helm (instrument for steering a boat or ship)
A 'rudder' is a flat wooden or metal piece fastened to the stern-post under the water. It can deflect the water so as to steer the boat in a particular direction, and it does this by being moved by the 'tiller', a horizontal bar fitted to its head. A 'helm' is a 'tiller', too, but also can be a wheel, especially in larger craft. If you take the 'helm', you are literally or figuratively in control.

rugby league see **rugby union**

rugby union/rugby league (form of rugby football)
'Rugby union' is the standard and most widespread form of the game, with fifteen players a side and always an amateur game. 'Rugby league', played largely in the north of England, Wales and southern Scotland, is a chiefly professional game with thirteen players (there are no wing forwards). There are some differences in the rules and scoring. In both games a try scores three points, but in 'rugby league' a successful kick at goal only scores two. If the ball goes into touch, the game is restarted in 'rugby union' with a line-out, in 'rugby league' with a scrum. Furthermore, in 'rugby league' a player can stand up when he is tackled and play the ball back with his foot. He can't do that in 'rugby union'. The two varieties are the result of a split in 1893, when the Rugby League broke away from the Rugby Union. The game still sometimes called 'rugger' is 'rugby union'. Both games are a development of football initiated at Rugby School, when one William Webb Ellis 'with a fine disregard for the rules of football as played in his time, first took the ball in his arms and ran with it, AD 1823' (commemorative plaque in Rugby School Close).

rush see **reed**

sable see **mink**

sabre see **foil**

safety/security (condition of being free from danger)
The words are sometimes used interchangeably, although there is a distinction. 'Safety' implies that danger, threatening or actual, is now past, and one has nothing to fear. 'Security' relates more to the future and suggests an absence of worry or concern about what will come or could come.

sago see **rice**

sailing/yachting/boating (sport or pastime of racing or moving over water in a boat)
'Sailing' usually implies a leisure sport, even a leisurely one. 'Yachting', with its yacht clubs and high-power sailing craft, is essentially a professional affair, and especially applies to racing contests. 'Boating' is the use of boats in general for pleasure, whether sailing boats (or yachts) or not. And of course there is absolutely nothing half so much worth doing as messing about in boats.

salvo see **round**

sarcasm/irony (expression of scorn or derision)
'Sarcasm', which is essentially harsh or cutting, may be expressed directly or ironically. Direct sarcasm occurs in such a remark as, 'You *would* miss the train, wouldn't you!' With 'irony' there is a contradiction between the literal and the intended meaning, at an elevated or merely a playful level. 'Lovely weather for ducks!' is an example of the latter, as are most remarks concluding '. . . I *don't* think!' 'Ironical sarcasm' is thus of the kind: 'Of course, you wouldn't know what it's like to spend all day cleaning and cooking, would you!'

sardine/pilchard (small fish sold canned in oil)
The 'sardine' in most European countries is the name for a young 'pilchard' (*Sardina pilchardus*), especially a one-year-old one. 'Sardine', too, is sometimes also used as a name for brislings or young sprats (*Clupea sprattus*) in Norway, where the 'pilchard' is unknown. The 'pilchard' itself is related to the herring, although smaller, thicker and rounder. The name of the 'sardine' may ultimately derive from the Mediterranean island of Sardinia, although the fish itself comes from a much wider catchment area, including the English Channel. The origin of the name of the 'pilchard' is not certain.

satsuma see **tangerine**

satyr see **faun**

saying/proverb (popular quotation embodying a familiar truth)

A 'saying' is an everyday, fairly homely thing, which may be colloquial and not even a complete sentence. Most clichés and hack-phrases are 'sayings'. Examples are rife – one only has to overhear or eavesdrop in a shop, bus or other public place to hear such expressions as 'You've got a one-track mind' or 'It takes all sorts'. A 'proverb' is less colloquial and normally a complete sentence, and is often of considerable antiquity, even to the extent that its original meaning may have been lost, or the original wording altered. This happened with, 'More haste, less speed', which is now loosely used as a cliché to mean, 'If you unduly hurry or skimp something, it will take you more time, not less'; originally it was, 'More haste than good speed', implying that something was done unnecessarily quickly.

scent see **perfume**

scheme see **plan**

schizophrenic see **psychopath**

school see (1) **department**, (2) **shoal**

sciatica/lumbago (pain in the muscles of the back or leg)
'Sciatica' (from the Greek word for 'hip-joint') is a pain down the back of the leg, from the hip down, originating from exertion that puts a strain on the lumbar or loin portion of the spine, where the sciatic nerve has its roots. 'Lumbago' is a fibromuscular injury in the small of the back caused by a sprain, sudden exertion or the like. Both therefore have either a painful or an etymological connection with the small of the back, the lumbar region.

scone see **bun**

scorn see **contempt**

scoundrel see **rascal**

scream/screech/shriek (piercing cry)
These similar-sounding words can be distinguished. A 'scream' is a loud, piercing cry, as of pain or fear, or a startled, high-pitched cry, not so loud (as when one is suddenly surprised by a hand placed on one's shoulder or

the unexpected appearance of a mouse). A 'screech' is a disagreeably shrill or harsh cry, as of an old crone or a 'villain of the piece' on the stage. A 'shriek' is sharper, briefer and usually louder than a 'scream', and is usually the prerogative of women and girls. It does not necessarily denote pain or fear, however, but more or less any sudden strong or uncontrollable emotion, as pleasure, surprise, joy, or amusement.

screech see **scream**

scrumpy see **cider**

sculpture/statue/torso/bust
(representation in stone or other material of human or animal)
A 'sculpture' is in fact *any* sculptured object in the round or in relief, whether representational or abstract. A 'statue' is a sculptured figure – or a cast or moulded one – of a person or animal, usually one that is life-size or larger. (Small 'statues' are statuettes or simply models.) Whereas a 'statue' is the figure of a complete person, a 'torso' is much more limited – it is the sculptured figure of a nude human trunk, especially one without the head or limbs. A famous example is the Belvedere 'Torso' in the Vatican. A 'torso' must in turn be distinguished from a 'bust', which is a 'sculpture' of the head, shoulders and upper chest of a person. Good examples are the 'busts' of Roman emperors at the British Museum in London.

scurf see **dandruff**

scythe/sickle (implement for cutting corn or grass)
The 'scythe' is the long one, with a curving blade on the end of a slightly crooked pole having two short handles at right angles. It is used – or was used – chiefly for mowing and reaping. The 'sickle' is the short-handled, short-bladed implement which is used either for cutting corn or, more commonly, for lopping overhanging branches, trimming shrubs, and hacking weeds generally. The 'scythe' has come to be regarded as the symbol of Father Time, who morbidly uses it to mow down the living when their hour has come. The 'sickle', by contrast, has become one of the two symbols

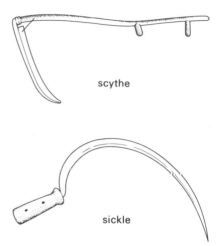

scythe

sickle

of Soviet Russia, where it represents the rural farmworker. (The complementary hammer stands for the urban industrial worker.) Traditionally, too, the 'scythe' has become familiar as an implement used by a man standing, while the 'sickle' is mainly associated with a woman bending – see the paintings of Millet. Both words come from a root meaning 'cut', as in 'section'; 'scythe' should really have no 'c', but it probably acquired it by association with the name of a kindred cutting implement, 'scissors'.

sea/ocean (region of salt water, usually defined and named geographically)
A 'sea' can be three things: a partially enclosed body of salt water, such as the Mediterranean 'Sea'; a definite part of an 'ocean', as the Sargasso 'Sea' (part of the Atlantic); a large body of inland water, when this is saline, as the Caspian 'Sea'. 'Oceans' are larger, of course, and fewer. For many years, the world was regarded as having five 'oceans': Atlantic, Pacific, Indian, Arctic and Antarctic. Today, however, only three of these are recognised: the Atlantic, Pacific and Indian. (The Arctic is now regarded as belonging to the Atlantic, of which it is a marginal 'sea', while the Antarctic is the Southern 'Ocean', divided into three portions – one for each of the three regular 'oceans'.) 'Seas' and 'oceans' in fact form a single integrated unit and are sometimes known collectively as the World 'Ocean'.

secondary modern school see **comprehensive school**

secretary see **president**

section/segment/sector (portion of a whole)
A 'section' is a part that is cut off or divided in some way from something, or regarded as a separate unit, as a military 'section' (see **corps**) or the final 'section' of a journey. The 'section' of a society or community is the part of it seen as having distinctive interests or functions of some kind. A 'segment' may also be cut off or separated, but is usually one of a number of pieces or parts that are marked off somehow, as the 'segments' of an orange or the divisions of a limb or the rings of a worm: the common or garden earthworm has up to 150 'segments'. A 'sector' of a society, as distinct from a 'section', is seen as having a single leader or controller, as the private 'sector' of industry, while in military terms a 'sector' is the portion of a front that is under the charge of a single commander. In geometry, a 'segment' is a part cut off from any figure, but especially a circle, by a line or plane, and a 'sector', more precisely, is the part of a circle that lies between two radii (see **radius**, if necessary) and the arc that joins them, like a slice of cake.

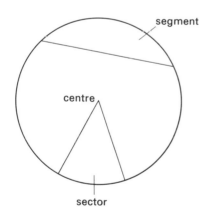

section see **corps**

sector see **section**

security see **safety**

segment see **section**

semolina/tapioca (floury food used for making milk puddings)
'Semolina' is the name of the large, hard parts of wheat grains that are left behind in the bolting machine after the fine flour has passed through. 'Tapioca' is a grainy foodstuff prepared from cassava starch by drying it on a heated plate while it is still moist. Puddings made from one or the other are notorious for turning up in nutritious school dinners, where they are usually regarded as having the same degree of palatability as **rice** pudding. (For what happens to the grains that pass through the bolting machine see **flour**.)

sense see **meaning**

senses see **faculties**

serial/series (set of successive articles or episodes)
A 'serial' is normally a story, play or the like that is told, written or broadcast in separate parts, which together make up the whole work. The word is actually the adjective of 'series', that is, a 'serial' story – one told in a 'series' of parts. A 'series', thus, is a set of individual articles or parts, each of which is complete in itself. In broadcasting, a 'series' is a set of programmes on a particular subject, so that there will be a common theme, but designed so that each one can be seen or heard either on its own or as part of the whole set. There may even be a number of 'series' on a topic.

series see **serial**

serpent see **snake**

set see **game** (portion of play forming a scoring unit)

settee see **couch**

shade see **shadow**

shadow/shade (dark area on the ground or elsewhere caused by an opaque or semi-opaque object intercepting the light)
A 'shadow' is either a single dark figure or

image, as the 'shadow' of a man, or else an area of relative darkness, as the 'shadow' of a building – the area which the building darkens by intercepting the light. Such an area will be fairly clearly defined. A 'shade' – usually the 'shade' – is a comparatively dark area with no particular form or limit, often regarded as providing shelter or relief from a light or heat that is too fierce, as the 'shade' of an old apple tree, where it is pleasant to sit. Of course, the 'shade' of a tree might also be its well-defined 'shadow'. 'Shade' is usually used with reference to the light of the sun, whereas a 'shadow' can be cast by any bright object, as a fire, a torch, or a candle. In some cases, however, the two words can be used more or less interchangeably, so that one can sit in the 'shadow' or sit in the 'shade'. Don't misunderstand someone, incidentally, when he says, 'Let's move a "shade".' He doesn't mean, 'Let's move into the "shade"', but, 'Let's move a little.'

shame/humiliation/mortification (feeling of guilt and embarrassment)
'Shame' implies a feeling of guilt mixed with regret: 'I did it, and I shouldn't have.' 'Humiliation' is the sense of being humbled, disgraced or shown up: 'I did it, I shouldn't have, and they let me know it; now I feel a real heel.' 'Mortification' – rather an impressive word – describes a sense of deep embarrassment with possible confusion: 'I did it, I made a proper mess of it, and now I feel terrible.' The word in its origin implies a 'death' or 'killing', as of one's pride or ego.

shares see **stocks** (divisions of a company's capital)

sheen see **gloss**

ship see **boat**

shoal/school (group of fish swimming together)
A 'shoal' is used of any fish, whereas a 'school', although also applicable to fish, tends to be reserved for marine mammals such as porpoises and whales. The word 'shoal' is not related to 'shoal' meaning 'submerged sandbank' but derives from the other half of this pair, 'school', which in spite of the fact that porpoises are intelligent

creatures and can be trained in captivity – they can imitate human voices as well as locate a variety of objects – comes not from the familiar educational establishment but from an old Dutch word meaning 'troop'.

shoe see **boot**

shore/beach/coast (edge of land beside a sea or lake)
'Shore' is a general word, often with an implied contrast to 'sea'. A 'beach' is a stretch of the shore with sand or shingle, especially at low tide, and is usually associated with swimming and bathing and seaside leisure activities generally. There are a number of shingle 'beaches' on the Sussex coast, but Beachy Head, the famous headland in East Sussex, is not so called because of the 'beach' below but because its name is French in origin: *beau chef*, meaning simply (but attractively) 'beautiful headland'. 'Coast' more or less equals 'shore', but the word applies to seas or oceans only, and is not used of a lake, however large it is. The 'coast' too, is normally regarded as the natural border or frontier of a country, which may have to be defended or protected, for example, from enemy attack, as implied in 'coastguard' and the name 'Coastal' Command for the RAF section which operated against enemy shipping in the Second World War.

shriek see **scream**

shrimp/prawn (edible crustacean)
The common 'shrimp' (*Crangon vulgaris*) is the smaller of the two, with a semi-

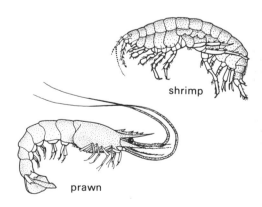

shrimp

prawn

transparent body, fanlike tail, and long whiplike antennae. The antennae of the 'prawn', however (by which is usually meant the *edible* 'prawn', *Leander serratus*), are much longer – one and a half times its own body length – and its largest pair of claws are on its second pair of legs, whereas the 'shrimp' has its largest pair of claws on its first pair of legs. Yet another difference is that 'shrimps' like to burrow in the sand between tides, whereas 'prawns' prefer rocky pools. In the USA, a jumbo 'shrimp' is about three inches long.

sick humour see **black humour**

sickle see **scythe**

sideboard/dresser (piece of furniture containing or holding plates and dishes)
A 'sideboard', as its name suggests, is a table or flat-topped chest standing at the side of the dining-room with dishes, plates, decanters and the like either on it or in it. The word essentially means a table placed at one side in a room where meals or dishes can be served or taken. A 'dresser' is a type of 'sideboard' specifically for the kitchen, also with shelves for dishes and plates. It sounds something like an item of furniture for the bedroom, but the connection is not with dressing but French *dresser*, 'to prepare' (i.e. food). A Welsh 'dresser' has a tall backboard with open shelves above its lower cupboard, and as a fine piece of furniture has come to be promoted not only to the dining-room but even to the sitting-room for the display of its own workmanship and the dishes ranged along its shelves.

sidesman/churchwarden (church official)
A 'sidesman' is an assistant 'churchwarden', whose special duty is usually that of taking the collection – when he may literally stand by the side of the 'churchwarden'. The 'churchwarden' is one of two officials elected annually – one by the parish priest, the other by the parishioners – to represent the lay members of the parish and to have special responsibility for the movable property in the church.

Siegfried Line see **Maginot Line**

simile/metaphor (figure of speech comparing one thing to another)
A 'simile' uses a direct comparison, however hackneyed, bizarre or inept, usually with the word 'as' or 'like', so 'cool as a cucumber' and 'like a bat out of hell' are both 'similes'. A 'metaphor' (from the Greek for 'transfer') is rather more subtle: it is saying that something *is* another, although of course it literally is not, so to speak of your mother-in-law (or whoever) as 'a real old gas-bag' or to call someone a 'red-bellied son of a yellow-livered caterpillar' (children are experts in the genre) is to indulge in 'metaphors'. A sustained form of this (a gas-bag filled with laughing gas, a caterpillar who will never turn into a butterfly, and more) is an 'extended metaphor'. A specially enjoyable form of it is a 'mixed metaphor', when two or more elements of the comparison are absurdly incongruous – often quite unintentionally so – as to 'set the ship of state on its feet', or the much quoted specimen allegedly perpetrated by the Irish politician, Sir Boyle Roche: 'Mr Speaker, I smell a rat; I see him forming in the air and darkening the sky; but I'll nip him in the bud.' Mixed 'metaphors' can, however, be used most effectively, with no comic effect, as 'take arms against a sea of troubles' (instead of 'host of troubles'), in Hamlet's famous 'To be or not to be' speech. Many 'metaphors' are proverbs, as 'Time flies', or clichés, as 'out of the frying-pan into the fire'.

sit-down strike see **sit-in**

sit-in/work-in/sit-down strike/go-slow/work-to-rule (type of strike)
A 'sit-in' is not so much a strike as an organised protest, especially against the policy or administration of a place. The protest consists in occupying an appropriate area and sitting in it until, in theory, the authorities change their attitude. Students dissatisfied with the policy of their college principal, for example, may organise a 'sit-in' in his office. A 'work-in' is usually understood as the take-over of a factory under threat of closure by its workers: they simply carry on working. A 'sit-down strike' is rather like a combined 'sit-in' and 'work-in', when workers refuse to leave the place where they are working as a form of protest or to stake a

claim. A 'go-slow' is another form of protest, when work is not stopped, as in an all-out strike, but is done at a deliberately slow pace. This is not quite the same as a 'work-to-rule', in which work is done not so much slowly as by the book, with instructions obeyed to the letter, especially trivial ones, which are normally waived in the interests of expediency. A 'work-to-rule' also means no overtime when this would be caused as a direct result of the 'work-to-rule' itself. It may have, certainly at first, little effect on the efficiency of the place, but is regarded as a suitable measure by a government office, for example, whose staff does not wish to be relocated in the wilds of Scotland as part of a redeployment or decentralisation policy. All these types of strike except the 'sit-in' are varieties of so called 'industrial action' – which is often more like industrial inaction.

skit see **parody**

skittles see **bowls**

slacks see **trousers**

slander see **libel**

slang/jargon (special type of speech or language)
The term 'slang' has two main meanings. First it applies to words or phrases, or particular meanings of words or phrases, that are regarded generally as being not standard English and that are often used, as the *Concise Oxford Dictionary* puts it, 'for picturesqueness or novelty or unconventionality'. Examples might be 'brolly' for 'umbrella' and 'canned' for 'drunk'. Secondly, 'slang' is the term for words or phrases as used specially by a particular class or profession, such as racing 'slang', thieves' 'slang', or school 'slang'. 'Jargon', apart from meaning 'gibberish' or 'debased language', is the term used to apply to the mode of speech employed by a particular group or profession *as a regular language* (which is where it differs from the second sense of 'slang'). One thus has scientific 'jargon', legal 'jargon', and the 'jargon' used by music critics, say. A form of 'jargon' that has become familiar to the public in general is bureaucratic 'jargon', with its lengthy, pompous and indirect mode of speech. Fortunately much of this, as found in government publications or official notices, is becoming obsolete. In his *Modern English Usage*, Fowler points out that 'slang' implies less dislike than 'jargon' – much 'slang' is quite endearing, in fact – and that 'slang' is commoner in sporting usage since many of the terms used in sport are also 'slang' in the first sense, i.e. are not regarded as standard English. An example of this might be cricket's 'hit for six', which is used generally to mean 'thoroughly surprise' – 'I really hit him for six that time.' A different distinction between the two is that 'slang' is usually short-lived – it dates very rapidly – while 'jargon', being more 'established', is much more durable in the language. However, both 'jargon' and 'slang' words may be quite old in origin: much legal 'jargon', for instance, is still in Latin, while the 'slang' word 'fence', meaning a dealer in stolen property, was known as long ago as 1600. The words themselves seem to be of unknown origin, although 'slang' may perhaps be related to 'sling'.

slapstick see **comedy**

slate see **tile**

slough see **marsh**

smallpox see **chickenpox**

snake/serpent (creeping, crawling reptile)
'Serpent', although basically meaning 'snake' – 'snakes' belong officially to the suborder *Serpentes* – is more common, perhaps, as a metaphorical word for a 'devious' person, or rhetorically (the old 'Serpent', and the like) to mean the Devil, than to apply to the scaly, limbless reptile commonly known as a 'snake'. However, a sea 'serpent', although normally regarded as a huge marine monster of some kind (but not yet scientifically identified), is also a (real) 'snake' of the family *Hydrophidae* that live in the sea. Subjectively, though, a 'serpent' is fearsome and powerful, while a 'snake' is cold and treacherous. As *Fowler* puts it, 'the "serpent" shines in the night sky; the "snake" lurks in the grass.'

snare see **trap**

snicker/snigger see giggle

snooker see billiards

snooze see doze

socialism/communism (political theory
that the community as a whole should own
and control the means of production)
'Socialism' (apart from the British sense
'policy of the Labour Party') is usually
thought of as having two meanings: (1) an
alternative to capitalism on the one hand
and 'communism' on the other, especially in
western society; (2) a stage on the road to
'communism', via class war and, ultimately,
revolution, especially in the Soviet Union
(this being the Marxist understanding of the
term). Soviet 'Communism' is thus a pro-
gression of both 'socialism' and Marxism (or
Leninist Marxism), and is a policy in which
property is vested in the community and
each works for the common benefit accord
ing to his capacity and receives according to
his needs. The term 'socialism' can in fact
cover a wide range of political, social
(obviously) and religious movements, from
'hard-line' Marxist 'socialism' to Christian
'Socialism' (which when it arose in the
nineteenth century did not demand common
ownership, as conventional political 'socialism' does) and the self-styled 'socialist'
governments of countries such as Ghana and
Indonesia which have little in common with
'socialism' as understood in the west. In
western society, thus, 'socialism' is contrasted with 'communism' in that the latter
involves revolution, but 'socialism' is without insurrection, revolution or other non-
constitutional activity. In 'communism',
too, the theory is that the state ultimately
withers away, while in most forms of 'socialism' the state continues to exist as an established system of political control.

sofa see couch

soft drugs see hard drugs

software see hardware

sole see plaice

solicitor/notary/commissioner for oaths
(member of legal profession)
A 'solicitor' is the one with whom most of us
have had personal dealings. Basically, he
advises clients on their legal rights, deals
with a whole range of legal matters from
conveyancing (buying and selling houses) to
proceedings in magistrates' courts, and puts
his clients in touch with a barrister if legal
action is necessary at a higher level than he
can deal with. (See also lawyer.) A 'notary'
is a 'solicitor' specifically appointed to deal
with such things as 'noting and protesting'
bills of exchange (he 'notes' on the bill –for
example a cheque – why it has not been
accepted or paid when presented), attesting
deeds and the like. A 'commissioner for
oaths' is another specific 'solicitor': one
authorised to administer the oath – oaths
are required on many occasions in law – to
someone making an affidavit, that is, a
written declaration on oath.

soliloquy see monologue

sonar see radar

soprano see treble

sound/noise (thing heard)
'Sound' is a general word for anything that
can be heard, as the wind in the trees, a dog
barking, or a supersonic aircraft breaking the
'sound' barrier. A 'noise' is usually thought of
as a loud, discordant or unpleasant 'sound' of
some kind, as the 'noise' of angry shouting or
a motorcycle revving. It can be qualified,
though, to mean more or less the same as
'sound', as in the phrase 'to make sympa-
thetic "noises"', that is, conventional remarks. E. M. Forster qualified the word in
his famous definition of Beethoven's Fifth
Symphony: 'the most sublime "noise" that
has ever penetrated into the ear of man.'

sound/strait/channel (narrow stretch of
water between two pieces of land)
A 'sound' often connects two seas or a sea
with a lake, and in some cases is the word for
the water between the mainland and an
island, as between the west coast of Scotland
and the Hebrides ('Sound' of Mull, 'Sound'
of Sleat). A 'strait' is similar, but more
obviously a narrow passage of water, as the

'Strait' of Dover (or Straits of Dover, since the word is often used in the plural with a singular meaning). A 'channel' is a wider stretch, as the English 'Channel', or Bristol 'Channel', or North 'Channel' between Northern Ireland and south-west Scotland.

sovereignty see **kingdom**

spa see **health resort**

spar see **mast**

specialist see **consultant**

species see **genus**

spectre see **ghost**

spine/thorn (pointed part of stalk, stem or leaf of a plant)
A 'spine' is a hard or woody outgrowth on a plant, as on gorse. It is not necessarily sharp. A 'thorn' is a pointed process that *is* sharp, as on a rose bush or hawthorn.

spinet see **harpsichord**

spirits see **wines**

spirt see **spurt**

spite/malice (ill will)
'Spite' is a petty expression of revenge or retaliation. 'Malice' is a more fixed state of mind – that of delighting in seeing harm done to others, whether gravely or flippantly. For '"malice" aforethought' see **murderer.**

sport see **game** (activity involving play)

spring/summer (season of growth and greenery and even warmth)
The question is not so much one of identification but of when, exactly, the one ends and the other begins. If 'spring' ends, for example, at the 'summer' solstice – which seems confusing enough anyway – and this is on 21 June, how can it be that Midsummer Day is only three days later, on 24 June? The answer lies in the definitions, since three different reckonings are in use. Astronomically, 'spring' is defined as beginning in the northern hemisphere at the vernal equinox, i.e. on that date when the sun crosses the equator and makes day and night to be equal in length. This is about 21 March. 'Spring' ends, and 'summer' begins astronomically, at the 'summer' solstice, which is about 21 June and the date when the sun is furthest from the equator and does not apparently move north or south. (The 'equator' here is the celestial one, not the terrestrial.) This means that 'summer' ends at the autumn equinox, which is about 21 September. But popularly, and in round months, 'spring' begins in March and continues for April and May, while 'summer' runs from June through to August. Or, if you don't mind not having an exact quarter of the year, you can start 'summer' in May – many people are only too glad to – and 'spring', even, in February (which is usually just wishful thinking). But according to either of these definitions, Midsummer Day on 24 June is hardly the middle of 'summer' by the calendar at all. The third explanation is a religious one: 24 June is John the Baptist's Day, and St John has always been associated in folk tradition with the sun's slow decline into winter. It was St John, after all, who said of Christ and himself, 'He must increase, and I must decrease' (John 3:30), and the days do indeed begin to shorten after 24 June. So when 'summer' starts for you depends on your viewpoint, and you can be guided by science, religion, or just plain sixth sense. (The whole thing is even further complicated by the fact that British 'Summer' Time starts around the first day of 'spring'.)

spurt/spirt (sudden flow or burst of something)
There used to be a distinction. 'Spirt' is the older form, meaning a gush, jet or flow of something, such as water or blood. The form 'spurt', which has now virtually ousted the earlier spelling, came to be used in a figurative sense, as a runner who puts on a final 'spurt' in a race. Now 'spurt' is used in all senses of the word.

squad see **corps**

squadron see **corps**

squid see **octopus**

stable see **stall**

stack/rick (pile or store of grain, hay or straw)
There is little difference between the two. A 'rick', however, may contain crops other than grain, hay or straw – peas, for example – and in addition is almost always thatched. A 'stack' may on occasions be unthatched. Possibly 'stack' is also the commoner word of the two.

stag/deer/hart/hind/doe/roedeer (animal with antlers)
The names all have specific applications. The 'stag' is the male of the red or any other 'deer' – the general term for the animal that annually sheds its antlers – especially one in its fifth year. A 'hart' is a male red deer, but *after* its fifth year. A 'hind' is the word for the female of the red deer, especially in, but also after, its third year. 'Doe' is a more general word for a female 'deer' (as the song in *The Sound of Music* reminds us), and is also used of the female of a hare or rabbit. A 'roedeer' is a small species of 'deer' (*Capreolus capreolus*) – seen in Britain in Epping Forest or the New Forest – which still lives in a wild state in many places of the world, even as far east as China.

stairs see **steps**

stalk see **stem**

stall/stable/loosebox/horsebox (living and feeding place for animals)
A 'stall' is normally a single compartment for one animal in a 'stable' or other lodging place, as a cow-shed. A 'stable' is usually a dwelling and feeding place of a horse, but can also be used for other animals, as cows. Both words are related to 'stand', since this is the basic attitude of the animal when inside. A 'loosebox' is an enclosed and covered 'stall' designed to confine an animal, especially a horse. A 'horsebox' is a van or trailer for transporting a horse or horses – a mobile 'loosebox', in fact. (A 'loosebox' is sometimes called a 'box stall', or simply a 'box'. Since a 'horsebox' can also be called simply a 'box' it is perhaps best to specify which kind is meant when first mentioning one or the other.)

star/planet (celestial body)
'Stars' are heavenly bodies similar in nature to the Sun. They are hot, glowing masses that produce their energy by thermonuclear reactions. 'Stars' outnumber 'planets' to the nth degree and our nearest star, which is in fact the Sun itself, is around 93 million miles from the Earth. 'Planets' are heavenly bodies that revolve in definite orbits around the Sun. There are nine known planets. These are, starting with the one nearest to the Sun: Mercury, Venus, Earth, Mars, Jupiter, Saturn, Uranus, Neptune and Pluto. All of them except Neptune and Pluto can be seen with the naked eye, especially Venus, which is also called, confusingly, the 'morning star'. The most important difference between 'stars' (that twinkle) and 'planets' (that do not) is that 'planets' shine by the reflected light of the Sun, whereas 'stars' shine by their own light. The word 'planet' originates from the Greek meaning 'wanderer'. Historically, the 'planets' were the Sun, the Moon, Mercury, Venus, Mars, Jupiter and Saturn, as these were the only heavenly bodies seen to change their position or 'wander' against the background of the 'stars'.

starboard see **port** (side of a ship)

start see **beginning**

statement see **account**

statesman see **politician**

statue see **sculpture**

steel see **iron**

steer see **ox**

stem/stalk (supporting body of plant)
'Stem' is a more general word, used for the main body of a tree, shrub or plant of any kind that supports its leaves and branches, and for the more slender body, attached to the main one, that supports fruit or flowers. Most 'stems' are thus also 'stalks', since a 'stalk' also supports leaves, fruit and flowers.

The word is more often applied, however, to a herbaceous plant, i.e. one with a 'stem' that is not woody and which dies down in winter. This means that a 'stem' is often larger and stronger than a 'stalk'.

steps/stairs (treads for one's feet when ascending or descending)
'Steps' is the more general word, although most 'steps' are external ones, as those that form a flight, or a single 'doorstep'. However, single 'steps' exist indoors as well, especially the ones that have to be minded when passing from one room to another – the underfoot version of 'Mind your head'. Ladders have 'steps', and so of course do 'step'-ladders, while a pair of 'steps' is not a ladder that has just two 'steps' but a ladder that has two corresponding sides (like a pair of scissors) and which does not need to be leaned against a wall. 'Stairs', by contrast, are almost always fixed indoor 'steps' on a 'staircase', and a single 'stair', on which children and animals sometimes like to stop and stare, is one of many on a complete set. The only common use for 'stairs' out of doors is as a landing stage by a river, as Horselydown 'Stairs' and George's 'Stairs' on the Thames in London just above Tower Bridge.

stickleback see **minnow**

stoat see **ferret**

stockbroker/jobber/broker (financial dealer)
A 'stockbroker' is an intermediary between the public and the 'jobbers' in the business of buying and selling stocks and shares. He acts as an agent for his clients and works for a fixed commission. He is usually a member of one of the stock exchanges. A 'jobber' – properly, 'stockjobber' – acts as a wholesaler dealing in stocks and shares. He, too, is a member of a stock exchange. He quotes two prices: a buying price and a selling price. The difference is called the 'jobber's turn' (selling is always higher than buying) and is his profit. His name comes from the fact that he does a job, or piece of work, for a profit. A 'broker' is a fairly general term for a middleman in some business, or an agent or commissioner of some kind. (The word may, of

course, be simply an abbreviation of 'stockbroker'.) There are specialised 'brokers', such as insurance 'brokers', who deal in services rather than goods. The origin of the name is obscure: it is not apparently related to 'break' or 'broke'.

stocks/pillory (old instrument of punishment)
The 'stocks' consisted of a framework with holes for the ankles and sometimes the wrists

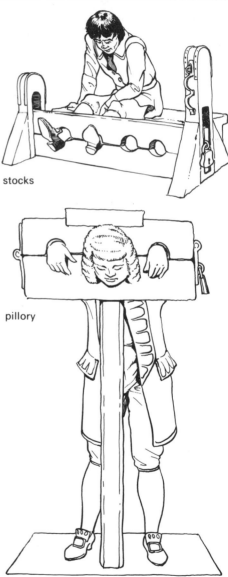

stocks

pillory

in which the offender was placed in a sitting position. The 'pillory' was an upright contrivance with holes for the head and hands, but not the feet, in which the criminal was held in a standing position. In both he was exposed to public derision, and could be assailed with verbal abuse or rotten fruit, to choice. In short, he would become a 'laughing stock' – which phrase derives from the former instrument. The origin of 'pillory' is uncertain: the word could perhaps derive from Latin *speculum in gloriam Dei*, 'mirror to the glory of God'. But such an etymology is speculative.

stocks/shares (divisions of a company's capital entitling their holder to profit)
The main difference is that 'shares' are issued in specified amounts, such as 25p, 50p or £1, while 'stock' is sold in undefined quantities (which may on occasion be divided into 'shares'). 'Shares' cannot be converted into 'stock' until they are fully paid. 'Stock' is also the term used for government loans. For types of 'shares', see **ordinary shares.**

stomach/belly/abdomen (organ of body in which food is digested)
A 'stomach' is a strange thing. As a word it is of unusual spelling and origin (the Greek for 'mouth', of all things), and is also one of the few words in English whose 'baby version' has become generally if colloquially accepted ('tummy'); as an organ it is of uncertain location and rather vague function – something to do with food, of course, but what? The 'stomach' is in fact situated a good deal further up in the body than most people think it is: more or less under the breast bone, rather than just above or below the belt. It is also only the first stage of digestion that takes place here, since most of the digestive processes occur in the small and large intestines. To make matters even more imprecise, we talk of 'stomach'-ache, not meaning a pain in the 'stomach'-ache, but discomfort in the bowels. So what is a 'belly' (sometimes thought of as rather a 'rude' word)? It is either synonymous with 'abdomen', which is the word for that part of the body which contains the 'stomach', bowels, and digestive organs generally, a sense reflected in the 'belly' landing of an aeroplane (made on its fuselage, or 'belly', without using its landing gear), or it means the same as 'stomach', in particular in the phrase 'an empty "belly"', or 'a full "belly"'.

stone/pip (hard seed of a fruit)
On the whole, 'stone' is used for the larger seeds, as of a plum or peach, and 'pip' of the smaller seeds, as in an apple or orange. However, 'stone' can be used of any hard seed, so that all 'pips' are 'stones'. Even so, fleshy fruits with small seeds are usually thought of as having 'pips'. The word is short for 'pippin', which of course is the name used in certain varieties of apple, as Cox's Orange Pippin and Ribston Pippin, both of which have 'pips' – or 'stones'.

Stone Age/Ice Age (lengthy era in prehistoric times)
The 'Stone Age' was the earliest of the three 'implement' ages: Stone, Bronze and Iron, and was itself divided into the Old Stone Age, or Palaeolithic (from about 3 million years ago to about 8000 BC), when implements were simply chipped into shape, Middle Stone Age, or Mesolithic (about 8000 BC to about 6000 BC), and New Stone Age, or Neolithic (about 6000 BC to about 2000 BC), when stone implements were ground and polished. In Europe the 'Stone Age' began about a million years ago and merged into the Bronze Age about 2000 BC. The 'Ice Age', or glacial epoch, when much of the northern hemisphere was covered with great sheets of ice, corresponds to the late Pleistocene (Greek 'most recent') epoch in the geological time scale which in fact largely coincides with the 'Stone Age' of archaeologists.

storm/gale/blizzard/tempest/hurricane/ typhoon (strong wind)
'Storm' is the general word covering all six and is often preceded by a specific, as a 'thunderstorm', 'snowstorm', or 'hailstorm'. If unspecified, and especially at sea, a strong wind is meant, often with rain. On the Beaufort Scale of windspeeds, a 'storm' stands midway between a 'gale' and a 'hurricane', with a speed of 55 to 72 m.p.h. A 'gale' is a wind with speeds between 39 and 46 m.p.h. 'Hurricanes' and 'typhoons' are tropical, revolving 'storms' with wind speeds of more

than 73 m.p.h. They are named according to the area of origin: 'hurricanes' start in the West Indies and 'typhoons' in the China Seas. A 'blizzard' is a 'snowstorm', usually a severe one, with a strong, cutting wind. The origin of the word is uncertain: perhaps it is connected with 'blow' or in some way imitative. A 'tempest', somehow a rather stately word, is a violent 'storm' of wind usually with accompanying rain, snow or hail. For some specifically devastating 'storms', see **whirlwind**.

stout see **ale**

stove see **oven**

strait see **sound** (narrow stretch of water)

street see **road**

stroke/heart attack/coronary (sudden disabling or even fatal attack)
A 'stroke' is the result of a blood vessel bursting in the brain – a cerebral haemorrhage – and destroying the surrounding brain cells by bleeding into them. This has the effect of cutting off the blood to the area of the brain beyond the haemorrhage, and leads to a paralysis in many cases. A 'heart attack' results from the failure of a section of heart muscle. (In turn it can be distinguished from heart failure, which is caused by the inability of the left or right or even both sides of the heart to pump enough blood for the body.) A 'coronary' is in full a 'coronary thrombosis', that is, the formation of a blood clot in the coronary artery (which resembles a crown – hence its name – and supplies the heart with blood). The three conditions thus have quite distinct causes.

style see **fashion**

subject/theme/topic (matter being considered in a speech or written account)
'Subject' is the general word for whatever is being treated or considered. 'Theme' implies an underlying concept that runs right through the matter and which is usually enlarged on or embroidered. 'Topic' is the 'theme', or 'subject', of a specific type of communication, often a brief or impermanent one such as a speech, a conversation, or an essay.

It often, too, relates to a question of the day or a current talking point. The word is unusual in being the English version of the Greek title of a work by Aristotle. This was *ta topika*, 'topics' (literally 'things pertaining to commonplaces'), which was a treatise reflecting discussions at the Athenian Academy.

suite/train/cortège/retinue (company of followers or attendants)
Four French words. A 'suite' usually applies to the followers or attendants of a royal personage. A 'train' is any band of followers, as a 'train' of admirers. A 'cortège' is normally the word for a funeral procession, and a 'retinue', as the term suggests, with its implication of people who have been 'retained' in service, is a 'suite' or 'train' of persons who officially attend or wait upon a dignitary of some kind.

sultana see **raisin**

summary/synopsis/précis (brief or concise account of something)
The difference is rather a fine one. A 'summary' is a brief account or abridgment, a 'summing up' of something, as a 'summary' of the day's play in a test match. A 'synopsis', from the Greek meaning 'seeing together', is a bird's-eye view of something, with an implied compression being made, as the 'synopsis' of a play, that is, not so much a brief account as a condensed one. A 'précis' is similar to a 'synopsis', but usually refers to a written work or extract that is itself somewhat lengthy or turgid and that really *needs* to be shortened for a particular purpose – if only as a school English language exercise. A 'précis' thus aims to make precise what is seen to be imprecise.

summer see **spring**

supplement/appendix/addenda (material added at the end of a book)
A 'supplement', which can be issued separately or incorporated in a book, is usually for purposes of comparing, improving, correcting or adding. In a sense it not only supplements but complements the main body of the book, that is, it makes it more complete. An 'appendix' is normally useful additional information without which, however, the rest of

the book is complete. In a reference work or dictionary, for example, an 'appendix' might be a table of some kind, or a list of symbols. An 'addenda' – strictly speaking the word is plural, with singular 'addendum' – is a kind of 'appendix' containing additional material which, given other circumstances, would have been incorporated in the main body of the book. An example might be new words at the end of a dictionary; if the publication of the dictionary had been a year later, they would probably have been in the main body of the book.

surgeon see **doctor**

Surrealism see **Futurism**

swallow/martin/swift (fast, agile bird feeding on insects in flight and nesting under eaves)
The 'swallow' is perhaps the most familiar of the three, with its long wings, swift flight, forked tail, and twittering call. The 'martin' is a member of the 'swallow' family, and in particular the 'house-martin', black above and white below, that builds and nests on the walls of houses, and the brown and white 'sand martin', which nests in sandbanks or sandpits. The 'swift' closely resembles the 'swallow', although it in fact belongs to another family (the one to which humming-birds belong). It can be distinguished by its very long wings and short, stumpy body and its extreme agility in flight: it can not only

catch insects on the wing but also drink, bathe and even mate. Unlike the 'swallow', too, its tail is not always forked.

swamp see **marsh**

sweater see **pullover**

swede see **turnip**

swift see **swallow**

swing/bop/boogie-woogie (form of jazz liable to periodic revival)
The heyday of 'swing', a form of 'easy' rhythmic jazz with a freely varied melody and simple harmonic accompaniment, was the late 1930s and early 1940s, otherwise 'the swing age'. This was the last great period of jazz proper before experimentation set in. 'Bop', short for 'bebop' (or sometimes 're-bop') was the highly syncopated type of jazz, with complex harmonies, that originated in America in the late 1940s. The word originated in an imitation of a typical musical phrase and in turn gave 'teeny-bopper' and 'weeny-bopper' as a term for a 'swinging' teenage or younger girl. 'Boogie-woogie' originated as a pre-war style of playing the blues on the piano, characterised by a persistent bass rhythm. It has since been revived and popularised several times and is by no means moribund. The actual word is of tantalisingly obscure origin. It is tempting to think of it as imitative in some way, but perhaps an American Negro slang word 'boogie' (meaning 'performer'?), with 'woogie' tacked on to rhyme with it, is nearer to the truth.

synonym see **homonym**

synopsis see **summary**

syrup see **treacle**

systems analyst see **computer programmer**

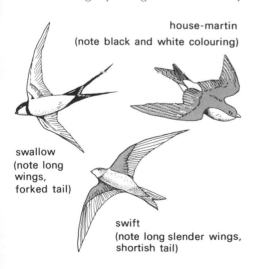

house-martin
(note black and white colouring)

swallow
(note long wings, forked tail)

swift
(note long slender wings, shortish tail)

tablet see **pill**

tact/diplomacy (ability to avoid offending others)
'Tact' suggests a delicate or sensitive touch (which is what the word literally means) in the handling of a situation where it is important not to offend or hurt. It usually implies, too, a personal wish not to offend. 'Diplomacy', which may or may not be personally motivated, suggests a skill in handling delicate matters, often in order to attain one's own ends without any complications or unpleasantness. A professionally diplomatic person is of course a diplomat, who originally held a diploma, or letter of recommendation that once was (literally) folded double (Greek *diploma*) – itself something of a diplomatic gesture.

tale see **legend**

talisman see **charm**

talon see **claw**

tangent see **angle**

tangerine/mandarin/satsuma (type of small orange)
'Tangerines' and 'mandarins' are very alike: they are both small, flat, loose-skinned (and relatively thin-skinned) and a deep orange-yellow in colour. 'Tangerines', however, usually have pips, while 'mandarins' – which is also the name for the canned variety – are seedless. 'Satsumas' are a type of 'mandarin', with the name being a commercially preferable one for the fruit, no doubt because it is more exotic. The names are geographical ones: 'tangerines' originally came from Tangier, 'mandarins' from China, where their colour resembled that of the robes of the Chinese officials called mandarins, and 'satsumas' originally came from

Japan, where the word is the name of a former province, also famous for its cream-coloured pottery.

tapioca see **semolina**

tar/pitch/bitumen/asphalt (black viscous substance used for surfacing)
'Tar', properly, is the dark, inflammable liquid obtained from the dry distillation of wood, coal or other fuel, and is used for preserving timber and iron and as an antiseptic, for example. Road 'tar' is actually 'pitch', which is in turn obtained from the distillation of 'tar', so that in road construction road 'tar' is used for sealing the wearing surface, which in many cases is constructed from 'tar' macadam (tarmac), a form of macadam or broken stone (as used originally by the civil engineer James Macadam) coated with 'tar'. A binder used for the surface layer of a road is 'bitumen', which is a tarlike hydrocarbon derived from petroleum, and also used is 'asphalt', which is a mixture of 'bitumen' and crushed rocks. 'Asphalt' is also used for roofing and in some paints, while in house construction it provides a protection against rising damp. All four words tend to be used loosely, however, to apply to a range of substances, both natural and artificial, in pure form or in combination, and the meaning will thus vary according to the context.

tart/pie/flan/pasty (dish of baked pastry containing fruit or meat)
A 'tart' usually contains fruit or at any rate something sweet, as an apple 'tart' or a treacle 'tart', or it is often small, with no top crust (as once was always the case), as a jam 'tart' or a custard 'tart'. A 'pie' usually contains meat or something savoury, as a pork 'pie' or a fish 'pie'. It is normally enclosed, as earlier it always was. Hence the difference between an apple 'tart' (open) and an apple 'pie' (enclosed). Compare, too, a mince 'pie' – not savoury, but enclosed. A custard 'pie', of course, is not intended for the table. It may start off as an edible 'pie', with flour and eggs, but finishes up with shaving cream or something equally inedible that simulates custard and is suitable for facial application. A 'flan' is usually open, with fruit – as opposed to a pasty, which is enclosed, with meat. Very

often, though, it is simply a pastry or sponge cake filled or spread with jam, fruit, cheese, or anything tasty and cookable. A 'pasty' is a chunky 'folded' 'pie', usually an individual one containing something savoury, such as meat or vegetables. A well-known type is the 'Cornish pasty', which is a pastry case filled with cooked minced meat and chopped vegetables, such as potato, cabbage and carrot, and eaten hot or cold. There are also sweet 'pasties', however, especially ones containing fruit, such as an apple 'pasty'.

tartan/plaid (characteristic cloth and pattern of Scottish dress)
'Tartan' is the name for the cloth, with stripes of different colours and widths at right angles to one another, that is used for the distinctive items of Scottish dress, especially the 'plaid' and the kilt. The cloth's design differs according to the clan that wears it. In this sense, the 'plaid' is the long, rectangular piece of cloth with such a design that Highlanders wear round their shoulders. 'Tartan' is thus not only the cloth but the design on it (so that a 'plaid' is made of 'tartan' and has a 'tartan' pattern). However, both words are loosely used interchangeably, so that 'tartan' can mean any chequered pattern (not necessarily the design of a Scottish clan), and 'plaid' can mean any chequered fabric (with a 'tartan' design). Such casual usage and even abusage is deplored by died-in-the-wool Scots, who are sticklers for the correct form.

tax/duty (levy enforceable by law)
'Tax' is a levy on such things as income (income 'tax'), property (wealth 'tax'), goods purchased or services rendered (value added 'tax', or VAT), or gifts made (capital transfer 'tax'). 'Duty' is a levy on such things as import or export (customs 'duty', excise 'duty'), the transference of property (death 'duty', probate 'duty'), and the legal recognition of deeds and documents (various types of 'duty'). 'Tax' is undoubtedly the kind of levy that concerns the general public more, with 'duty' applying to business and commerce in many cases, or chargeable in specific instances. If there is any discernible or significant difference, it is that 'tax' tends to be levied on actual objects (income, property, goods, gifts), and 'duty' on an action or process of some kind (importing, exporting, selling, manufacturing, attesting).

teacher training college/college of education/institute of education (higher educational establishment for the training of teachers)
'Teacher training colleges', or just 'training colleges', are now officially known by the less precise title of 'colleges of education'. They were establishments where, at any rate to 1975, teachers were trained, on a three-year course, to teach in primary schools. In 1975, however, the system of teacher training began to be radically reorganised. Many 'colleges of education' have now merged with each other or been integrated with the rest of higher education with training places concentrated in polytechnics, colleges of higher education and universities. The whole change is because of a general move towards a graduate profession, that is, teachers with degrees in education, not diplomas. 'Institutes of education' are something quite different. They are establishments within a university which supervise and co-ordinate the academic work of the 'colleges of education' in a particular area, at the same time approving syllabuses and conducting examinations. They are closely linked with the faculty or department of education attached to the university which trains graduates as teachers.

technical college/polytechnic/college of advanced technology (specialised further education establishment)
A 'technical college' or 'tech' is an establishment specialising in technical subjects such as mechanical engineering with the aim of preparing its students for industry. 'Polytechnics' provide all types of courses (full, part-time and 'sandwich') in a wide range of subjects at all levels. They complement universities and colleges of education in this respect. The present 'polys' are those that have been formed since 1967 from either 'technical colleges' or colleges of technology. The 'colleges of advanced technology' ('CATS') were set up in 1956. They originally were ordinary 'technical colleges' chosen to concentrate on advanced work. In 1965 they were elevated to university status.

tempest see **storm**

tenor/baritone (male singing voice)
The 'tenor' is the high natural male voice, although there is in fact a higher one, the countertenor (see **treble**). The range of a 'tenor' is roughly from the A below middle C to the A above. The 'baritone', until quite recently spelled 'barytone', is the next lowest male voice, intermediate between 'tenor' and bass and having a range approximately a third lower than a 'tenor'. Of all male singing voices, the 'tenor' is the rarest and the 'baritone' the most common. (It derives from the Greek for 'heavy tone', the 'bari-' being as in 'barometer', which measures atmospheric pressure or 'heaviness'.)

test see **trial**

theft/larceny/robbery/burglary (crime of stealing)
According to the Theft Act, 1968, a person is guilty of 'theft' if he 'dishonestly appropriates property belonging to another with the intention of permanently depriving the other of it'; that is, it is immaterial whether taking the property is for one's own gain or benefit or not. This same act repealed the Larceny Acts of 1861 and 1916, in which 'larceny' had to involve so-called 'asportation', that is, the 'carrying away' of property with the intent of stealing. Since 1968, therefore, 'larceny' has not legally existed. 'Robbery' is basically stealing with force, actual or threatened. 'Burglary', once the crime of housebreaking at night (i.e. between 9 p.m. and 6 a.m.), has also been redefined by the recent Theft Act. The Act has eliminated the 'breaking' element of 'breaking and entering' with intent to commit a felony or of 'breaking' out of a house after a felony, and has abolished the night v. day distinction. 'Burglary' now is entering any building or part of a building as a trespasser with intent to commit certain offences (such as stealing, or inflicting grievous bodily harm) or, having entered, committing or attempting to commit such offences. 'Aggravated' 'burglary' involves a firearm – even an imitation one – or any weapon of offence, or explosives.

theme see **subject**

theory/hypothesis (untested idea or opinion)
A 'theory' is an explanation of something that has become more or less established or accepted as accounting for known facts or phenomena, as Einstein's 'theory' of relativity or the Darwinian 'theory' of evolution. A 'hypothesis' is a conjecture or supposition made in order to explain facts or phenomena – a starting point, in fact, or basis, by which the truth may be reached. Avogadro's 'hypothesis', that equal volumes of gases under the same conditions of temperature and pressure contain equal numbers of molecules, was first made in 1811. It was generally accepted after 1858, so that today it is more generally known as Avogadro's law. The two terms are therefore really opposite in meaning – respectively facts demanding an explanation, and an explanation leading to the facts – although loosely they are both used to mean 'view' or 'idea': 'I have a "theory" about that', 'Yes, but that's only a "hypothesis".'

thorn see **spine**

three feet square see **three square feet**

three square feet/three feet square (measurement of an area)
'Square' units of measurements are used to express the total area of any surface, whether the figure measured is itself 'square' or not (so that a circle can have its area expressed in 'square inches', say). 'Three' (for example) 'square feet' thus expresses the area of a surface of a figure of any shape, such as a table runner three feet long and one foot wide. 'Three feet square', however, is a surface measurement of a 'square' figure three feet by three feet, in other words nine 'square feet'. The two terms are sometimes confused, either because the numerical expression 3 ft² is taken to be the same as 3 sq. ft, or because the distinction is wrongly taken to be between 'square' and cubic measures. (See **weight**, and the illustration on p. 119.)

tiara see **crown**

tiddler see **minnow**

tied house see **free house**

tile/slate (thin slab used for covering roofs) A 'tile', traditionally coloured red, is made of baked clay. A 'slate' is a plate of fine-grained grey, green or bluish-purple rock that can be easily split. 'On the "slate"' is a characteristically British way of saying that a debt has been recorded ('I always go to this pub as they have a "slate"', an English host once said to a mystified American guest); to be 'on the "tiles"' is to be out on a spree, even a debauch. So doubtless one could have a night out on the 'tiles' on a 'slate', if one knew the

three square feet (for example)

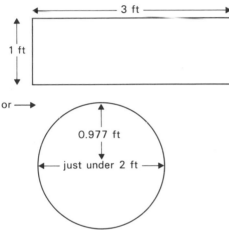

a circle of radius approx. 0.977 ft will have an area of 3 sq. ft

three feet square (only possibility)

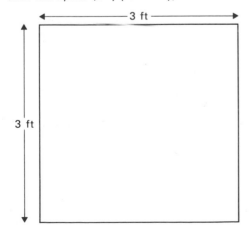

right hostelry. Such are the delights of the English language.

tiller see **rudder**

tiredness/weariness/fatigue (feeling of having used up one's strength or energy) 'Tiredness' is the fairly normal sensation experienced by someone at the end of a full or busy day, when a good proportion of one's mental or physical resources has been used up and one feels ready to rest or sleep. 'Weariness' implies a prolonged sensation of 'tiredness', so that one's strength has been worn out and one is constantly 'below par' and listless. 'Fatigue' is not so much prolonged 'tiredness' as an excessive degree of it, so that one is 'done in' and must immediately stop and rest (and probably sleep).

titter see **giggle**

TNT see **dynamite**

toad see **frog**

tolerance/toleration (degree of allowing something of which one does not approve) 'Tolerance' suggests a lenient or charitable attitude, as towards the expression of some kind of minority right of which one does not really approve. 'Toleration' implies allowing or bearing something that one does not agree with or approve of, as a 'toleration' of loud music or (by a non-smoker) of someone smoking in a non-smoking compartment of a train.

toleration see **tolerance**

tomb see **grave**

tongue/palate (organ of taste in the mouth) The 'tongue' is the true organ of taste, since it contains the taste buds. To say that something tickles your 'palate', or is agreeable to the 'palate', as particularly a wine, is really to miss the mark, since the 'palate' is the roof of the mouth, which has no taste buds. However, 'palate' has meant 'sense of taste' since the early sixteenth century (hence 'palatable') and we are now stuck with the anatomical misnomer.

topic see **subject**

tornado see **whirlwind**

torso see (1) **sculpture**, (2) **trunk**

tower/turret (high structure on top of a building)
A 'tower' can be either a complete building, as the 'Tower' of London, or a high structure on a building, as the square 'tower' of a church or the round 'tower' of a castle. A 'turret' is a small 'tower' (a 'tower-ette'), which can either rise from the ground or project from a wall, especially at the corner of a main building such as a castle. 'Turret' is also the word for the revolving armoured 'tower' housing a gun and the gunners on a ship, or in an aircraft or tank.

town/city (sizeable populated area)
A 'city' is generally larger and more important or older than a 'town'. More precisely, it is a 'town' that has been created a 'city' by charter, and especially one with a cathedral. In the USA a 'city' is a municipal corporation occupying a clearly defined area. It may have a smallish population (just as an American village may have a sizeable one), so the number of inhabitants only is no guide to the status of a place, as it is in Britain. London, a 'city' if ever there was one, itself contains the 'City' – its business and commercial centre, governed by the Lord Mayor and Corporation.

track/pan/zoom (movement of a film or television camera)
A 'track' is made by a camera in any direction, as forwards or sideways, when in operation, the whole camera moving bodily together with the cameraman. (It very often does this actually on tracks.) A 'pan' – derived from 'panorama' – is a movement of the camera in such a way that a moving person or object is kept constantly in view, especially by swinging the camera horizontally. A 'zoom' is made – with a 'zoom' lens – so as to make a person or object seem either to approach (at the same time growing in size) or to recede (diminishing in size).

trade see **occupation**

train see **suite**

trap/pitfall/snare (device for catching animals or humans)
A 'trap', strictly speaking, has a spring, as a 'mousetrap' or a 'mantrap'. A 'pitfall', rather obviously, has a pit for the prey to fall into. A 'snare' is a device for entangling birds, rabbits or other unwary creatures in order to capture them. Literally, the contrivances are not difficult to distinguish. Figuratively, however, they must be applied more precisely. A 'trap' is usually a scheme planned by one person to catch another, as a 'trap' for the unwary or the 'trap' you nearly fell into when you said that. The latter would not be a 'pitfall' in the metaphorical sense, since this is a concealed danger, error, or source of disaster or 'downfall', as a newspaper editorial that avoids the usual 'pitfalls' (the usual errors). A 'snare' is similar, but figuratively suggests enticement or inveiglement or temptation. 'Kingdoms are but cares, State is devoid of stay; Riches are ready snares, And hasten to decay,' wrote Henry VI in the fifteenth century.

treacle/syrup/molasses (sweet, sticky foodstuff)
All three are by-products in the process of refining sugar. 'Treacle' (called 'molasses' in the USA) is removed at the second stage of refinement. After further refinement and bleaching, 'syrup', sometimes called 'golden syrup', is extracted. (Golden Syrup is a familiar trade name for a brand of this used in making cakes. Its manufacturers define it as 'partially inverted refiners' "syrup"'.) 'Molasses' (in the USA, 'treacle') is what is removed at the *first* stage in the process of refining sugar. The kind used for human food comes from cane sugar; the 'molasses' that is bitter and unpleasantly flavoured and used as a feed for farm animals comes from sugar beet. It can also be used to make alcohol, such as rum. 'Molasses' the word comes ultimately from Latin *mel*, 'honey'.

treble/soprano/alto/contralto (high singing voice)
'Treble' is traditionally applied to boys' voices and musical instruments of high pitch, as a 'treble' recorder, while 'soprano' is used of women's voices. An adult female

'treble' voice has a range approximately from middle C to 'top' A (a thirteenth above it). Lower than this is an 'alto' voice, whose range is roughly from the F below middle C to the D a ninth above it. This is in fact the lowest woman's voice, and is called a 'contralto' when applied to the voice of a female soloist or operatic singer. An 'alto' voice can also be applied to a similarly low register of a boy's voice, although of a man an 'alto' voice is an artificially high one – a falsetto – similar in range to a countertenor. (The difference here is that the countertenor is not a falsetto voice but a natural extension of the upper tenor voice.) The range of a male 'alto' is approximately the same as a female – possibly a tone or two lower. (For notably deeper voices see **tenor**.) Usage is fairly firmly established, therefore, although the words themselves are unusual. 'Soprano' comes from Italian 'above', since the 'soprano' voice is the highest. 'Treble' is something of a mystery. Three of what? Singing in thirds, or a voice pitched a third above another? The origin is not too clear. Perhaps once boys sang what was the third part, that is, the higher notes. In fact 'soprano' can also apply to a boy's voice as well as to a woman's although this use is now somewhat dated, as 'Ernest Lough, the boy "soprano"', who with 'O, for the wings of a dove' tugged at the heart-strings of thousands in the 1930s. 'Alto', paradoxically, comes from the Italian for 'high', since the reference is not to the female voice but the male. The term 'contralto' derives from fifteenth-century Latin *contratenor altus*, indicating a voice that is predominantly above the tenor. The two words were subsequently blended, in the Italian form, as *contr'alto*.

trial/test (attempt to ascertain or establish something)
'Trial' basically indicates trying, as international horse 'trials', where horse and rider try to give of their best, or a piece of equipment available for ten days' free 'trial', to enable a would-be purchaser to see how it works and whether it is what he needs – by trying it out. A 'test' is a more demanding thing: a 'trial' under approved or fixed conditions, or a final 'trial' after a series of experiments. A 'test' pilot thus flies, and subjects to various tests, an aircraft that previously may have undergone a series of 'trials' on the ground only. 'Trial', indeed, often indicates an initial try-out, and 'test' a final one: compare a 'trial' run and a 'test' run in a car.

trip/journey/voyage (course of travel)
A 'trip' nearly always implies 'there and back', whether on foot or by transport, for business or pleasure, short or long, hurried or leisurely. A 'journey' is a longish 'trip', usually by land or air rather than sea, but not necessarily with the 'there and back' idea as a 'journey' by train to Scotland or by air to New York. 'Voyage' primarily suggests travel by sea, and moreover for pleasure, as a cruise. This means that a 'voyage' is normally relatively long in time or distance, with no idea at all of the return section of the travel.

troop see **corps**

trot/canter/gallop (gait or pace of a horse)
A horse's slowest pace, at an average of four and a half miles an hour, is a walk. It is a four-beat gait, with legs moving in the order (for example) near (i.e. left) hind, near fore, off (right) hind, off fore. The 'trot' is the next fastest pace, but a two-beat gait, in which the animal lifts each diagonal pair of legs alternately – near fore and off hind almost simultaneously, followed by off fore and near hind. This means that at times, noticeably at a fast 'trot', the horse will be altogether off the ground. The next fastest pace is the 'canter', whose name is popularly thought to come from 'Canterbury', since it was the pace adopted by medieval pilgrims as they rode to Canterbury Cathedral to pay homage at the tomb of St Thomas à Becket. (Another version traces the word back to Latin *cantherius*, meaning 'gelding' or 'riding-nag'.) This is a three-beat gait, with first the near hind, off hind, and near fore on the ground practically together, then the off fore on its own, and the final beat being the complete suspension of the animal in the air. A 'gallop' is a fast 'canter' – around thirty miles an hour – so that all four feet are off the ground in each stride, and the horse really makes a series of low leaps.

troubadour see **minstrel**

trousers/pants/slacks (garment for lower half of body)
'Trousers' are always an outer garment or an only one (as pyjama 'trousers'). They come in a variety of shapes and sizes, such as short 'trousers' ('shorts') and long, men's and women's. 'Pants' is chiefly an American word for what in Britain are 'trousers' or 'slacks'. The term has a certain circulation, however, in spite of the fact that it also means 'underpants' – for which the preferred American word is 'drawers'. (Those anxious to further Anglo-American relations must take care not to get their knickers in a semantic twist.) 'Slacks', which can look quite smart and stylish, in spite of being designed for 'slack' or casual wear, are either a male garment, especially for sport, or, more commonly, a female one, although a 'trouser' suit – not a 'slack' suit – is an exclusively feminine affair.

truism see **commonplace**

trunk/torso (upper half of human body)
In spite of 'trunks', as for swimming, your 'trunk' is your whole body apart from your head, arms and legs. A 'torso' is usually the word for the 'trunk' of a human statue (see **sculpture**), but can also be used of a person, often with reference to an idealised or statue-like body: 'He much admired his rippling torso.' A 'trunk', too, can be used of the body of an animal, but with care, of course, when the animal happens to be an elephant.

trunk road see **motorway**

tune/melody (series of notes that 'make sense' in music)
The two terms mean almost the same, although 'tune' is quite often used for the upper part in a piece of music, together with an accompaniment, while 'melody' is a more technical word in musical theory, seen as distinct from harmony, rhythm, and so on. Subjectively, a 'melody' is a more poetic and meaningful thing, while 'tune' frequently applies to a rather trivial or superficial line of music. Hence such phrases – which bring out this difference – as 'a haunting "melody"', but 'whistling a happy "tune"'. And more than a few girls are called 'Melody' – even the word itself is melodious – but is there any girl named Tune?

turf/peat (type of fuel found in boggy soil)
'Peat' is the basic substance, that is, the combustible soil that consists of partially decomposed vegetable matter as found characteristically in bogs, typically in Ireland – where a piece of it is called a 'turf'. (In Scotland a piece of 'peat' is simply called 'a peat'.) 'Turf' also, of course, means a grass covering in general, with *the* 'turf' meaning a race course, and a piece of such grass, as used for laying a lawn, for example, is *a* 'turf'. An alternative word for 'turf' in this last sense, but one which is usually avoided because of its undesirable connotations, is 'sod'.

turner see **carpenter**

turnip/swede/parsnip (root vegetable)
All three tend to be something of an unfavourite with children, who may or may not acquire a taste for them in adult life. The 'turnip' and the 'swede' both belong to the genus *Brassica*, which also includes such non-root vegetables as the garden (and common) cabbage and the more exotic kohlrabi. The 'turnip' has a fleshy globular or elongated white-coloured root, while the 'swede' – strictly speaking, part stem and part root – is similar, although somewhat larger, but with white flesh or yellow. (If the latter, it is known as rutabaga.) The 'parsnip' has a longish carrot-type root which is pale yellow in colour. In spite of their unattractive taste, the vegetables have rather interesting names. The 'turnip' was formerly a 'neep', as it still is in Scottish parlance – compare the traditional Burns Night dish of haggis and 'bashed tatties and neeps' (mashed potatoes and 'turnips') – with the 'tur-', however, something of a mystery. The 'swede' really does – or did – come from Sweden, and is properly a Swedish 'turnip'. It was brought from Sweden to Scotland in the eighteenth century (1781–2, to be exact). The 'parsnip' was originally a 'pasnep' but the 'nep' became 'nip' by association with 'turnip'. The word ultimately derives from Latin *pastinum*, 'dibble' (a two-pronged fork for planting and digging).

turret see **tower**

tweeter see **woofer**

tweezers see **forceps**

twilight see **dusk**

type I error/type II error (type of error in statistics)
A 'type I error' is a 'rejection of the null hypothesis in statistical testing when it is true'. A 'type II error' is an 'acceptance of the null hypothesis in statistical testing when it is false'. (Both definitions as given in *6,000 Words: A Supplement to Webster's Third New International Dictionary*, 1976.) It is of course *very* important to distinguish between these.

type II error see **type I error**

typhoon see **storm**

UHF see **high frequency**

ukelele see **guitar**

ultra-violet rays see **X-rays**

umpire see **referee**

undercroft see **vault**

underdeveloped countries see **developing countries**

United Kingdom see **England**

untruth see **lie**

uprising see **revolt**

V1/V2 (type of German flying bomb)
The 'V1', nicknamed the 'buzz bomb' and 'doodle bug', was the pilotless aircraft or flying bomb launched against England in the Second World War by the Germans. Of the 8,000 or more launched in the period 13 June 1944 to 29 March 1945 about 2,500 landed on London. The 'V2' was not an aircraft but the first military long-range rocket or ballistic missile. It was nearly twice the length of the 'V1', but had a longer range and was nearly ten times faster than the'V1', which flew at an average of 360 mph. Over 10,000 'V2s' were manufactured, of which about half failed to go off or exploded prematurely. A total of 4,300 were launched; of the 1,402 aimed at Britain, 517 landed on London. The 'V' stood for German *Vergeltungswaffe*, 'retaliation weapon', the retaliation being in return for British bombing raids on Germany.

V2 see **V1**

vaccination see **inoculation**

vagabond see **vagrant**

vagrant/vagabond (tramp or other homeless person)
Many tramps these days – those that still exist – like to think of themselves as 'travellers' or 'wayfarers' or something, but probably not as tramps or 'vagrants', which latter word has a connotation of disrespectability or dishonesty. A 'vagabond', related to it in origin, implies a tramp who is also a permanently dishonest or thieving person – he steals to survive. The word is not used much today, although legally a 'vagabond' is a 'person who wanders about and has no dwelling' and who will become, if he commits one of a number of particular offences, a 'rogue and "vagabond"'. (The definition is that of the Vagrancy Act, 1824, still in force, which classifies 'vagrants' themselves as 'idle and disorderly persons', 'rogues and

"vagabonds"' or – in charming but correct legal terminology – 'incorrigible rogues'.)

valour see **courage**

vampire/werewolf (human being transmogrified as a murderous beast)
At a popular level (where it best flourishes), a 'vampire' is the reanimated corpse of a person improperly buried, and as such is supposed to suck the blood of people as they sleep. 'Vampire' bats, named in their honour, do actually feed on the blood of animals – and even man, if conditions are favourable. A 'werewolf' is a more or less orthodox human male by day, but at night turns into a wolf (retaining human intelligence), and in this guise devours animals, humans or corpses – an omnivorous orgiast. Both creatures owe most of their gruesome popularity to the invention of the cinema and the art of the horror film, as do their brothers in crime, Frankenstein and Dracula. The 'vampire' bequeathed its name to the 'vamp', the female exploiter and seducer of men (but not to the verb 'vamp', meaning 'improvise musical accompaniment', which derives from Old French *avanpie*, 'fore part of the foot', of all things). And as if all this wasn't enough, there is a sinister link between the two creatures, since 'werewolves', after death, are believed to turn into 'vampires'!

vanity/conceit/arrogance (undue self-pride)
'Vanity' is empty pride, the desire for admiration based on a personal achievement or attraction or quality. 'Conceit' is a heightened version of this, even an exaggerated expression of it: putting yourself over as very clever, smart, good or whatever when you're not. 'Arrogance' is an assumed superiority, an overbearing pride: setting yourself up on a higher level than other mere mortals because of your supposed superiority to them. The three are thus in increasing degrees of presumptuousness – and insufferableness.

varnish/lacquer (preparation giving a glossy surface)
'Varnish' is a resinous solution used to apply a hard, shiny, transparent coating to a surface such as wood or metal. (Nail 'varnish' may be transparent or coloured, of course.) 'Lacquer' can be used to mean a coloured 'varnish' of shellac applied as a coating for brass, but usually the word is taken to apply to a nitrocellulose finish brushed or sprayed on a surface to form a protective film. The colour is provided by an added pigment, which in the case of a clear 'lacquer' is omitted. 'Lacquer', like 'varnish', also has a use in cosmetics – as a hair spray.

vaudeville see **musical**

vault/cellar/crypt/undercroft (underground room or chamber)
'Vault' is the word either for a place of storage under a building, usually a commercial one, as a bank 'vault' or a wine 'vault', or for a place of interment under a church or in a cemetery, as a family 'vault'. It can also mean apparently the opposite: not an underground room but one with overhead arches – but many underground vaults have arches, too, and this is the common link. A 'cellar' is often a more domestic storage place, as a coal 'cellar' or, again, a wine 'cellar'. A 'crypt' or 'undercroft' – the words are virtually synonymous – is a cell or 'vault' under a church regarded as a private or secret burial place in particular, as distinct from 'vault' as a more general word (also denoting a place larger than a 'crypt'). 'Crypt' is related to 'cryptic', i.e. 'hidden', while an 'undercroft' is a croft – basically the same word as 'crypt' – that is under the church. All the words are useful as the name of a restaurant or wine bar, especially a basement one, since they nicely conjure up wine and an 'olde worlde', historical atmosphere, or even a rather mysterious or spooky one.

vehicle licence see **driving licence**

vein/artery (main blood vessel)
The 'veins' are the vessels that carry the blood *to* the heart, while 'arteries' take blood *from* it to the rest of the body. Loosely, 'vein' can mean blood vessel in general, as in 'He claims to have royal blood in his veins'. In figurative use, an 'artery' is a main or trunk road, whether thought of as taking traffic to a city or from it, while 'vein' is often used

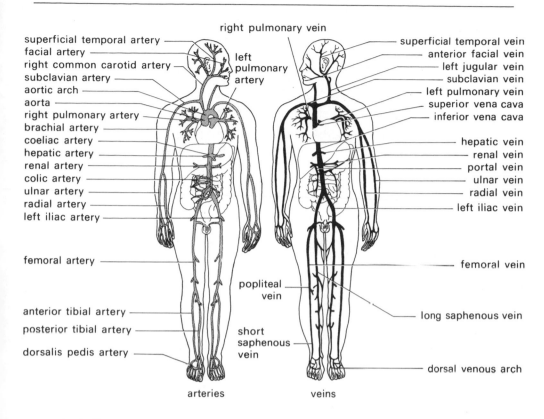

right pulmonary vein

superficial temporal artery
facial artery
right common carotid artery
subclavian artery
aortic arch
aorta
right pulmonary artery
brachial artery
coeliac artery
hepatic artery
renal artery
colic artery
ulnar artery
radial artery
left iliac artery

left pulmonary artery

femoral artery

anterior tibial artery

posterior tibial artery

dorsalis pedis artery

popliteal vein

short saphenous vein

superficial temporal vein
anterior facial vein
left jugular vein
subclavian vein
left pulmonary vein
superior vena cava
inferior vena cava

hepatic vein
renal vein
portal vein
ulnar vein
radial vein
left iliac vein

femoral vein

long saphenous vein

dorsal venous arch

arteries   veins

metaphorically to mean 'mood', as a remark made 'in humorous vein'.

vendetta see **feud**

verandah see **balcony** (platform in front of a house)

vermouth/bitters (bitter-flavoured alcoholic drink)
'Vermouth' is a white wine flavoured with wormwood or other aromatic herbs. French 'vermouth' is dry, and Italian sweet – the latter being the 'it' that goes with gin. The word is actually the same as 'wormwood', deriving ultimately from the German (*Wermut*). Martini is a cocktail of gin, French 'vermouth' (or Italian), with added orange 'bitters' and the like. 'Bitters' themselves are liquors impregnated with bitter herbs or roots, either to give the appetite or digestion a lift or simply as flavourings. In the latter case they are usually called after their flavour, as orange 'bitters', peach 'bitters'.

Campari is a well-known brand of Italian 'bitters', which can be drunk with or without soda. 'Bitters' (plural) is of course nothing to do with that peculiarly English beer called bitter (singular), for details of which see **ale**.

verse see **poetry**

vertigo see **dizziness**

VHF see **high frequency**

viaduct see **aqueduct**

vicar/rector/parson/curate (clergyman)
A 'vicar' is a parish priest, historically in a parish where tithes were appropriated, or where he was acting as priest in place of the 'rector' or 'parson', i.e. acting 'vicariously'. A 'rector', by contrast, was a parish priest in a parish where tithes had not been appropriated – that is, they went to him. A 'parson', properly, was the holder of a benefice who had full possession of its rights. In other

words, he was a 'rector'! The term is now used, sometimes somewhat condescendingly, of any clergyman. A 'curate', now an assistant clergyman, especially one working with a parish priest, is historically the title for the clergyman who had the 'cure' or charge of a parish – otherwise a 'vicar' or 'rector'. (They order these matters rather better in France, where le curé is the parish priest, and le vicaire his assistant.) The residences of the first three became respectively the vicarage, the rectory, and the parsonage. For some reason there is no 'curacy' – not as a residence, at any rate.

view/vista/panorama (extensive prospect)
A 'view' is a sight generally, especially from a high vantage point, as of a landscape or valley. A 'vista' is a 'view' seen through a long avenue of some kind, as between rows of trees or buildings. One of London's 'vistas' is the view of Buckingham Palace seen from Admiralty Arch up Pall Mall. (Unfortunately, the focal point is partly obscured by the Queen Victoria Memorial.) A 'panorama' is an all-round 'view', or at least a 'view' over a wide area, as of Paris from the top of the Eiffel Tower. (The word is Greek for 'all view'.)

village/hamlet (small populated place)
A 'village', which one almost always associates with the country, although some, as Dulwich 'Village' in London and Greenwich 'Village' in New York, have long merged with a city, is traditionally larger than a 'hamlet' but smaller than a town. It is usually thought of as having less than 1,000 inhabitants and its own parish church. In the USA, a 'village' –which may have well over 1,000 inhabitants – is a small municipality with limited corporate powers. This means that 'hamlet' is a rather more versatile word: at its vaguest it can mean any small 'village', especially a pretty one, and at its most precise – which is not very – it means a settlement smaller than a 'village' with no parish church but belonging to the parish of a nearby 'village' or town. Somewhere in between these two a 'hamlet' can also be a word for a small group of houses in a particularly remote or isolated country area. The word literally means 'little ham', i.e. 'small homestead', but 'ham' now exists

only in place-names, as Hampstead, Hampton and Oakham.

violet/purple/mauve/cerise/magenta/ maroon (shade of blue mixed with red, or red tinged with blue)
Colours can be subjective things, especially when they are blends or shades of other colours, as these are. However, seen as far as possible objectively: 'violet' is the colour at the opposite end of the spectrum to red, produced by a small amount of red with blue, and typically is the colour of violets (the 'purple' ones, that is); 'purple', the royal colour, is more or less halfway between red and blue, with a variation either way, giving reddish 'purple' or bluish 'purple'; 'mauve' is a bright but delicate pale 'purple' of bluish hue, as sometimes seen rather indelicately on a drinker's nose (it is also a reddish-'purple' aniline dye); 'cerise' is cherry-coloured, but red cherries rather than black or yellow (and also a textile dye, also known as fuchsin, forming a red solution in water); 'magenta' is a brilliant crimson, that is, a deep purplish red without any yellow in it; 'maroon' is a brownish crimson or reddish chestnut colour.

viper/adder (poisonous snake)
The 'viper' and the 'adder' hardly need distinguishing, since they are one and the same snake – the only poisonous one in Britain. However, the genus Vipera covers a number of 'vipers' apart from the British one (Vipera berus), such as the horned 'viper' (Vipera cornutus), and Russell's 'viper' (Vipera russellii) of India – the latter responsible for a number of human deaths. On a wider scale, the whole family Viperidae consists of about 150 species of 'viper', found in many countries round the world. Both names have unusual origins, since both contain an error. The 'viper' (or 'adder') is so called as it was thought to be viviparous, that is, bringing forth its young alive. It nearly is – but not quite, since its young, when born, are enclosed in an egg-type membrane which they immediately hatch out of. This means that the snake is strictly speaking not viviparous, but ovoviviparous. A small inaccuracy, therefore. The 'adder' (or 'viper') also has a name that is slightly wrong: it ought to be 'nadder', but the 'n' was taken to belong to

'an' and became wrongly separated ('an adder' instead of 'a nadder'), as in fact also happened to one or two other words, as 'auger' (which should be 'nauger'), 'apron' ('napron') and 'umpire' ('numpire'). (The opposite happened to 'a newt', which should be 'an ewt'.)

virginals see **harpsichord**

viscount see **duke**

vista see **view**

vitamin A/vitamin B/vitamin C/vitamin D/vitamin E (chemical substance in food necessary for good health and growth)
'Vitamin A', or retinol, is found in liver, yellow and green vegetables, cod liver oil and eggs, among other things. It is essential for normal growth of the skeleton and is well known for its role in preventing night blindness (via the carrots with which it is popularly, although not exclusively, associated). There are various kinds of 'vitamin B'. One of the best known is 'vitamin B_2', otherwise riboflavin, found in milk, eggs, kidney, liver and eggwhite and important for a healthy skin and eyes. 'Vitamin B_1', or thiamine, is influential on mental attitude, muscle tone and appetite, and found to a large extent in yeast and pork. Deficiency of it causes beri-beri. The most recently (1948) discovered vitamin is 'vitamin B_{12}', or cobalamin, particularly important in the nervous system and needed by all cells in the body. Deficiency can occur in vegetarians, since it occurs only in animal foods (liver, kidney, lean meat, milk, eggs, cheese) and not in any plant foods. 'Vitamin C', or ascorbic acid, is one of the cheapest and easiest to manufacture, although it is found naturally in fruits, especially citrus fruits, and vegetables – including potatoes. A deficiency of it, as is classically known, produces scurvy. It plays a vital part in the process of building and maintaining bones and teeth and in wound healing. (Some claim it can prevent the common cold, but this is still disputed.) 'Vitamin D' is the 'sunshine vitamin', actually provided by sunshine – in which sense it is not a true vitamin, since it does not gain access to the body through what is eaten. It does exist, however, in milk, fish,

eggs, butter and margarine. It is a great bone-builder and maintainer, and can prevent rickets. 'Vitamin E' is contained in most foods, especially vegetable oils and whole grains. Health food fanatics therefore get more than their whack of it. Its main claim to fame is that it prevents sterility, although its exact effectiveness in this direction is not proven. The actual word 'vitamin' – originally 'vitamine' when invented in 1912 – is a misnomer, since the substance does not contain an amino-acid. (The 'vit-' part is Latin for 'life'.) When the mistake was discovered, the final 'e' was dropped to try to avoid suggesting a connection with 'amine'. There are other vitamins and vitamin-like compounds with other letters, but these are the ones most familiar from the 'blurb' on the packets of various foodstuffs.

vitamin B see **vitamin A**

vitamin C see **vitamin A**

vitamin D see **vitamin A**

vitamin E see **vitamin A**

vogue see **fashion**

volley see **round**

volleyball see **netball**

volts/watts/amps/ohms (units of electricity)
'Let's put a hundred bulb in – that'll be brighter', we say, or 'Surely everywhere's 240 now?' 'Watts' in the first case, of course; 'volts' in the second. What *is* a 'watt'? But perhaps we should start with a 'volt'. This is a unit of electric potential – the one that makes electricity 'move'. Technically it is defined as the difference of potential between two points on a conducting wire carrying a constant current of one 'ampere' when the power dissipated between these points is one 'watt'. Thus, an 'amp' is a unit of current, an 'ohm' a unit of resistance and a 'watt' is a measure of energy expended (as we half expected from our light bulb). The four are thus interdependent. 'Volts', 'watts', 'amps' and 'ohms' are named respectively after an Italian, a Scot, a Frenchman and a

German, all physicists (Alessandro Volta, André-Marie Ampère and G. S. Ohm) except the Scot James Watt, who was an inventor and engineer. (They were, however, all born in the eighteenth century and all died in the nineteenth.)

volume see **weight**

voyage see **trip**

war/battle (period of open hostility and combat between nations or other opposing forces)
A 'war' is a larger, generally longer affair, as the Hundred Years 'War', Vietnam 'War' or Trojan 'War'. A 'battle' is usually more localised, and is a fight or combat either at a place or for a place, as is indicated in the names of such engagements as the 'Battle' of Agincourt, 'Battle' of Hastings or 'Battle' of Brandywine (all at these places), or the 'Battle' for Iwo Jima or 'Battle' for Kohima in the Second World War. (Most battles are named 'of' a place, although many were really 'for', such as the 'Battle' of Stalingrad and even the 'Battle' of Britain.)

warranty see **guarantee**

wasp/hornet (flying insect with an unpleasant sting)
The 'wasp', with its vivid black and yellow warning colours, formidable sting, predilection for fruit and sweet things, and curiously narrow waist, needs no introduction. So what is a 'hornet'? At its vaguest it is the word for any large kind of 'wasp', especially one with a serious sting. More exactly, it is the name sometimes given in Britain to the 'wasp' known as *Vespa crabro*, although a looser division between the two is to call all

members of the genus *Vespa* a 'wasp', and all those of *Vespera* a 'hornet'. (In the USA these two genera are more often known respectively as yellow jackets and 'hornets'.)

watts see **volts**

weariness see **tiredness**

weasel see **ferret**

wedding/marriage (act or ceremony of marrying or state of being married)
'Marriage' is the state of being married, entered into as a result of a 'wedding' – or a 'marriage'. What difference is there? Both words mean 'ceremony of marrying'. 'Wedding' is the more emotive term, conjuring up a memorable ceremony, an emotionally charged gathering of the two families and their friends, and a subsequent reception and honeymoon. 'Marriage' is a more formal word to denote the legal or religious ceremony that sanctions the conscious (and usually deeply committed) decision of a man and woman to live as husband and wife. The word thus anticipates the married state to follow. The difference between the words can be seen in such typical expressions as a 'white "wedding"' and '"wedding" bells' on the one hand (festivities and fun), and '"marriage" ceremony' and 'banns of "marriage"' on the other (formalities and a commitment to the future).

weight/volume/mass (unit of measurement of a body)
To take 'mass' and 'weight' first: 'mass' is the measure of the inertia of a body, in other words the resistance it offers to having its speed or position changed. 'Weight', however, is the result of the pull of gravity and depends on geographical location. This means that 'weight', for example, could be zero – as in space – but 'mass' is a non-varying property (except, as specialists in these things will hasten to point out, at speeds approaching that of light). Put mathematically, if m is the 'mass' of a body, and g its acceleration due to gravity, its 'weight' w is given by the equation $w = mg$, and is expressed in kilograms, newtons or other units (one pound of 'weight' is the equivalent of 4.445 newtons, and one kilogram of

'mass' at the earth's surface weighs about 2.2 pounds, or 9.8 newtons). 'Volume' is the size, measure or amount of anything in three dimensions, that is, the space occupied by a body or substance expressed in cubic units, as the cubic inch, fluid ounce, or gallon. (Cubic measurements must not be confused with square measurements: see **three square feet**.)

werewolf see **vampire**

wheat see **corn**

whelk/winkle (edible shellfish)
The 'whelk' is the larger of the two, with a pale-coloured spiral-shaped shell about three inches long. The 'winkle' is smaller and fatter, with dark rings on a grey shell about one inch high. Its proper name is 'periwinkle' – nothing do with the blue flower so called, although the word may have been influenced by the flower's name. (The 'peri-' may derive from Latin *pinna*, 'mussel', but this is only a possibility.) 'Winkles' are traditionally winkled out (the verb comes from the creature) from their shell with a pin or special 'winkle-picker'. There is, apparently, a subtle difference in taste between the two, but what it is exactly, only a gastronomic gastropodophile can say.

whin see **gorse**

whinny see **neigh**

whirlwind/tornado/cyclone (destructive revolving wind)
A 'whirlwind', as its name implies, is a mass of air whirling round in a cylindrical or funnel shape. When this happens at sea, the result is a waterspout. A 'tornado', occurring typically in West Africa or America, is a funnel-shaped whirling wind that travels along a narrow track causing great damage. In effect it is a form of 'cyclone', which is the term usually applied to a violent hurricane of restricted diameter in general, and which embraces not only the 'tornado' but also the hurricane, the typhoon, and the Australian willy-willy. All these winds occur in tropical regions, with the term 'cyclone' applying in extra-tropical regions to a region of low barometric pressure, i.e. a 'low', as opposed

to an anticyclone or 'high'. For more winds and weather, see **storm**.

whiskey see **whisky**

whisky/whiskey (spirit distilled from malted barley)
The difference is mainly in the spelling: 'whisky' is from Scotland ('scotch'), 'whiskey' from Ireland, though there are also corresponding variations in the manufacturing process. (The latter spelling is also the American one.) Both words derive from Irish and Scottish *usquebaugh*, in turn from *uisge beatha*, 'water of life'. Clearly the Celts are a race with a fine, fiery spirit. . . .

whist see **contract bridge**

white magic see **black magic**

White Paper/Green Paper/Blue Book
(official government publication)
Government papers of all kinds presented to Parliament are called 'White Papers'. Lengthy 'White Papers', such as the reports of royal commissions, are bound in blue paper covers in book form and are called 'Blue Books' (or sometimes Blue Papers). A 'Green Paper' is a type of tentative 'White Paper'. It sets out the proposals for a future government policy that must first and foremost be discussed (rather than be regarded as a commitment to a particular action). It is printed on green paper to distinguish it from a 'White Paper'. In the USA a 'Blue Book' is a (non-governmental) book in blue covers giving details of US government officials, or other prominent persons. (The non-governmental Black Papers that arose in Britain in the late 1960s to criticise educational policies had a name patterned after the 'White Paper'.)

whitewash/distemper (solution suitable for painting on walls or ceilings)
The difference lies mainly in the composition and application of the substance. 'Whitewash' is a solution of quicklime or whiting and size for brushing over walls and ceilings to make them clean. 'Distemper' is a water paint (as distinct from an oil paint) containing powder colours and is used mainly for painting internal walls and scenery.

Wild West see **Middle West**

wines/spirits (type of alcoholic drink)
When is a wine not a wine? There is no doubt about the well-known table 'wines' of France and Spain, say, or Germany and Italy. But what about sherry or port, for example? These are fortified 'wines', so called – fortified in fact with brandy – so that they have an alcoholic content of around 20 per cent as against the traditional table 'wines' whose content is around 10 per cent. Madeira, muscatel and marsala are other fortified 'wines'. 'Spirits', with an alcoholic content of 40 per cent or more, are distilled liquors in which the concentration of ethyl alcohol (the intoxicating agent) has been increased above that of the original fermented mixture. So although fortified 'wines' are fortified with brandy, a 'spirit', they are not themselves classed as 'spirits', which are the familiar 'hard' drinks such as gin, vodka, whisky and rum. Fortified 'wines' in America are usually known as dessert 'wines'.

wink/blink (brief closing of the eye)
A 'wink' is usually a rapid closing and opening of one eye done deliberately to convey some signal or meaning, as a friendly greeting or a 'glad eye'. A 'blink' is an involuntary rapid closing and opening of both eyes, either as a natural process frequently repeated to lubricate and cleanse the eye or as the result of a sudden blow or shock or dazzling light.

winkle see **whelk**

wit see **humour**

witch doctor/medicine man (tribal
magician having powers of healing)
There is little difference in the function of the two – although a 'witch doctor' can both heal *and* harm. The chief distinction is in their area of operations: the 'witch doctor' is found among African tribes, the 'medicine man' lives among the American Indians. (The Canadian city of Medicine Hat is said to be named after a 'medicine man' who lost his hat while fleeing from Blackfoot warriors who had massacred his tribe.)

wood/forest/grove/copse/coppice
(collection of trees)
A 'wood' is smaller than a 'forest', is not so primitive, and is usually nearer to civilisation. This means that a 'forest' is fairly extensive, is to some extent wild, and on the whole not near large towns or cities. In addition, a 'forest' often has game or wild animals in it, which a 'wood' does not, apart from the standard quota of regular rural denizens such as rabbits, foxes and birds of various kinds. Many newer 'forests' in Britain are of planted trees, while the famous 'forests' of medieval Britain, such as the New 'Forest' (created by William the Conqueror, as a royal hunting ground, therefore decidedly old), although originally partly 'man-planted', are now regarded as natural extensions of their former confines. A planted 'wood', as distinct from a natural one, may often be recognised from the predominance of one particular species of tree. A 'grove' is a smallish group of trees and is normally cleared of undergrowth; it may also contain fruit or nut trees, as an orange 'grove' or a walnut 'grove'. 'Copse' is simply a shortened form of 'coppice', and is a small 'wood' of undergrowth and small trees that are grown to be cut from time to time.

woofer/tweeter (type of loudspeaker)
These attractively juvenile names are respectively for a loudspeaker that will reproduce low-frequency sounds, and one (smaller) that will reproduce high-frequency sounds. Both form part of a hi-fi unit or music centre, for example. See also – on the same sort of lines – **wow**.

work-in see **sit-in**

work-to-rule see **sit-in**

world/earth (planet on which we live)
The 'world' implies not just our terrestrial globe but the people who inhabit it. Someone who sails single-handed round the 'world', therefore, will doubtless have his or her exploit reported all over the 'world'. The sense 'mass of population' is used more narrowly in such terms as the Western 'World' or the Third 'World' (for definition of which see, if necessary, **developing countries**). The 'earth' is more the globe

seen either as a scientific entity, specifically astronomically (the planet 'Earth') or geographically (the 'earth' and its natural resources), or, from a religious viewpoint, as contrasted with heaven and hell (it was the 'earth' God created in the beginning, not the 'world'). In general, too, 'earth' is a more lofty or poetic word than 'world', especially where the senses are the same: compare 'the people of the "earth"' and 'the people of the "world"'.

Worship see Lordship

wow/flutter (perceptible variations in pitch in sound reproduction)
Both words are imitative. 'Wow' is slow fluctuation of pitch, most clearly detected in long notes. 'Flutter' is the term for rapid variation in pitch or in loudness. Both are caused in irregularities in the speed of the turntable or tape, either in recording or in playing. (Neither should be confused with woofer and tweeter, which are similar types of jokey name but relate to something different.)

X-rays/infra-red rays/ultra-violet rays/ gamma rays (invisible rays used in medicine or for special applications)
'X-rays', so called as their original nature was unknown, are the ones discovered by Roentgen in 1895 and widely used to examine the interior organs of a person or the nature of an opaque object. They are of a shorter wavelength than light. 'Infra-red rays' are ones beyond the visible red rays at one end of the spectrum. They are largely used in photography, in heat therapy, and for night-viewing devices, such as for military surveillance. 'Ultra-violet rays' are the opposite: beyond the visible violet rays at the other end of the spectrum, with a wavelength between visible light and 'X-rays'. One of their most popular uses is for so-called 'sun lamps', which produce an artificial suntan. 'Gamma rays' are streams of gamma radiation, that is, electromagnetic radiation of shorter wavelength and higher energy than 'X-rays', especially that portion of the electromagnetic spectrum that has a frequency greater than about 3 by 10^{19} hertz. They are so named since they were

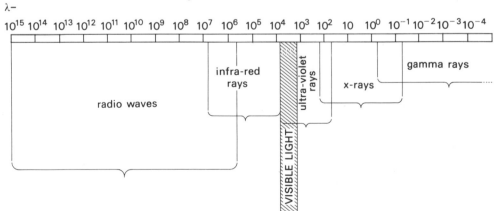

Wavelengths in electromagnetic spectrum

$\lambda = 2\pi c/\omega$, where λ is wavelength, c is speed of light, and ω is frequency (of oscillations of electric and magnetic fields)

discovered (in 1900) as a third component of the radiation from radioactive materials, the others being alpha-particles and beta-particles (and alpha, beta and gamma being the first three letters of the Greek alphabet). 'Gamma rays' have uses in radiotherapy and in the detection of flaws in metal castings. The respective wavelengths of all these rays may be seen in the diagram.

yachting see **sailing**

yard see **mast**

yearning see **longing**

zebra crossing see **pedestrian crossing**

zone see **belt**

zoom see **track**

For Reference

Not to be taken from this room